Praise for *Augmented Analytics*

An essential read for any organization embarking on analytics transformation. The detailed coverage of Augmented Frames alone is worth the price of the book. Packed with technical depth and practical insights, use cases and code samples, this book clearly lays out the path to becoming a data-driven organization in the era of AI.

— *Donald Farmer, principal, Treehive Strategy*

Augmented Analytics comes at the right time in mid-2024 to provide much needed clarity to both business decision makers as well as Data and AI managers and practitioners alike on how to reach the next level of analytical maturity. It is full of pragmatic advice and sound foundational knowledge on applying the concepts of Augmented Workflows and Augmented Frames. Readers equipped with this knowledge will be in a better position to connect all the "analytical" dots to design and execute digitization projects in the enterprise.

—*Karl Ivo Sokolov, managing partner for Data, Specific Group*

Augmented Analytics is your guide to transformational insights. Crafted with wisdom, this handbook offers practical guidance for navigating analytics transformation, whether you're an analyst or a leader. Essential reading for insight-driven decision making.

—*Noro Chalise, data scientist, QSystems AI*

Augmented Analytics

Enabling Analytics Transformation for
Data-Informed Decisions

Willi Weber and Tobias Zwingmann

Beijing · Boston · Farnham · Sebastopol · Tokyo

Augmented Analytics

by Willi Weber and Tobias Zwingmann

Published by O'Reilly Media, Inc., 1005 Gravenstein Highway North, Sebastopol, CA 95472.

O'Reilly books may be purchased for educational, business, or sales promotional use. Online editions are also available for most titles (*http://oreilly.com*). For more information, contact our corporate/institutional sales department: 800-998-9938 or *corporate@oreilly.com*.

Acquisitions Editor: Michelle Smith
Development Editor: Sarah Grey
Production Editor: Clare Laylock
Copyeditor: Shannon Turlington
Proofreader: Emily Wydeven

Indexer: nSight, Inc.
Interior Designer: David Futato
Cover Designer: Karen Montgomery
Illustrator: Kate Dullea

June 2024:   First Edition

Revision History for the First Edition

2024-05-31:   First Release

See *http://oreilly.com/catalog/errata.csp?isbn=9781098151720* for release details.

978-1-098-15172-0

[LSI]

Table of Contents

Foreword

When it comes to artificial intelligence (AI) and analytics, the explosion is almost tangible. People are starting to dream about dashboards that show the brightest futures and algorithms that change the way we work. The possibilities are endless.

The shift to analytics is forcing us to reinvent the way we think, the way we work, and the way we collaborate—with humans and with AI. Everyone wants to know how to take advantage of all these opportunities. How can we outperform our competitors? How can we make the most of what we already have? And how can we prepare for a future that we can't even imagine now?

Of course, tools will help: algorithms, generative AI, models, transformers, and more. But the basis for answering these questions is not tool-driven. To successfully manage this change, it is important to identify your organization's specific needs, audiences, and potential and to develop a tailored implementation plan.

This book will help you identify the potential to implement analytics in your own unique business environment—and find your own ways to bring it to life. It provides a solid framework, with plenty of room to customize. Most importantly, it will show you the limits of trainings and upskilling and offers you a good way of bringing analytics right where it brings value: augmenting the workflows of your target groups.

In addition to infrastructure improvements, it's worth looking at the people who are shaping the change in organizations around the world: the softer, more human side of analytics is critical to success. This includes empathy, understanding, enthusiasm, excitement—but also perhaps fear, uncertainty, or skepticism. It is therefore essential to integrate, support, involve, and train every role. More than ever, "it's all about the people." And it's not only about the people being trained. People who love AI and data analytics bring their enthusiasm and innovations to work every day, and their passion and euphoria can spread quickly, inspiring colleagues and helping to overcome obstacles.

As an analytics transformation manager, I am very excited to be a part of this story, together with Tobi and Willi. In my role at HDI Global, I was able to shape the analytics transformation through various initiatives and formats and had the chance to see its impact with my own eyes. Seeing the endless potential and, most of all, empowering so many people to take an active part in this change were (and are) great experiences. I am excited to bring our own transformation to the next level with augmented analytics as its enabler. Most of all, I'm excited about continuing to be with people with understanding, empathy, and passion as they go even further through this transformation.

Readers, I wish you the best of luck in making the most of these infinite possibilities. With this great book as your guide during your own transformation, I am convinced that you will help your organization find the best way forward.

— Christiane Busche
Analytics Transformation at Data Analytics
HDI Global
January 2024

Preface

Becoming data-driven is an ambitious goal—yet, from our perspective, there is not a single company that hasn't in some way embarked on this journey in recent years. They all have different goals and approaches, and basically a different understanding of what *data-driven* really means, but they have started.

The questions everyone needs to ask are about why you're doing this, what you plan to do, and how you'll achieve this goal. Are you striving for a good, stable business intelligence (BI) ecosystem? Do you want to scale your analytics capabilities across the organization? Do you understand analytics and its related potentials as part of your business assets, which absolutely need to be aligned with your business strategies? Depending on your organization's goals and ambitions, these questions—and, ultimately, your journey to analytical maturity—will vary.

It's important to also understand where you are on this journey: are you still at the beginning, halfway through, or almost to the end? Whatever's on your agenda, your ambition, your strategy, and the journey to becoming a data-driven organization inevitably leads to a fundamental, often far-reaching transformation. This transformation will change how you process data and deal with the resulting insights, what you use them for, how they influence business decisions, and above all, how these insights affect people and change their actions. We call this the *analytics transformation*, whether or not it is part of an overarching digital-transformation initiative in your company. This is so specific, important, and extensive that it requires its own strategic roadmap and a comprehensive approach.

Think about the last trip you took. We work through every journey in iterations, whether it's a road trip through Europe, your personal career, or the transformation of your company. A journey needs milestones, waypoints, junctions where you decide to go left or right, and pauses where you recapitulate the journey so far, develop new strategies, and prepare for the next stage. Whatever kind of journey you've embarked on, you'll always need the same basic things: the right equipment, resources, and environment; the right skills; and above all, the right mindset.

The same goes for your company's analytics transformation. You'll need wide-ranging skills to address your environment and tooling, drive the transformation, and bring your aspirations to life. You'll need all relevant business stakeholders involved, and at least a few of them must be passionate about the journey. But most important, without the right mindset, there will be no successful transformation.

One evening, around bedtime, Willi's phone pinged him with a new article that caught his attention: "Ten Unsung Digital and AI Ideas Shaping Business" (*https://oreil.ly/pu4aV*) by Kate Smaje and Rodney Zemmel. The article ended up giving him a sleepless night. The ideas that Smaje and Zemmel discuss are shaping digital and analytics transformations in the modern business landscape, even though they don't necessarily dominate the headlines. These ideas address all the aspects we touch on in this book: business, culture, value, strategy, technology, AI, awareness, leading by example, process, competency, collaboration, operating model, executing initiatives, scaling solutions, rapidly adapting to changing market conditions, and the need to combine all of these to be successful. Augmented analytics is a significant part of addressing each and every one of these, if not always a direct solution.

That was a sleepless night for Willi, who realized that the concepts and possibilities we describe in this book are farther reaching and more important for transformation than even we had realized. For the first time, it felt like all of our ideas had come together into a comprehensive whole.

He read every single question raised in the article and answered them multiple times: once for each idea. Here are some of Smaje and Zemmel's questions:

- Are you using software to build products, services, or businesses that create a true competitive advantage for your business?
- What specific initiatives on your roadmap directly support scaling?
- Have you identified the specific roadblocks to achieving scale, and are you clear about how to deal with them?
- Are you developing those hard-to-copy capabilities (processes, workflows, automations) that power the products and services you need to build and improve?
- Do you have a clear view of which emerging technologies could most enhance your competitive differentiation?
- What standards and best practices do you have in place for building data products across the organization, and are they easily accessible by relevant teams?
- Have you identified the most important roles in your business that could benefit from a generative AI copilot?
- How quickly are you able to conceive of, build, and launch a new product or service?

- How much value have your digital and AI initiatives generated in the past six months?
- How well is your digital-twin platform integrated into your product, solution, or business development?[1]

It has become clearer and clearer that augmented analytics is what connects these ideas and makes them work together. AA allows businesses to literally be "rewired" (thus fulfilling the metaphor of the book on which the previous bulletpoints are based, *Rewired: The McKinsey Guide to Outcompeting in the Age of Digital and AI* by Eric Lamarre, Kate Smaje, and Rodney Zemmel [Wiley]). AA is the enabler that brings business and analytics together.

That's why we're showing a way forward that deals with more than just the hard, technical aspects of an analytics transformation. If you really want to transform your organization successfully, you need to take a much broader approach.

It will not be enough to establish infrastructure, develop BI and analytical products, and ensure good data governance. You also need to consider adaptation with dynamic business strategies, the changing organization, diverse people and processes, and finally, the cultural environment in which you want to operate. We cover all these topics because only their combination will lead you to a point where you can successfully introduce augmented analytics to achieve a higher level of analytics maturity and transform from a data-driven business into an *insight*-driven one.

Are standard data-driven methods, such as reporting, data-science models, and self-service BI, really meeting organizations' needs in a rapidly changing business environment? Given the scope of the changes they are intended to inform, their effectiveness is severely limited. This book challenges you to rethink the paradigms of analytics transformation and take them a step further—to a place where augmented analytics closes the gap between data and strategic insights like never before.

For example, in commercial insurance, new topics like augmented underwriting and augmented portfolio steering are starting to dominate the insurance-industry headlines and will become standard over the next few years. Other industries and their workflows will follow and experience the seamless integration of insights.

In fact, augmenting our human capabilities with technology has always been a key driver of innovation and progress. We learned to control fire and cook food, amplified our physical capabilities with the wheel, and developed the printing press, providing wider access to knowledge than ever before. We've been creating more capable versions of ourselves since the Ice Age.

---

1 Sample questions from the article "Ten Unsung Digital and AI Ideas Shaping Business," Kate Smaje and Rodney Zemmel, *McKinsey Digital*, January 9, 2024, *https://oreil.ly/T_Udr*.

Today, our entire digital lifestyle is based on augmentation. We choose shows on streaming services recommended by algorithms. On the road, our navigation systems suggest the fastest routes, augmenting our knowledge of directions. Restaurant ratings help us find the best options, supplementing our preferences. And the next frontier is augmenting our own intelligence.

This is particularly important for businesses. To explain why, let us share a little story. Back in late 2022, at a conference of high-profile European data leaders, one speaker projected a picture similar to Figure P-1 on the wall. It became the whole conference's key talking point because literally every company in the room was facing the situation it depicts.

Figure P-1. Data experts in the total workforce

What's happening here? In most businesses, there's a group—usually a minority—of what we call data experts or data professionals. Depending on the company's analytical maturity, they usually account for between 10% and 20% of the total workforce.

During the last few years, employers have spent a lot of energy on empowering this group: providing them with better tools, building them labs, and so on. Expectations for their output have been high, and some companies did find their "high-value" use cases. But this approach has reached its limit: transformation isn't about empowering this minority anymore. Now it's about empowering the other 80% of the organization and unlocking more data-driven use cases (not always high in individual value, but many in number). How can you achieve this?

The goal here is not to turn every knowledge worker (shown on the right in Figure P-1) into a data expert (on the left). It's not about turning every accountant into a data analyst. The hard truth that most organizations need to swallow is that most accountants do not *want* to become data scientists. They want to stay accountants. Instead, it's about turning those accountants into *better* accountants—and the same holds true for virtually every knowledge-worker role.

This book shows you how to achieve that—and how to do so at scale.

Who Should Read This Book?

This book covers many aspects, both methodological and technical, of the broad topic of analytics transformation. The methodological topics are particularly foundational for understanding analytics maturity while the technical topics help you increase that maturity.

The book is especially valuable for experienced analysts and for people in strategic and managerial positions who are responsible for some facet of an analytical or digital transformation. Engineers and other roles concerned with implementing and integrating analytics solutions will, however, appreciate the technical concepts and frameworks we provide to help start enhancing workflows in your organization, complete with a minimum viable product (MVP).

In summary, this book is for anyone who understands that, while you can separate analytics into its technological, methodological, and business components, you can make use of them effectively only when you have a comprehensive perspective.

You will see in these pages many transformative concepts and ideas that have a strong strategic character. You will also see technical implementations in dedicated analytics programming languages, such as Python and R. But even if you are not an analytics professional with programming skills, this book is for you: we explain all concepts, including the technical implementations, in a way that business professionals can understand while providing a complement for people who would like to dive deeper technically.

Learning Objectives

By the end of this book, you will understand the following:

- The importance of aligning technological advances with dynamic business strategies and organizational processes
- The critical components of an analytics transformation and how they relate to overall business strategy
- How augmented analytics bridges the gap between traditional analytics environments and insight-driven decision making
- The fundamental roles of the organization's culture, skills, and mindsets as prerequisites for successfully adopting augmented analytics
- The relevance of analytical roles and a holistic use-case approach
- The limitations of traditional approaches to analytics
- How augmentation can move your organization forward and make workflows more efficient

- The challenges of implementing augmented analytics
- How to introduce augmentation into the enterprise infrastructure
- How combining analytics with software-engineering techniques can kick-start your first analytics-augmentation MVPs

You'll also be able to:

- Assess your organization's current analytical maturity and identify areas for improvement
- Evaluate and adapt your analytics strategies in response to evolving business needs and market trends
- Develop a strategic roadmap for analytics transformation tailored to your organization's unique needs and goals
- Address the technological, organizational, and cultural challenges associated with analytics transformation
- Develop methodological and technical concepts for your individual augmentations
- Implement augmented analytics infrastructures and integrate them into your business processes

Navigating This Book

Now that you understand the intention of this book and its goals, let's outline its structure in more detail and show you how it reflects the needs of readers from both the methodological and the technical worlds.

The first section, which is the less technical part of this book, addresses the organizational and transformational foundations of analytic transformation holistically and explains the concept of augmented analytics in detail. The second section of the book, which starts at Chapter 5, makes a seamless transition into the technical aspects of implementing augmented analytics and integrating it into your analytics ecosystem in an architecture-independent way.

Let's take a closer look at each chapter:

- Chapter 1, "The Business Transformation", makes a general case for the importance of analytics in today's business landscape. We look at how different industries are increasingly moving to incorporate analytics as part of their corporate culture.

- Chapter 2, "The Analytics Problem", explores the importance of defining the right purpose for your analytics transformation. We lay out the framework a company needs—from cultural, infrastructural, and organizational perspectives—to reach the point of organizational maturity where augmented analytics can have the greatest impact.

- In Chapter 3, "Understanding Augmented Analytics", we break the concept down into its core components, explain its benefits, and describe how it enables transformation and helps you overcome hurdles. We explain the main task of integrating augmented analytics into workflows and address the enablers and challenges of augmentation.

- Chapter 4, "Preparing People and the Organization for Augmented Analytics", focuses on the human and organizational aspects of using augmented analytics in a targeted and sustainable way.

- Chapter 5, "Augmented Workflows", looks in detail at how to augment workflows with analytics, including identifying appropriate workflows and balancing automation with human integration. It also addresses technical challenges and infrastructure.

- Chapter 6, "Augmented Frames", is a deep dive into the technical implementation. It introduces the concepts of augmentation engines and workflows through a distributed API infrastructure, with a strong focus on quick prototyping, generating insights, and integrating those insights into user workflows.

- Finally, in Chapter 7, "Applied Examples", we present practical applications of augmented analytics, including improving underwriting processes, improving forecasting processes in Agile projects, and accelerating the distribution of sales information. These tangible examples illustrate the transformative potential of augmented analytics and should inspire readers to look for parallels in their own domains and get started with their own prototypes.

Conventions Used in This Book

The following typographical conventions are used in this book:

Italic
Indicates new terms, URLs, email addresses, filenames, and file extensions.

`Constant width`
Used for program listings, as well as within paragraphs to refer to program elements such as variable or function names, databases, data types, environment variables, statements, and keywords.

O'Reilly Online Learning

 For more than 40 years, *O'Reilly Media* has provided technology and business training, knowledge, and insight to help companies succeed.

Our unique network of experts and innovators share their knowledge and expertise through books, articles, and our online learning platform. O'Reilly's online learning platform gives you on-demand access to live training courses, in-depth learning paths, interactive coding environments, and a vast collection of text and video from O'Reilly and 200+ other publishers. For more information, visit *https://oreilly.com*.

How to Contact Us

Please address comments and questions concerning this book to the publisher:

O'Reilly Media, Inc.
1005 Gravenstein Highway North
Sebastopol, CA 95472
800-889-8969 (in the United States or Canada)
707-827-7019 (international or local)
707-829-0104 (fax)
support@oreilly.com
https://oreilly.com/about/contact.html

We have a web page for this book, where we list errata, examples, and any additional information. You can access this page at *https://oreil.ly/AugmentedAnalytics*.

For news and information about our books and courses, visit *https://oreilly.com*.

Find us on LinkedIn: *https://linkedin.com/company/oreilly-media*.

Watch us on YouTube: *https://youtube.com/oreillymedia*.

Acknowledgments

From Willi

Writing down all of these ideas came at the best time for me personally, and I am grateful to have contributed to the development of augmented analytics as a field.

First, I would like to thank my beloved wife, Kathrin, who always supports me in my projects and gives me the freedom I need to try new things. At least 50% of my success and the benefit of my work rests on your shoulders. Thank you very much.

Looking back on my professional career, which has shaped my behavior, my attitude, and my passion for data analytics, I can think of three mentors who have guided me through different stages of my career. Surprisingly, each of them was my supervisor.

Eugene Neigel, Head of Corporate Information Management, CEWE Stiftung & Co. KGaA, was my first supervisor after my apprenticeship as an IT specialist. He ignited the spark of passion for data analytics in me. Starting with the first BI and OLAP systems, he showed me how data is an elementary asset for distribution and sales.

My second mentor was Alexander Schlei, Head of NatCat Services, HDI Global SE. He helped me discover my ability to get very creative in developing analytics products, assessing risk, and creating pricing solutions. We established one of HDI Global's most important NatCat processes and developed the first computationally intensive natural-hazards modeling.

Finally, Dr. Dirk Höring, Executive Board Member, Short Tail, HDI Global SE, is the person who believes most in me and who promoted me to manager. He has helped me combine my technical and methodological skills with strategic and visionary thinking and with inspiring and leading people.

My first mentor ignited my passion, the second supported me in realizing my ideas, and the third made me someone who develops strategic and visionary approaches. (I'm just realizing the similarity to analytical maturity levels, which we cover in Chapter 2!) I thank each of you for your commitment and continuous support, and for the trust and the freedom you have given me to realize my ideas. Ultimately, you have also helped to make this happen.

From Tobias

After finishing my last book, *AI-Powered Business Intelligence* (O'Reilly), in late 2022, I promised my family (and myself) that I wouldn't write another book for six months at least. About three months later, I was sitting with Willi in a nearby restaurant, sipping a beer, and brainstorming the idea of writing a book on augmented analytics. At this point, the decision to embark on this new project was mutual and effortless. And for the rest, I convinced myself that being "just" a coauthor would be a good enough argument for halving the break I had originally planned.

I want to thank first and foremost my beloved wife Çiğdem for always supporting and pushing me throughout this journey and for being my anchor in the everyday chaos of juggling raising the three most beautiful kids in the world together, running a business, writing a book, and staying mentally sane. I love you!

A big shoutout to Anett and Gülten, for again winning the World's Best Grand-mothers award; to Remzi for entertaining the kids; and to Erdem Gül for running the best restaurant in Hannover and hosting the best family breakfasts. I'd also like to thank my grandmother, Sigrid Zwingmann, who won't be able to read this book in English, but I know she'll be happy to see her name in it. And finally, Klaus-Dieter Zwingmann, who unfortunately didn't get the chance to hold this book in his hands, but I'm sure he would have enjoyed it very much.

We both would like to thank the entire team at O'Reilly for making this book possi-ble. A special shoutout goes to our developmental editor, Sarah Grey, for always being an amazing writing coach with great feedback, extraordinary attention to detail, and the ability to cut through our fluff so that the good stuff could shine! Special thanks also to our acquisitions editor, Michelle Smith, for trusting in us, providing guidance, and making this book happen. And last but not least, to our production editor, Clare Laylock, for turning a bunch of wild manuscripts into such a beautiful book and breathing life into it! We cannot express enough how much we appreciate your help.

Reviewing a technical book is almost as difficult as writing it. Therefore, we would like to thank our technical reviewers Christiane Busche, Donald Farmer, George Mount, Karl Ivo Sokolov, Prashanth Southekal, and Michael Zimmer for their valua-ble feedback, which has greatly improved this book. And special thanks to Frank Schultheiss for collaborating on the Agile Forecasting use case in Chapter 7.

## CHAPTER 1

The Business Transformation

As we write this book in 2024, the business landscape is marked by increasing adoption of digital technologies and practices, often referred to as "business transformation" or "industrial transformation." This transformation is not the first one. So far, the world has seen three industrial transformations, each driven by new technology: steam power (beginning in roughly the 1760s), electricity and mass production (from the mid-1800s to the 1910s), and computerization (from the late 20th century to the present). This chapter will explain what's different about the current transformation compared to previous ones and why we believe that augmented analytics (AA) is so well positioned to solve the problems that many businesses currently face.

Augmented analytics simply means providing people with access to technology that gives them the analytical leverage they need to accomplish the business task at hand in a better way. If you've heard this term before, you might associate it with automated forecasting in Tableau dashboards; that's not what we're doing here. AA requires a much more holistic approach to really take off. We will dive deeper into defining AA in Chapter 3.

Before we do that, let's zoom out a bit and explore the external driving forces that make using AA a necessity for staying competitive in today's world.

Why Businesses Are Transforming

We're currently in the computerization and information age, and many experts believe that AI will drive the next phase of this industrial transformation. So what makes this phase of business transformation more special than previous ones? We believe there are four main factors at play, which we'll examine one by one in this section.

Factor 1: The Speed of Change

Digital transformation is happening much faster than previous transformations, requiring businesses to be agile and adapt quickly. For example, steam power took several decades to fully transform the economy. Mass production took roughly half a century. And computerization took about 20 to 30 years. In contrast, the digital transformation is happening in just a few years for some industries. To be clear, most companies and organizations are just not built for that pace; you need exceptional leadership and organizational agility to succeed in this environment.

For businesses, this rapid pace of change has led to increased pressure to keep up and stay competitive. Every bookstore around the corner suddenly has to compete with companies like Amazon; every taxi company has to compete with Uber, which offers exceptional customer service built on top of world-class data analytics. But the competition doesn't come only from disruptive players. Even traditional businesses have started to disrupt themselves. Consider the shift toward Industry 4.0 in manufacturing, which includes adopting smart factories and Internet of Things (IoT) devices to optimize production processes and improve efficiency.

Factor 2: The Convergence of Multiple Technologies

Previous industrial transformations were driven largely by one or two key technologies, such as steam and electricity. But digital transformation involves integrating technologies like AI, cloud computing, data analytics, and IoT into manufacturing, which on their own have the potential to disrupt entire industries.

The advancements of the 2010s and 2020s in computation, networking, and storage have resulted in new technologies and services that have significantly changed the way businesses operate. This makes the current phase of digital transformation much more complex and multidimensional. It's extremely hard to predict where the ship is heading and navigate the waters successfully. Disruption can happen practically overnight, as we saw in the consumer electronics and retail spaces, or it can take years. For example, while renewable energy started disrupting the energy sector around 20 years ago, it's still far from being the dominant energy source in most countries.

Factor 3: The Importance of Data

Digital transformation often requires fundamental changes in business models and in the way organizations think about data. In previous industrial revolutions, data "just happened": you knew how many cars you sold, how much material you needed, how many employees you had, and so on. You analyzed data in hindsight to improve processes. Don't get us wrong—this alone was a big deal. It has fueled an entire business-intelligence software industry in the golden age of computerization, including database vendors and visualization tools. However, in the digital age, data has evolved from something that happens to something that *must* happen.

The volume of data created, captured, copied, and consumed is still growing at an unprecedented pace, according to a 2022 McKinsey report (*https://oreil.ly/atX1g*). As Figure 1-1 shows, this trend has been taking place for more than a decade and is predicted to keep up its momentum.

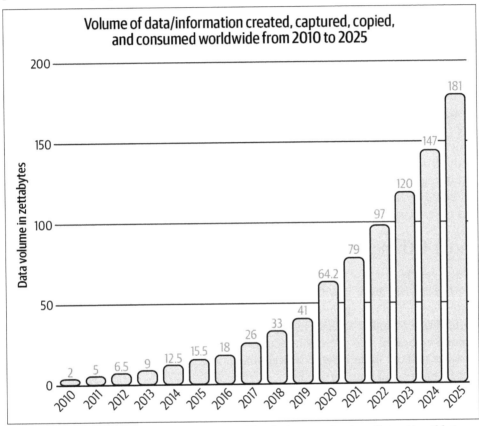

Figure 1-1. The growing amount of data worldwide (source: Statista (https://oreil.ly/ p7b-T))

Most organizations have found a way to tackle the sheer volume of data with modern technology: cheap storage, high-performance compute, and low-latency networking power have enabled a new wave of offerings that both consumers and businesses alike love and embrace, such as streaming services, social media platforms, and ecommerce sites. Adoption of these new services has not only fueled the digital ecosystem but has also literally generated the fuel to drive it: data.

Yet most of this data is not clean, tabular data that can easily be analyzed but rather unstructured data, such as text, images, and videos. Businesses generate unstructured data all over the place—for instance, through social media, customer interactions, and IoT sensors. In many cases, technology is only helpful to a certain extent; human analytical skills are required to make sense of the data. Most businesses still struggle with this growing complexity.

So companies have to think strategically about which data they need to collect, how they will collect it, and what insights they can gain from it (which, in some industries, can even happen in real time). This requires a whole new paradigm about data and often drives a need to add new roles to a company.

Some people (*https://oreil.ly/PX9qM*) compare data in the current economy to oil in the "old economy" as a driving resource. But we think this is actually a bad comparison. Unlike oil, data doesn't get used up when it's consumed. Instead, we get even more data the more we interact with it. Nor is data a scarce resource: it can be generated and collected in numerous ways. The only parallel that holds true is that both oil and data are worth much less when they are not refined. Both resources need a thorough process of cleaning, preparation, and governance before they can be used for commercial purposes. In a way, every company has to learn these skills, even if it has never worked with data before.

Factor 4: Changing Consumer Behavior and Customer Centricity

When people first saw the iPhone, they never wanted any other phone again. "Who needs a stylus?" Steve Jobs famously asked at the iconic 2007 iPhone launch keynote (*https://oreil.ly/hihIc*), pointing his finger in the air. Since then, consumers have gotten used to touch screens instead of mechanical keyboards or plastic pens. The iPhone embraced and anticipated customers' needs, but it would never have been possible without underlying technical innovations like multitouch display, high computing power, and long battery life.

Since then, numerous other industries have had their own "iPhone moments." For instance:

- Shopify showed small shop owners that running their own ecommerce store doesn't have to be hard or expensive.
- Tesla showed car buyers just how well electric vehicles can perform—and how fun and effortless driving can be.

- Amazon Prime changed the way people shop, making one-day delivery the norm and raising the bar for customer-service expectations.
- Netflix revolutionized the way we consume video content, introducing binge-watching and personalized recommendations based on viewing history.

These are just a few examples. We aren't endorsing the underlying brands or services—we just want to show you that digital transformation spans all industries and is often driven by the changing behaviors and expectations of consumers.

Industries Heavily Impacted by Digital Transformation

McKinsey researchers investigated (*https://oreil.ly/u3arB*) Big Data's impact on different industries in a 2011 study, which is the source for Figure 1-2. (While technology has changed a lot since then, its importance in these industries has not, and the key challenges have remained surprisingly steady.) Table 1-1 describes some example industries that have been extraordinarily affected by the current business-transformation processes, their key challenges, and how they leverage data and analytics to address these challenges.

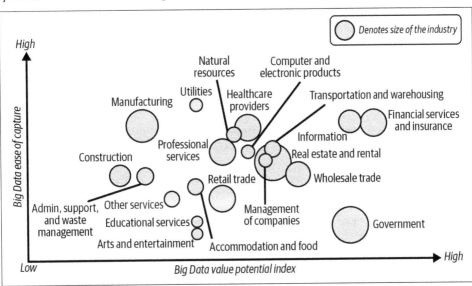

Figure 1-2. Industries heavily impacted by big data and analytics (adapted from McKinsey (https://oreil.ly/BAin9))

Table 1-1. Industries affected by digital transformation, their challenges, and how they use data and analytics

Industry	Why affected	Key challenges	Use case examples
Agriculture	Meeting growing food demand while addressing sustainability concerns	• Maximizing crop yield • Optimizing resource usage (water, fertilizer) • Finding skilled workers • Complying with sustainability standards	• Precision farming • Real-time monitoring of crop growth and soil conditions • Automation • Identifying patterns for optimal resource usage
Commercial insurance	Powerful dynamics can be observed on the insurance market. New technologies need to be handled with new technical products and analytics solutions.	Handling industrial Internet of Things (IIoT) demand, B2B processes, data-driven underwriting, and pricing	• Commercial efficiency in marketing and sales • Excellence in pricing and underwriting • Cost reduction in claims management • Reduction of expenses in optimizing operations
Finance	• Emergence of fintech • Increasing customer demands for personalized, cheap, and digital financial services	• Legacy technology infrastructure • Regulatory hurdles • Security concerns	• Real-time fraud analytics • Credit-risk modeling • Support for investment decisions • Automated report generation
Healthcare	• Aging population • Increasing demand for personalized and efficient healthcare services	• Finding skilled workers • Cost containment • Meeting regulatory standards	• Personalized medicine and treatment plans • Predictive diagnostics • Automation • Identifying potential cost savings through data analysis
Information technology	IT plays a critical role in driving digital transformation across all industries.	• Keeping up with emerging technologies • Managing data security and privacy concerns	• Process automation • Enhanced cybersecurity • Data-driven decision making
Manufacturing	• Increased cost pressure and higher expectations for quality • Globalization of production and supply chains	• Reducing downtime • Optimizing supply chain • Improving product quality • Reducing waste	• Predictive maintenance • Real-time monitoring of production processes • Optimizing supply chain logistics • Optimizing planning
Transportation	• Decarbonizing traffic • Emerging automated and shared mobility options	• Developing new business models • Addressing regulatory and safety concerns for automated mobility • Improving operational efficiency	• Optimizing transportation routes • Predicting demand • Reducing fleet downtime • Assessing environmental impact • Ensuring safety and compliance

Industry	Why affected	Key challenges	Use case examples
Utilities	• Decarbonization and decentralization • Increasing demand for renewable energy sources and grid stability	• Cost-effectiveness • Grid stability • Integrating renewables into the grid	• Demand forecasting and load balancing • Optimizing energy production and distribution • Grid management

The Consequences for Your Business

In the past, transformations primarily centered on optimizing processes and cutting costs. For example, lean manufacturing and Six Sigma, which were all about improving efficiency and reducing waste, were popular trends during the last industrial revolution. These frameworks were mainly driven from an internal perspective: *what can we do better and cheaper?* No one was asking about the "what" and the "why" of customers' needs.

Today, however, companies need to be laser-focused on customers and their needs, which involves understanding their journey and creating a seamless experience for them. Why? Because it's possible. Thanks to digital technology, companies can easily collect large amounts of data about their customers and analyze it to get insights into their behaviors, needs, and preferences. As a result, customer-centricity has become an essential component of staying competitive in today's market. As we will explain in Chapter 2, analytics is an excellent way to support organizations with managing this transformation—and at the same time is the biggest challenge in itself.

According to a recent Gartner study (*https://oreil.ly/n9msV*), fewer than half of data and analytics leaders reported that their team is actually providing value to their organization. The core problems cited by respondents were that analytics has hit a dead end and that making data-driven decisions often turns out to be "too complicated" or "too technical" for the average employee.

Innovation has consistently shown us that the way to spur mass adoption of any technology is by making it simpler and easier to use. Think back to the early days of computing. The very idea of operating a computer was daunting to most ordinary people. Computers were reserved for technically inclined professionals who could navigate through intricate programming commands. Then came the graphical user interface, the desktop, and—perhaps most pivotal of all—the mouse. These seemingly simple inventions transformed computing from a specialist's arena into everyone's playground. People who were once intimidated by lines of code could now point, click, and drag. These innovations bridged the massive gap between complex technology and the average user.

Similarly, mobile phones used to be for calling and texting. But the introduction of user-friendly touch screens, intuitive interfaces, and app ecosystems transformed them into ubiquitous, indispensable tools for everything from photography to navigation to banking. These shifts in technology demonstrate a fundamental principle: to achieve widespread adoption, technology needs to be intuitive and easy, and it needs to cater to the user's natural inclinations and behaviors.

The analytics world is no different. People who use analytics but who are not data professionals form the majority of the workforce: about 80%. These individuals might never be interested in diving deep into complex data sets, sifting through raw data, or understanding intricate analytics tools. Instead of making them come to the world of data, we need to bring data to them.

There's No Analytics Transformation Without Augmented Analytics

Your authors have a strong opinion: analytics that don't leverage modern techniques like AI and automation will not suffice for running a profitable business. Why? Because you won't be able to scale out analytics to the full workforce of the organization.

Consider the three big ideas of Big Data: volume, velocity, and variety. Traditional analytics mainly tackled volume. With modern tech and affordable storage, we can now also handle massive amounts of data quickly and inexpensively, solving velocity. What businesses are really still struggling with is the third V: variety. The challenge of getting insights from complex data is only getting harder.

Imagine a medium-sized company that gathers a tremendous volume of data from numerous sources: internal systems, customer interactions, social media, third-party providers, and more. Each data source has its own structure, format, and level of reliability, and there's a myriad of data types: structured data such as sales figures, semistructured data like customer feedback, and unstructured data like social media comments.

This complexity is compounded when the company tries to draw insights from its cross-functional data. Say the marketing team wants to understand the impact of a recent promotional campaign on sales. This requires integrating and analyzing data from marketing and sales systems and, potentially, external data, such as market trends and competitor activity, within a certain time frame.

Getting actionable insights here is beyond the capabilities of traditional analytics. You can't figure all of this out in a manual Excel spreadsheet or a static, overloaded business intelligence (BI) dashboard. The company's data is a good representative of today's data: messy, contradictory, and difficult to make sense of.

While technical challenges factor in, the difficulty of making sense of it all is due above all to a lack of analytics maturity. Only a few "data experts" handle these topics—and, in some organizations, the "data experts" are just the best Excel users.

A Data-Driven Culture

Having the best tools and technologies is great, but without the right mindset, they're of little use. A *data-driven culture* is an organizational culture in which data isn't just appreciated—it's *required*. It's a culture where questions like "What does the data say?" are standard. For analytics to truly make an impact, organizations need to foster a mindset that's curious, analytical, and always hungry for insights.

Most companies still lack this kind of data culture, though. Indeed, most still struggle with basic *data literacy*, which Gartner (*https://oreil.ly/uG8gj*) defines as the ability to read, interpret, understand, and communicate data effectively. According to a 2020 Qlik study (*https://oreil.ly/67NS5*), "Only about 24% of business decision-makers, from junior managers to the C-suite, feel fully confident in their ability to read, work with, analyze and communicate with that data." That means that most workers do not yet have sufficient skills to analyze and interpret data.

Fortunately, with the right culture and maturity, organizations can tap the full potential of data to guide decisions and strategy.

The "People Problem" and the Limits of Upskilling

During the first three industrial revolutions, employers had the advantage, with a lot of control over their employees and little competition. Taylorism (*https://oreil.ly/Wdc-4*) could never have happened in a world where employees could easily find alternative work. Today, though, the leading economies (the United States, Europe, Japan, and so on) have a completely different problem: a "people problem." They face an aging population and a shrinking workforce (*https://oreil.ly/jWCK7*). So what does that mean for digital transformation? It's simple: you can't just replace your workforce. Even if your business had the economic power and local labor laws allowed it, there wouldn't be enough human capital available to close the gap.

It's vital to leverage the workforce you have, including people's unique skillsets and contributions. But because a lot of these workers don't have the necessary digital or data-literacy skills, it's essential for every business to create a culture of learning and upskilling. We're not talking about a three-day workshop here: getting people ready for the digital age and staying competitive require hard technical skills as well as collaboration, adaptability, and a continuous-learning mindset.

Upskilling the workforce is therefore probably the largest cultural change that every major business will go through in the 2020s and 2030s. Gartner Research predicts that this cultural shift will make the biggest difference in whether digital transformation efforts succeed or fail.

But here's the hitch: upskilling your workforce probably won't solve your problem. In fact, we believe that most businesses will never succeed in upskilling *all* their workers, especially with regard to data analytics. It's time to accept that, just as not everyone wants to or can be a programmer, not everyone wants to or can be a data person. Instead, we need to empower them with technology, so they can do their jobs better and in a data-driven way. But how is that possible? Some organizations create separate analytics teams, essentially spinning up an internal consulting firm. But this leads to further separating concerns rather than democratizing the company's data capabilities.

The solution is to meet people where they are. Expecting universal advanced analytics expertise across all roles is unrealistic. Instead, give employees tools and interfaces that augment their existing data skills and capabilities. This pragmatic approach recognizes the limits of mass upskilling while still enabling broader data usage.

AA aims to bring analytics to the people, rather than forcing them to become analysts. Just as the mouse made computers user-friendly, AA aims to make data analytics accessible, intuitive, and (most important) actionable for the majority. This is the transition from a data-driven to an insight-driven approach.

Conclusion

You've seen how and why business transformation is happening, and you know that leveraging data and insights at scale is a cornerstone of managing this transformation and staying competitive in global markets.

Scaling analytics across an organization requires more than just upskilling employees and investing in new tools. It requires a paradigm shift in how we approach analytics. Just as the mouse bridged the gap between users and computers, AA can bridge the analytics adoption gap, helping organizations to make better, more informed decisions at scale.

Before we dive deeper into the solution—augmented analytics—let's make sure you understand the need for analytics and the analytics adoption gap. We'll see you in the next chapter!

## CHAPTER 2

The Analytics Problem

As we briefly discussed in Chapter 1, analytics has become an indispensable capability in today's transforming business world. As data volumes grow exponentially, organizations' ability to collect, process, analyze, and glean insights from data is more critical than ever before for staying competitive.

Analytics serves as the bridge that connects raw, unstructured data with meaningful, actionable insights. It enables organizations to shift from relying on intuition and past experiences to making decisions using a data-driven approach. With analytics, organizations can precisely measure outcomes, perform attribution analysis, optimize processes, predict future trends and events, and simulate scenarios. Powerful analytics capacities allow organizations to be more proactive and forward-looking and inform how they develop and improve their products, services, and business models. Analytics is everywhere—or, at least, it should be.

This chapter will help you understand the importance of doing analytics, determine your organization's analytics readiness, and cross the chasm that prevents your company from being data- and, ultimately, insight-driven. But what does "being insight-driven" even mean?

We will explain more about the concept of being data-driven versus insight-driven in this chapter. To be fair, though, there is no single, universal definition of "being insight-driven." What works for a tech startup might not apply to a traditional manufacturing company, given the diverse nature of industries, business models, and companies' sizes, goals, fields of action, processes, and data sources.

Thus, we aren't going to spend our time establishing a one-size-fits-all definition. Figuring out what drives the highest value for your organization will be your personal homework. But we will not leave you to face this challenge alone! Any company can use the general framework provided in this chapter to craft its own analytics journey.

Everything you do should stem from a good purpose. Let's begin by exploring what *your* purpose for analytics could be.

Finding Your Analytics Purpose

Why should your organization learn to use data to make better decisions? There may be many reasons, such as industry competition, a need for accurate forecasting and decision making, or improvements to operational efficiency. Regardless of the trigger, the analytics journey often starts with realizing that leveraging your data can provide valuable insights and a competitive edge. Let's begin by looking at some general triggers that apply across various industries.

Competition and Customer Expectations

Customers today, especially technologically proficient customers, expect personalized experiences and tailored, appointment-based offers that meet their individual needs and preferences. To provide this effectively, businesses must embrace data analytics to identify and improve relevant processes and areas of operation.

Operational Efficiency

Inefficiencies lead to increased costs, so improving overall efficiency is always one of the main drivers for adopting AA. This includes improving processes, workflows, and communications, identifying bottlenecks, eliminating redundancies, and streamlining operations. As you'll learn later in this book, the most impactful changes for your business are not necessarily the extravagant use cases that completely transform everything. Often, it's the small improvements in process and operational efficiency that truly make a difference.

Finding the initial purpose for initiating transformational change is very likely to fall into this field of action. Be aware, understand the processes, and develop your acumen for improving processes with data analytics.

Availability and User Friendliness

In the past, improving data quality was challenging and costly. Analytics tools were difficult to use, computational power was constrained, and limited external data was available. This made it easier for companies to justify their lack of transformational efforts.

But data storage and computation capabilities have advanced a lot. Memory capacity has significantly increased thanks to cloud computing, and the necessary platforms and applications are readily available for use, even by the general public. Companies now can leverage advanced data analytics fully—there's no reason to hesitate. This is called *data liberalization*: the guided open consumption of all data by all stakeholders.

Innovation

Emerging research shows (*https://oreil.ly/53XJA*) that data analytics plays a pivotal role in fostering innovation within organizations. Data can uncover new market trends, customer preferences, and emerging opportunities, prompting companies to innovate new products and services.

It's about learning from historical insights and using data analytics to run simulations and as-if machines to evaluate innovations at the earliest stages of development (e.g., the ideation phase). You will understand this in more detail in Chapter 5 when we introduce the concept of augmented workflows.

Finding your purpose in innovation is essential for many organizations. While operational efficiency focuses on improving current processes, innovation strives to create something new and distinctive that will ensure your company's success—perhaps not today, but in the future.

Regulatory Compliance

Businesses operating in regulated industries, such as healthcare and finance, have the obligation to maintain precise records, conduct audits and reporting, and prove compliance with regulations such as the General Data Protection Regulation (GDPR); Health Insurance Portability and Accountability Act (HIPAA); environmental, social, and governance (ESG) requirements; and others. This obligation often triggers tasks and operations that are necessary but are not directly beneficial to the business model. Allocating valuable resources toward these activities can adversely affect a company's overall performance, so streamlining and supporting these processes is a common purpose for analytics transformations in these industries. In organizations where there is resistance to transformational change or the C-level has little awareness of the importance and value of data analytics, regulatory compliance can be the "trump card" that convinces the leadership.

How to Start Your Analytics Journey

Never start your data-driven journey without a valid goal. Your goal is the foundation for all subsequent activities. Without it, you will inevitably lose focus and lead those activities in the wrong direction. This will cost a lot of money, time, and effort; in the worst cases, it could destroy the trust of colleagues, stakeholders, and customers as well as the reputation of your company.

Your task, then, is to find your purpose and describe it in a way that aligns with your organization's goals and values. We don't want to discourage you now, but it won't be easy: you'll need a very good business understanding of your organization's end-to-end processes, or at least a very good enterprise-wide network that can help you find your purpose and prioritize it in an overarching context. We recommend that you reach out for external support from consultants or experts, activate your network, attend conferences, and talk with other professionals in your industry who have experience with their own data-driven journeys.

Industry Examples

Let's look at how this plays out in a few major industries.

Ecommerce

In the ecommerce industry, the abundance of online data offers valuable information about customer behaviors, preferences, and purchasing trends. Businesses in this sector are primarily focused on improving user experience, boosting conversion rates, and optimizing their product offerings to meet customer demands. They can utilize data to tailor recommendations based on customers' browsing and purchasing histories, leading to improved customer satisfaction and increased sales. They can also use it to enhance pricing strategies and maintain a competitive edge.

Healthcare

The healthcare sector possesses a vast amount of patient information derived from electronic health records and medical devices. Healthcare facilities can employ data analytics to predict patient admission rates, allocate resources efficiently, and decrease wait times. Similarly, pharmaceutical corporations aim to optimize drug-development processes by reducing the time and costs involved. The driving force is the desire to enhance patient care, optimize hospital processes, and facilitate data-informed diagnoses and treatment options.

Manufacturing

Manufacturers aim to enhance efficiency and minimize downtime. The trigger for this sector is often the need to implement predictive maintenance on machinery using sensor data, ensure optimal operational conditions, and prevent breakdowns. Manufacturers also use data-driven insights to optimize production processes, reduce waste, and improve product quality. For example, an aircraft manufacturer might utilize data analytics to predict aircraft engines' maintenance needs, thus reducing flight cancellations and enhancing safety.

Financial Services

The financial sector is motivated by the necessity to mitigate risks, detect and prevent fraud, and optimize investment strategies. This drive is often influenced by regulatory requirements and the goal of strengthening customer confidence. Financial institutions use advanced algorithms based on data analysis to detect and prevent fraud and to gain insights into customer behavior and preferences, so they can offer personalized financial recommendations and product offerings.

Government

Government institutions, particularly those that deliver public services, can benefit greatly from data analytics in various areas. They utilize data for planning, allocating resources, and understanding citizens' needs and preferences. Most are under pressure to ensure transparency regarding accountability, processes, and decisions, so they use crucial data to track and report on government activities, budgets, and outcomes. Using analytics, especially generative AI, can also support policymaking.

Commercial Insurance

The insurance industry's needs include evaluating risk accurately, identifying fraudulent claims, optimizing pricing strategies, and improving internal processes. There is also growing demand from brokers and customers for appropriate, transparent, and efficient insurance coverage in the changing business-to-business (B2B) landscape. Research conducted by McKinsey (*https://oreil.ly/JbKE8*) highlights the transformative potential of advanced analytics in industrial insurance.

Adopting data analytics can revolutionize various aspects of a company's core business and end-to-end insurance processes. For instance, analyzing customer behavior and preferences allows companies to target the right customers with personalized offerings and identify cross-selling opportunities. Data analytics also facilitates market-research analysis, to identify new opportunities in evolving markets or explore avenues for market expansion. Additionally, it enhances the underwriting process by enabling more accurate risk assessment, coverage determination, and pricing strategies.

Companies can enhance their service processes, such as claims management and customer support, by improving efficiency and accuracy. This includes optimizing how they handle claims routing and resolving customer inquiries. By focusing on policy-settlement improvements, insurers can improve workflows and streamline internal processes and overall operations. The potential for commercial insurers is significant, so it's important not to overlook these opportunities to leverage core business capabilities.

Insurance companies can develop innovative services that enhance the insurer-customer relationship and add value, such as informative service portals that serve as a one-stop shop for relevant information. Finally, insurers can leverage their data expertise to create entirely new business models, such as introducing risk-free premium products tailored to new target markets; providing insights and support for site surveys, exposure analysis, and assessments of natural catastrophes and climate-change impacts; and meeting local authorities' ESG requirements.

The Concept of Analytical Maturity

If you've discovered your purpose and recognize the significance of becoming data-driven, congratulations on completing the first vital step in your journey. This is a significant milestone that should not be overlooked or underestimated.

Now that you've determined the "why" of your data-driven journey, it's time to focus on the "what." What are the next steps? Well, that depends where you are. And "where you are" is best described by a concept called an *analytical maturity model*.

An analytical maturity model tries to capture an organization's "readiness" to use its data to get insights and improve business performance. One common framework is the four-tier maturity framework on data drivenness (*https://oreil.ly/0dgIz*), first introduced by Ramnath Vaidyanathan, VP of product research at DataCamp, as the Infrastructure, People, Tools, Organization, and Processes (IPTOP) framework (*https://oreil.ly/sR59Q*). Many companies use this framework in various modified forms. We, too, have modified it for this book. We have incorporated our own experiences; for instance, we have found for ourselves that certain aspects are crucial to succeed in one or another of the individual maturity levels. Thus, the content, descriptions, focus, and even names we present here may differ from those in the original IPTOP framework, though the basic idea is the same.

This framework describes four stages an organization must go through to become data-driven. These four stages, shown in Figure 2-1, are Data Reactive, Data Active, Data Progressive, and Data Fluent.

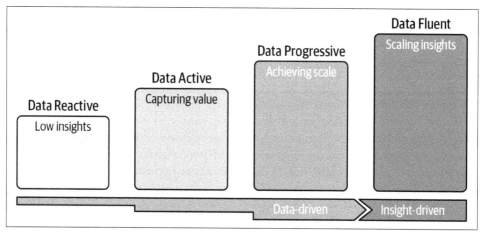

Figure 2-1. The four-tier IPTOP analytics maturity framework (https://oreil.ly/sR59Q)

You can loosely map this four-tier IPTOP framework to the impact of analytics across an organization, as described by the McKinsey maturity model (*https://oreil.ly/kCT20*).

Let's examine the stages:

Stage 1: Data Reactive
> Organizations at this early stage use analytics selectively and on an ad hoc basis. Data is not widely shared or used across the organization. The organization gains some insights but struggles to view data as a valuable asset. Data might be present, but it isn't seamlessly integrated, making data sharing a challenge across various segments. We like to call this stage *Data Reactive*.

Stage 2: Data Active
> Organizations at this stage have a stronger commitment to analytics and capturing value. Frontline staff use data more effectively in their roles. Senior leaders champion the cause, pushing for better data and analytics capabilities. However, data-driven decisions are not yet pervasive. Silos persist across units. The organization, as a whole, still has a few hurdles to overcome. We will refer to this stage as *Data Active*.

Stage 3: Data Progressive
> In this stage, achieving scale with analytics becomes a high priority with dedicated resources. It's no longer a "nice to have" but a "must have." Typically, there's a central unit or department, like an analytics center of excellence, that drives some strategic use cases and encourages data-driven decisions on a larger scale in the organization. Staff are empowered to adopt analytics, and there are typically various analytics training programs in place. We call this stage *Data Progressive*.

Stage 4: Data Fluent
> Organizations in this stage are all in on becoming insight-driven. You might wonder: what is insight-driven versus data-driven? In short, it's a mindset shift of who is able to draw conclusions from and make better decisions based on data (see the sidebar "Data-Driven Versus Insight-Driven" for more information). At this stage, analytics is tightly integrated into operations. Data is a strategic asset. Silos dissolve as functions integrate analytics. Decisions at all levels rely on insights from data. Decision making is insight-driven, and continuous learning is embedded in the organization's DNA. That's what we call *Data Fluent*.

These levels build on one another: you can't reach a level without mastering the previous one.

Data-Driven Versus Insight-Driven

What's the difference between being data-driven and being insight-driven? Let's start with the similarities. Both concepts are about making better decisions based on data. However, by our definition, the difference lies in *who* is making those decisions and what level of data expertise they need to achieve this. Data-driven decisions often involve making decisions based on "raw," complex or lightly preprocessed data, which typically requires a data professional like a data analyst or data scientist to make a valid decision based on that data. Insight-driven decisions, on the other hand, give people with lower levels of data literacy even more preprocessed and semantically enriched data (a.k.a. information) to help them make better decisions.

Consider this simple example:

- In a *data-driven* approach, data analysts would analyze sales data to suggest better inventory decisions.

- In an *insight-driven* scenario, a marketing manager would be presented with the insight that "Product X is popular with 25- to 34-year-olds in the summer" when planning their next advertising campaign, allowing them to make informed decisions quickly and easily.

To recap, data-driven decisions need a higher level of data literacy. They rely on individuals with specialized skills to interpret raw or minimally processed data. This approach is grounded in the direct analysis of data sets, often involving statistical methods, data mining, and machine learning techniques to uncover patterns or trends.

Insight-driven decisions, in contrast, are accessible to a broader audience with varying levels of data literacy. This method emphasizes providing preprocessed, semantically enriched information, making it easier for nonspecialists to understand and act upon that data— something that AA delivers at scale.

Both concepts build on each other, and the journey from data to insight often takes a lot of time and energy, but the goal is not to be data-driven but to be insight-driven. Only insight-driven strategies offer a competitive advantage, as they bring the insights to the players in the company who need them to achieve greater excellence in their processes.

As you scale analytics from one stage of data maturity to the next, you need to consider four key dimensions—*strategy, people and organization, data ecosystem,* and *cultural change*—collectively known as the SPEC framework (Figure 2-2).

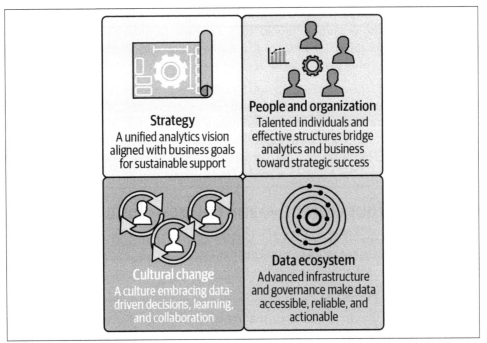

Figure 2-2. The SPEC framework

Let's look at each of these dimensions:

Strategy
> The organization needs a compelling, aligned, enterprise-wide analytics vision and strategy that includes business opportunities, is closely linked to the business strategy, and can be supported efficiently and sustainably.

People and organization
> An effective analytics organization has key functions that successfully bridge analytics and business, filled by people with the breadth and depth of talent needed, and can leverage these effectively to achieve its strategic goals. It adopts operating models that promote analytics across the organization. People are the foundation for creating a culture where everyone understands the value of data and the importance of continuous professional development.

Data ecosystem
> The ecosystem of a mature data-driven organization enables its analytics strategy with best-in-class processes, data architecture and infrastructure, tools, data-security frameworks, and data governance. Data is collected, explorable, reliable, understandable, compliant, and actionable across the organization. People of all skill levels can use various methods to work with data, from common descriptive models to predictive and prescriptive models, on an appropriate platform.

Cultural change

The organization's culture should fully promote flexible, data-driven decision making, exploration, learning, and internal collaboration. Failure is seen as a learning opportunity and a necessary step toward success.

Without each of these levers, no analytical transformation can succeed. They are equally important and partially interdependent. Most importantly, the culture described here can take root only if the business's strategy is aligned with how it applies analytics and if the business fully supports employees in developing their analytical skills. The business's data ecosystem must be sufficient to support the business strategy and the experience level of the workforce.

Determine Your Current—and Future—Data Maturity

To help you evaluate where you stand in your analytical maturity, let's examine the four levels in more detail and how the SPEC dimensions appear in each one.

Stage 1: Data Reactive

Data reactivity is the first and lowest maturity level. A *Data Reactive* organization is beginning to gain insights, but it uses analytics only rarely and in areas with a natural need for data, such as accounting and risk management.

Current status

Analytics capabilities at this stage are limited to basic, standard reporting for management and regulatory authorities. Only certain departments have access to data. The company as a whole has no awareness of the benefits of using data or the importance of data skills. These domains are often starting to really leverage analytics and build a basic level of excellence in their field, but (and this is important to understand) they do not view analytics as strategic leverage or as primarily driven by overarching business demand.

Strategy. At this stage, there is no strategic alignment between business and analytics. Senior management rarely considers analytics in business decisions, and there is no sustainable vision of how to use it for business goals. Analytics is not business led or integrated into the frontline of the business at even a rudimentary level.

People and organization. Because of the loose connection between strategy and analytics, the organization is structured around operationals. There is no dedicated center of excellence for analytics in place to streamline activities and raise awareness of the benefits of using analytics professionally.

Most employees have little or no data literacy. A few colleagues in the business units can perform basic descriptive analyses on an ad hoc basis. People who are directly involved in analytics are experts hired for that purpose, who built their skillsets outside the company and were hired for that knowledge. They are often far away from the core business and can use their own work in limited and specific ways. The problem is often that it is not so much their skills but their vision that is limited. They are often concerned only with how they can use analytics for their own challenges. These experts often use specific tools for a specific purpose that is limited to that case. These tools and techniques are rarely transferred to larger projects where they would broaden the scope of the project and help others realize their own ideas technologically. Most people see the work of analytics experts as a mysterious, arcane, complicated, ultra-specific matter that no one else really understands.

Data ecosystem.   The data infrastructure is limited to absolute necessities at a basic level, with little capacity or investment allocated to it. Unconnected databases are in place to meet basic management and regulatory reporting requirements; reporting is inadequate standard reports and mainly based on limited ad hoc analyses.

Processes are highly departmentalized and are designed with retuned, decentralized legacy tools, with no comprehensive alignment between them. There is no comprehensive data strategy, and no one has addressed the issues of unified infrastructure; a common, coordinated data-governance approach; or centralized, trusted data storage.

Cultural change.   Domains with analytical capabilities are often separated from one another. They operate autonomously, in silos, and use different methods and approaches. No one takes ownership or pushes the organization to expand and unify its analytics capabilities. Decisions are mainly made based on gut instinct. There is no data culture to begin to drive business success through data analytics.

Why is it so important to get past this stage? This is the bare minimum to meet the requirements of analytics. Companies at this stage will have a very hard time sustaining their business success over the long term. It will be difficult for them to expand their capabilities, optimize the organization, or develop new use cases. Such companies are increasingly unattractive to potential employees, especially young employees, who demand modern technologies and processes.

The key levers are people, skills, and culture. A few early adopters can provide momentum, spreading awareness as well as best practices and procedures throughout the company and making others aware of the importance of this issue. It is best if these early adopters are in management or, better yet, at the C-level, to influence the organization and strategically incorporate analytics into the business strategy.

Technological investments in data infrastructure and tools are necessary, but according to Sudaman Thoppan Mohanchandralal, Chief Data Officer at Allianz Benelux (*https://oreil.ly/yF-TQ*), *people* drive the success of data and analytics initiatives.

Moving to the next level

Figure 2-3 outlines some of the fields of action involved in moving to the next level.

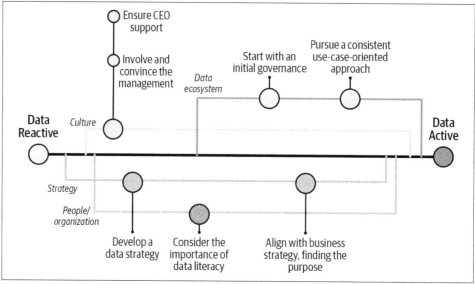

Figure 2-3. Actions on the path from Data Reactive to Data Active

The biggest imperatives include:

Drive change from the top down

Companies with high-performing data initiatives report higher levels of direct executive support. Involve management to drive ownership of this issue and build awareness and support at the C-level. The top-down approach is the key differentiator between companies that are ahead in maturity and those that are far behind, according to a 2016 McKinsey survey (*https://oreil.ly/coMBn*).

Highlight important use cases

Pilot use cases to give people a glimpse of the possibilities. When you achieve individual successes or create advanced insights with data, make those achievements visible to the whole organization. These are the "first lighthouses," and they can win you weighty supporters and fans who will carry their positive impressions into all corners of the organization. Do not underestimate this effect.

Start with initial governance

Get a sense of where things stand in each department or domain. How are the domains working with data? What are their use cases? What kinds of data do they use frequently and for what purpose? What are their processes? Try to identify parallels so that your first initiatives can align certain tasks across domains.

Develop a data strategy

Focus on creating a strategy to achieve a comprehensive data infrastructure. Make sure to address data collection, storage, and processing. Scope out the organization's data-infrastructure requirements and determine what initiatives will be needed to modernize the underlying IT infrastructure to support those requirements. Think about initiatives for tackling data governance and improving data quality.

Emphasize data literacy

The key components of scalable data strategies are learning and professional development. Start by identifying people who have the right mindset to drive change. Assess what capabilities your organization already has and incorporate the skills of subject matter experts (SMEs) to identify and formulate the right requirements. Start small; identify or hire a few professionals who can use analytics to optimize their operations. Take a close look at your IT department; you'll find people with excellent coding and automation skills there.

At this level of maturity, don't overinvest in specialized data professionals like data scientists. In the beginning, you will only need them rarely. Instead, focus on data engineers and analysts.

This brings us to Stage 2: Data Active.

Stage 2: Data Active

At the *Data Active* stage, the organization is starting to capture value from its data. This is the stage of awakening. The organization is still weak in analytical maturity, but it is aware of its past problems and intent on improving. Because leveling up from Data Active to Data Progressive is one of the most important steps in this journey, this section will be especially detailed.

Current status

A limited but slightly increasing number of people outside the usual data-driven domains have the skills and data access to perform analysis and uncover value-driven insights. Early adopters are experimenting with approaches to advanced analytics. There are some pilot models for descriptive analysis, but there is little connection or alignment among them.

Strategy. For the first time, the analytics transformation has full management support. The C-level is fully committed to the relevance and importance of data analytics—a very important milestone. Domains are rethinking their recent approaches and evaluating their data processes to draw out their needs and requirements. The organization now realizes the value of data and analytics for its strategic goals.

People and organization.   A data strategy is in place, but data skills are still heavily concentrated in the BI and data management departments and are not being taught to the entire value chain. The organization is highly centralized—a necessity at this level of maturity to ensure sound data provision and management. Experts in a few different domains are working on the first initiatives to leverage data. Some departments have better data access and can use new infrastructure faster than others, giving them an unfair advantage in driving key strategic initiatives.

Data ecosystem.   A foundational data ecosystem has been established, but only key experts understand how to access data. Data storage is still siloed. The data experts do not yet have a comprehensive data-governance approach or a reliable company-wide data-provisioning system.

Core reporting capabilities are based on solid infrastructure. Most data work is still done with spreadsheets. Initial implementations of advanced analytics tools are in place but are used only for ad hoc analysis; coordinated integrations and appropriate operational approaches to ensure a robust analysis run have not yet been established.

Cultural change.   The company's data culture is in its infancy. Most of the organization is not yet convinced of the benefits of data analysis. Early adopters in forward-looking departments are experimenting with solutions for their use cases but are not working to establish an approach for other departments or eliminating silos, so the gap between different units will become wider. There is no center of excellence.

The main problem at this stage is that, while the organization has begun many initiatives around awareness and infrastructure, it has not developed an organizational model to bring all these loose threads together. Now it needs to establish a center of excellence for data analytics to align the tasks of the ongoing transformation.

Moving to the next level

The path to data maturity is a long one; it usually takes several years to reach the next stage. The organization must still focus on the foundations: investing in infrastructure and developing sponsorship at the management level.

To move to the next level, you'll need to take the actions described in Figure 2-4. These actions are all about firmly anchoring analytics within the organization, including employee involvement and changes in behavior and mindset from the top to the bottom of the organization.

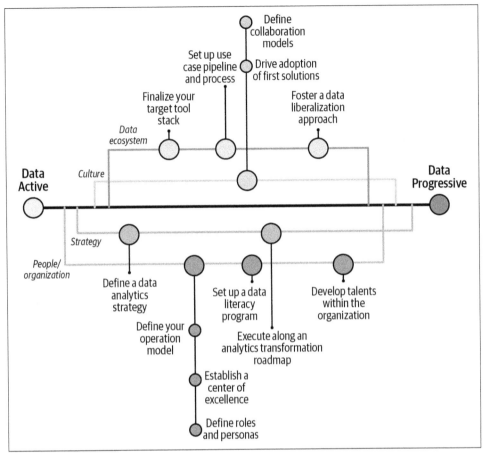

Figure 2-4. Actions on the path from Data Active to Data Progressive

The biggest imperatives include:

Stick to your purpose

Whatever your goal, everything you do must be connected to that goal. Directly linking activities to your defined purpose drives adoption as well as investment and budget decisions. Clearly state why what you're asking for—a specific initiative or investment, an additional employee—is important to achieving the company's goal. Be specific and avoid overgeneralizing. Single out one aspect of your goal, perhaps a strategic pillar in the business strategy, and then explain how your proposal directly contributes to that specific aspect.

Develop an analytics strategy

In stage 1, you developed a data strategy; now it's time to think about an *analytics* strategy. This is where you look at the value of applying data analytics and the cultural implications for your organization. This strategy will be your guide through the transformation. It must be aligned with the business strategy, and it ideally should involve all functional domains and be approved by top management.

First, establish your status quo. What do you need to improve to reach your goals? What are the gaps keeping you from reaching the next level?

Second, define individual action items to make those improvements—again, always with your overarching purpose in mind. Use the SPEC dimensions to bundle them for a better overview and to help you distribute responsibilities if necessary.

Third, organize the tasks into a roadmap with milestones and initiatives. Divide it into three or four phases. To do this, separate the most basic activities that will drive your transformation from the more advanced activities that build from these basics. Define what each phase needs to accomplish to achieve excellence in your overall data-driven journey. Creating a coordinated strategy roadmap not only serves to sort and structure the upcoming transformation but also makes it visible across the company, even to those who are not yet directly affected. Such visibility makes your activities more credible, which will help when you're ready to tackle complicated or difficult tasks that affect already overstretched departments.

Foster an experimental spirit

We noted that at this stage, some experienced practitioners, especially in advanced business domains, are beginning to leverage the newly created data sources and extend them with their own data and information. These experiments often form the nucleus of new approaches and methodologies that can be developed in later stages. The first advanced analytics approaches will probably come from domains close to the core business, but they're likely to be disorganized and siloed. Synergies may be difficult to leverage. However, that doesn't mean you should try to stop or contain them—let people experiment! They are doing valuable groundwork and helping to test the analytics strategy and identify new needs.

Invest in foundational technologies

We just advocated letting the domains experiment with analytics and data. But we recommend two additional measures.

First, involve the business units very early on in exploring and testing use cases: if the business units are part of the solution, that drives adoption and awareness. We have often seen technical departments explore use cases with the best of intentions but often with the belief that they might be of interest to different areas. Then they start implementing something and produce results that no one really needs or ever requested. The way to avoid this pilot trap is to do some research to familiarize yourself with the technology and methodology. All use cases should be purpose-driven. Get buy-in from early adopters; these people exist, so be sure to identify them early.

Second, set up a solid preliminary production runtime. At this stage, your environmental conditions won't be appropriate yet, but if you want to convince business stakeholders to contribute again and help drive the transformation, give them a result they can use.

Don't wait for ideal conditions to get started

You may be wondering when to start working with data to create value. Should you wait until the organizational structure is mature enough to create an appropriate environment? No—our recommendation is don't wait. There is no perfect setup. The organization will always be chasing you, and you'll discover new needs that will later affect how you set up the organizational and technical environment. You can't build an environment from scratch with what the organization *theoretically* knows about data analytics.

Start your journey with what you have. Figure out which methodology is right for you and which tools are appropriate, and get going. For example, if you don't have a cloud-based integrated development environment (IDE) for Python or R, use a local IDE. Just remember that everything you produce needs to be transferable to other runtimes and processes, so make sure your solutions can eventually be aligned with the new setup. Support the organization in moving in the right direction but be open to adopting other infrastructural choices.

Create a center of excellence

One of the most important tasks at this stage is to create a *center of excellence* (CoE) for analytics. This is a dedicated unit that has the necessary vision to organize and manage this important change. In fact, you might need several CoEs working hand in hand: for example, a CoE for data management and BI or a traditional data office with a focus on data governance. At the very least, we recommend establishing a CoE for data analytics.

Different CoEs focus on specific tasks. CoEs do not have to be separate units or departments, but it is typical to have a bundle of capabilities under a separate responsibility. CoEs for BI, analytics, automation, innovation, robotics, generative AI, and so forth are common across the data, analytics, and digitalization space.

The CoE establishes an end-to-end process for managing the transformation and sustainably integrating analytics into the company. It advises and guides the business units through the transformation and supports them in their roles. This unit is usually also responsible for designing the analytics strategy. It has the most leverage and influence on the transformation of any department. (We'll do a deep dive into the CoE in Chapter 4.)

Building analytics awareness must become a habit

Leaders need to show everyone the importance of using data to make decisions. They should explain what it means to be data-driven and who should make decisions based on what data. Ideally, they should take the lead in narrowing the core analytics use cases for their business and fostering a mindset that values facts over guesswork while recognizing that this is a journey, not a switch that can be flipped.

Develop a change-management program

No matter how big your company is or what kind of operational model you will use in the end, during any analytics transformation, something within the organization will change—and you will have to prepare people for this. Every role requires an individual approach to introducing the change. (We'll discuss roles within the transformation in Chapter 4.) This is an extensive task, and you will need support from a transformation-management team. At the very least, you'll need one person who is skilled in change management.

Create an upskilling strategy

Investing in the mindset of the people in your organization is one side of the coin; the other side is developing and shaping their capabilities. Data literacy is key to realizing the full potential of analytics, so investing in education is essential to reaching the next level of maturity. As you define roles, you also need to plan how to upgrade people's knowledge and skills.

You'll need to address three areas of knowledge: business understanding, mathematics and statistics, and the use of tools and programming. Each role will require a different depth and breadth of knowledge in these areas, and thus a different approach. A data analyst will need a much deeper understanding of programming than a knowledge worker in human resources; conversely, that knowledge worker will understand their business more deeply than a data scientist ever will.

You must approach dealing with these different needs properly and take a unique approach to each need. You will see that this will be quite a challenge and a balancing act. Without a well-thought-out strategy, you run the risk of overwhelming some users while not providing enough depth for others to fully perform. The result may be that they lose interest and neglect their strongly required data literacy. Invest the time and capacity to provide appropriate education for each role.

Support collaboration

Even if your workforce has the right mindset and a perfect balance of skillsets, these won't be worth much if you don't create an environment where people can work together. While it's not a new insight that "teamwork makes the dream work," in reality, it's a challenge.

Early maturity in analytics transformation implies lower overall cultural maturity in the organization, which means you're likely to face silos and rifts between different business units, with some ahead and others behind. This is normal. Everyone is focused on doing their jobs, and there's little room for extra activities on the side. But this must be overcome.

One approach is to nurture a spirit of research and curiosity about the field of analytics. You can use this to build the first bridges between the CoE and the business units. In the next chapter, we'll introduce a role that we believe is imperative to this transformation: the analytics translator. But, of course, you need much more than one role for a successful transformation.

It's important to foster collaboration and create a sense of belonging. Put formal mechanisms in place to support a collaborative way of working, such as shared events and processes and strategic alignments. If professionals in other domains are curious about the opportunities that data analytics can offer, keep the barriers to entry low.

Focus on data quality

Data quality will be central to everything you do in the data ecosystem. All the technological improvements and infrastructures you develop won't stop your insights from being worthless if your data is insufficient and incomplete.

In our experience, when people have little awareness of the value of good data, they won't invest time and effort in improving data quality. Even worse, IT input systems often do not take this into account, skipping necessary validators and constraint specifications to avoid annoying users with inputs that seem to be unnecessary. Poor data will slow your transformational process. Data quality contributes indirectly but intensely to the success of your transformation.

Data quality is a subfield of data governance; it encompasses a set of processes, responsibilities, and practices that also covers areas like data security, data compliance, data lineage, and master data management. It's a very broad topic, so divide and conquer. Start with a small, specific data-quality initiative, ideally one that's directly related to one of your pilot use cases. You might analyze only the completeness of the data fields in your data for a specific domain, then set up reporting that shows managers which objects are incomplete and need improvement.

As you do this, be transparent about where you stand on data quality and availability. Show people what efforts you are making to fill in missing data and how improving data quality can drastically change the outcome of a use case. Employees need to be convinced that the data they enter into inventory systems every day will be important in the future.

Modernize your data stack

Building a state-of-the-art tool stack is essential at this stage. Without a solid technical foundation, you cannot convince your company of the possibilities that advanced data analysis offers.

The technology must be holistic to ensure an end-to-end approach. Use a layered architecture to separate data collection from data transformation and reporting. Consider alternative approaches to data processing: you don't have to stick with your old transformation and reporting tools just because that's how you've always done it. Reporting, from online analytical processing (OLAP) reports to modern dashboards, also seems like an evolution, but in the end, you'll need a much broader approach to meet the demands ahead. You'll need analytics applications that fuse traditional software applications with analytic computing capabilities and that communicate and consume data in new ways. Will you need to deliver data in unusual ways? If so, how about using API infrastructures in addition to the usual SQL interfaces in your new data warehouse?

Consider, too, whether a data warehouse is the best solution for your needs. In terms of familiarity and ease of data access, sure; in terms of rapid deployment and flexibility to handle unstructured or semistructured data, maybe a data lake, data lakehouse, or data mesh approach would be better. We're not in a position to say; you'll need to assess your organization's needs to build your tool stack. For getting deeper in touch with this topic, we recommend the book *Deciphering Data Architectures* by James Serra (O'Reilly).

Cloud-based systems are currently standard; data lakes with programmatic pipelines in, for example, Python are a recommendation from our side. If a data warehouse should be part of the systemic solution, really consider if you need extract, load, and transform (ELT) or extract, transform, and load (ETL) tools or if you could solve the same problems with programmatic approaches. Try to make yourself independent from any particular vendors and stay flexible. Their tools that promise an all-encompassing solution come with the price in that they end up being the legacy systems of tomorrow. Instead of investing in expensive all-in-one analytics tools, invest in people who can develop and code. Your analytics infrastructure will need runtimes and IDEs for professional analytics development.

As you look for the best option for data storage, keep lower operations and IT costs in mind. Consider next-generation data hosting, self-service tools, and automated data-quality routines.

See this transformation as the next stage of your company's evolution

Honestly, this is our favorite piece of advice. As we mentioned earlier, do everything with a purpose. If you are in some way responsible for driving this whole data-driven journey, then it's especially important to do it with passion. Your authenticity and ownership are the final touches that will make the transformation a success. People will associate you and your team with it. You are the face of the transformation and its role model, so do everything you do with conviction. If you're not ready for that, give this responsibility to someone else.

Don't underestimate the impact: transforming into a data-driven company is one of the most important changes a business can experience. What you do here will be your legacy!

This shift from Data Active to Data Progressive is absolutely essential. Table 2-1 summarizes the key actions you need to take.

Table 2-1. Key actions in transitioning from Data Active to Data Progressive

Strategy	• Align business strategy with analytics initiatives. • Define your analytics strategy and roadmap. • Start with the first use cases. • Create a execution infrastructure for use case.
People and organization	• Define roles in the transformation. • Determine needed upskilling and awareness for different roles. • Define an operation model for your organization. • Establish a CoE.
Data ecosystem	• Extend your data-quality efforts. • Set up your target technology tool stack. • Establish a reporting/frontend target landscape. • Foster data liberalization. • Extend your data ecosystem's analytics capabilities beyond the common BI infrastructure.
Cultural change	• Create an inclusive, collaborative environment. • Focus on understanding, conviction, adoption, and value.

Stage 3: Data Progressive

Becoming a *Data Progressive* organization is a real achievement and an important milestone.

Current status

In this stage, the majority of your organization is participating in the analytics transformation of and deriving sufficient value from data for day-to-day business decisions. You've laid the foundation for further development by building your data ecosystem. Data is largely accessible, and you've established a pipeline of use cases as well as an organizational model that enables all roles to reap the benefits of analytics.

Data Progressive organizations have at least one data-savvy person on every team, regardless of that team's function, who can analyze data, report on it, reason with it, and center use cases around it. Data is accessible, well categorized, and easy to find. Data is seen as a strategic asset, and there is broad awareness of analytics, but data literacy is not yet enterprise-wide.

Strategy. All business units are aware of the benefits of data analytics and are hiring (or considering hiring) people with the right skills to use data analytics for their business needs. Managers, in particular, understand the changes that the transformation will bring and are encouraging their teams to be open to adopting and applying data analytics.

Data analytics has a place in all business strategies. The company has a compelling, aligned, enterprise-wide analytics vision and strategy. These are fully focused on business opportunities, linked to business strategy, and supported by a quantified use-case roadmap. Overall, data is seen as a strategic asset, and analytics awareness is spread throughout the organization. Data liberation is an established concept in your organization, and all business units have agreed to promote the open exchange of data across silos, where it can be used in the business and where it is needed for decision making.

People and organization. The organization as a whole is well prepared to move to the final stage of maturity. There is a CoE that supports the business with analytics across multiple dimensions. It helps the business units to implement use cases, progress in analytics maturity, and drive the analytics transformation. Each area has at least one data-literate person who can apply analytics to their area. Data literacy is a company-wide concept; in theory, all employees could participate in analytics, but in reality, only a limited number are truly involved and able to make data-driven decisions.

Data ecosystem. Data is largely accessible, and the data infrastructure is mature. Most data is easily discoverable, understandable, or actionable across the organization. You have a modern tool stack and the foundation for a framework that democratizes working with data. Data governance has become more mature, and processes have been established to ensure data quality. Most data is compliant with regulations, and data lineage, master data management, and a data catalog have been implemented. The organization has developed descriptive, predictive, and prescriptive data models, using a variety of methods and techniques and following best practices in model development. A use-case approach is in place to support efficient discovery and implementation of the most impactful analytics projects, adding selective, domain-specific value. (We'll discuss this more in Chapter 5.)

Cultural change. A Data Progressive enterprise has mature processes for streamlining data-talent workflows but is still creating ways of working that will operationalize and effectively use analytics cases. As a result, the processes for scalable data work are not yet transferable across the enterprise. There's still plenty of silo thinking, but a significant number of employees have the right mindset to drive change once the environment fully supports the final stage of maturity.

Moving to the next level

Here are the main fields of action to move into the next stage, data fluency:

Improve data quality and governance

Liberalizing your data comes with the burden of investing in data governance and, in particular, data quality. The more you use data, the more important it is that people are confident in that data. Only with that confidence can you move beyond gut-based decision making.

To convince people to contribute, invest in comprehensive data-quality processes and make it easier for business users to troubleshoot quality issues. You may need a mix of voluntary and mandatory mechanisms to ensure a minimum level of data quality. Consider implementing a reward system, rigorous monitoring, or even restricting a business unit's ability to act if its data quality falls below a certain threshold.

For example, if an insurance company's data on customers' risk characteristics is of poor quality, the company may need to plan for an additional reinsurance buffer. That company might give individual business units less capacity to write new business until data quality is up to standard. However, don't involve business users so much in correcting past data-quality problems that they become overwhelmed by the effort and fail to see the benefits. Good processes can help you to automate data-quality improvements on the basis of experience or external information.

Invest in operationalization capabilities and tooling

As more business processes and products use advanced analytics, ML models, and generative AI (gen AI), it's important to continuously monitor, integrate, version, and explain these models. DevOps and MLOps capabilities need to be considered as analytics is still evolving. Building models in production is increasingly important to scale analytics, and you'll need ops capabilities to ensure that your data products and solutions operate reliably and sustainably in production.

It's important to think of analytics solutions as software products. A reliable runtime is even more critical than developing the most accurate model; how available your solutions are will determine how many people adopt and use them. Allocate resources to hire new data professionals on a wide range. This is when DevOps professionals and software developers should join the CoE, alongside data engineers, analysts, and scientists. Stage 3 is the appropriate time to bring them in; earlier in the process, you won't have the culture, ecosystem, and data availability in place to realize the full benefit of their work.

Make data easy to find

Your data needs to be not only collected and accessible but also trustworthy, reliable, actionable, and easily discoverable, especially for nonprofessional data users. You'll typically achieve that by using an enterprise data catalog. A great resource for this is *The Enterprise Data Catalog* by Ole Olesen-Bagneux (O'Reilly). Discovery and cataloging tools were born out of the growing pains of Data Progressive organizations. These tools provide powerful search capabilities; comprehensive views of record ownership, lineage, metadata, structure, and interoperability; and programmatic capabilities to scale data-quality checks and descriptions and drive enterprise-wide key performance indicator (KPI) calculation rules and patterns. However, these tools are of most interest to users with strong analytical acumen in each area. They will not help activate and leverage the analytics maturity of most nonprofessional data users in your organization, but they will help those who are able to in some way apply analytics themselves. Later, we will discuss whether it is really necessary to actively engage all knowledge workers in data analytics.

Lower the barriers to working with data

Provide data liberalization frameworks for your data professionals and aspiring analysts from the business units. For example, the CoE at HDI Global has developed an extensive infrastructure of R packages that provide a streamlined way to move and transform data around the data infrastructure as well as repetitive data preparation and calculations, algorithms, logging mechanisms, UI optimizations, visualization themes, R Markdown templates for different types of reports, and custom functions to optimize different parts of analytical processes and data workflows, including internal knowledge management. This doesn't replace the standard data pipelines; it just helps the CoEs handle data and algorithms for dedicated business requirements quickly and efficiently.

Integrate analytics in your business workflows

Spoiler alert: this is the real focus of the book. Applying data analytics to your workflows is the difference between Data Progressive and Data Fluent.

Breaks and interruptions in the workflow of knowledge workers will always prevent you from realizing the full potential benefits of data analytics. In all of your infrastructure design decisions, consider how to integrate analytics results into your software and tools. For example, include web API infrastructure for analytics delivery in your data ecosystem's design to enable easy access to insights.

But you'll also need to put a lot of effort into driving the interaction in the surrounding systems. You'll need agile capacity in development teams as well as strong ownership on the business side—leaders willing to push the organization to integrate analytics solutions. So you need to build strong business ownership.

Roll out organization-wide data training fit for all data personas

At the earlier maturity levels, we discussed data literacy as a mandatory key initiative. There, we focused on analytics awareness for managers and data literacy for interested business users. At the Data Progressive stage, however, you need to address *all* roles. That means the majority of employees in your organization: the people who incorporate analytics and insights into their daily decisions. You will need specific, tailored formats for their training, education, and professional development. Consider breaking this group down into more specific personas by role and domain.

Be aware that data training is not enough to make this group data-driven and data literate. A much broader concept—and maybe even the opposite of training—will get them there, as you'll understand when you read Chapter 3.

In addition, invest in training your data experts. Keep them up-to-date on new methods and technologies but also help them bolster their weaker skills. In particular, teach them how to drive adoption. In our experience, data experts are generally highly motivated and, at best, true experts in their field. But to truly become a data-driven company, everyone needs to broaden their skills and contribute to the transformational capabilities. Sure, you will have established a role bridging analytics and business, but transforming a business is not a one-way street; all stakeholders need to change to this goal, so driving adoption is an issue that affects all roles.

Encourage a culture of learning

Companies need to reward a culture of continuous development and contribution to the analytics journey if they are to build and sustain data literacy and responsibility across all analytics functions, according to McKinsey research (*https://oreil.ly/cRIo4*). This includes creating safe spaces for active learning and development; encouraging novel, data-driven approaches to problem-solving; and promoting hands-on learning.

This also means rethinking the roles of managers. The data analytics transformation requires employees to develop themselves and take new professional paths, and for this, they need the support of their managers and leaders. This calls for the managers to adopt a different mindset. In a retraining world, a manager empowers employees to do things on their own.

Measure data competencies over time

Find ways to track and measure learning activities in your organization. Don't just focus on new skills like mathematics, statistics, and programming—focus on business knowledge, too. For analytical insights to be valuable, the problem statement has to be clear, and the people seeking insights (including the analytics professionals) must be able to understand the underlying business case. A skills and knowledge management database can be useful for hosting and organizing learning as well as for monitoring and analyzing people's skills; here, knowledge graphs are the perfect technology for analyzing skills. People and skills are connected in massive graphs, and it is immediately possible to see who in the organization has a particular skill.

Conduct regular assessments to track which skills are becoming more sophisticated or spreading throughout the organization. Following on from the reward system, think about using ranks in data roles and perhaps in business personas to outline a development path that people can follow to improve their skills and increase their employability. Ranks can act as a motivator and make increasing skill levels transparent.

Consider decentralizing

As data liberalization and data literacy mature, you need to consider a more decentralized approach to data analytics. A CoE with a strong centralized approach is best at the Data Active stage. To add real value and get the whole organization involved and participating in analytics, you need to loosen the reins while maintaining a strong CoE. You'll need a strategic roadmap on how to implement decentralization. We'll discuss this further in Chapter 4.

Let's step up now to the pinnacle of the maturity model: data fluency.

Stage 4: Data Fluent

In a *Data Fluent* organization, everyone knows how to access, use, and leverage the data they need to make the most of their actions. This could mean:

- Analysts using analytics languages to streamline complex data workflows
- Marketers using a gen AI language model as they create an ad campaign announcement
- Sales managers accessing BI dashboards to draw conclusions about a campaign's progress
- Executives pulling insights from a knowledge repository to make data-driven decisions
- Underwriters getting enhanced insights within their underwriting tool
- Executives bringing new analytics ideas and taking a clear ownership position
- Data professionals using the latest tools and techniques to further liberate data and drive innovation across the organization

What unites these individuals is a shared belief in and commitment to the importance of using data to make decisions and solve problems.

Current status

At this stage of full maturity, data analytics has become part of the enterprise-wide cultural DNA. Self-evident collaboration is overtaking siloed thinking, and integrated, insight-driven decision making is becoming the norm.

Strategy. Data analytics is a vital component in any business strategy, serving as a solid foundation. Analytics initiatives aim to achieve the highest standards of performance. The organization has developed operational models with short, efficient iterative processes that allow it to adapt swiftly in response to emerging opportunities and techniques. The business strategy positions the analytics transformation as a catalyst for collaboration; it fosters a culture of ownership and encourages clearly defined responsibilities. Using analytics is a mandatory capability in all business domains.

People and organization. Silos are being dissolved in favor of a collaborative mindset. All employees, especially new hires, in all business units are expected to have an analytical mindset and strong awareness of and proficiency in analytics. Their skills and advanced data literacy allow them to leverage and take clear ownership of data analytics products. The organization encourages decentralized approaches and actions as well as a decentralized operating model (see Chapter 4 for more on that). The CoE is more and more a sparring partner and consulting unit, empowering the business domains to define their positions and roles in the decentralized model.

Data ecosystem. In the organization, there is a shift from taking advantage of *data liberalization*, which is defined as the guided open consumption of all data, to an approach of *data democratization*, where especially nontechnical business units take responsibility for acting as data providers with commitments and governance. People outside IT and the CoE are using and leveraging the data technology ecosystem. A distributed but highly networked data infrastructure is in place, with corresponding accountability and governance. There are company-wide standards for how to handle data, processes, calculations, and results.

For all new data sources, the standard approach is to use operationalized, end-to-end data processes, event streaming, and automated, self-service data provisioning. Taking care of data quality is now a habit. Processes and data are fully documented in the data catalog and lineage inventory systems. People from all business units use knowledge repositories as reliable resources to enrich domain-specific insights.

Cultural change. Fostering collaboration and empowerment and breaking down silos results in an environment where employees from all departments can take ownership of data and insights. This proactive culture values continuous learning and adaptability, feeding into the organization's ability to respond quickly to changes. Thanks to this cultural shift, the organization faces challenges with a more open mindset. People see transformations as important and necessary aspects of the organization's development.

Moving to the final stage: Crossing the analytics chasm

While a lot of companies eventually make it to stage 2, Data Active, only some manage to reach stage 3, Data Progressive. And very few companies get to stage 4, Data Fluent. Although it is hard to get exact research data for this phenomenon, it's something that we observe over and over again. And the TDWI Business Intelligence Maturity Model (*https://oreil.ly/S180Q*), which can be loosely mapped to the four-stage maturity model we're using in this book, further supports this observation by the stylized frequency distribution of how many companies are present in each stage, as shown in Figure 2-5.

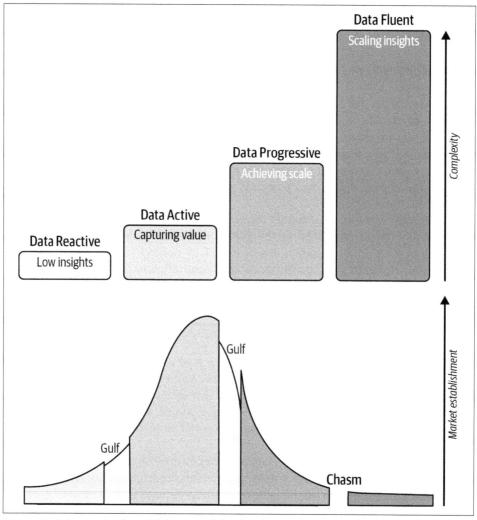

Figure 2-5. Impact and establishment of the four steps of analytical maturity

Even though this model focused more on the maturity of BI solutions at the time, it revealed that few companies have gone the last mile and brought their maturity to excellence. It takes effort to approach and successfully master each stage.

Now, the important thing is not so much how many companies are in what stage. The important takeaway is that there are three gaps that become increasingly harder to cross, the more you increase your analytics maturity levels.

Why is that? Because of the growing complexity of analytics adoption across the broad majority of your workforce. The more people you need to "win" internally, the harder it is to foster this change. This, by the way, doesn't apply only to analytics, but to every technological innovation.

So far, the standard approach for organizations to reach stages 2 and 3 has been *self-service BI*. Self-service BI extensions became popular as a way to improve users' overall understanding, use, and adoption of analytics delivery. Self-service BI also became an important milestone in a company's pursuit of excellence in analytics and thus business operations.

But self-service BI is always limited by users' level of analytics maturity. If users are not skilled (or willing) enough to do analytics, even the best BI tool won't make a change. What's more, moving to a self-service BI system is always a break in the current workflow that most business users simply don't want to make. Instead, they want insight at their fingertips, no matter what process or software they are in: writing an email, conducting a web conference, creating an order document, or pricing a customer contract.

Let's give some special attention to the last gap: the analytics chasm between stage 3 and stage 4. Why is this chasm so hard to bridge? Two things come into play here.

First, although the goals of the higher levels are defined, the path to getting there becomes increasingly unclear and abstract, no doubt in part because the absolute level of maturity cannot be precisely determined, and there are far fewer good practices to describe it. While reaching stage 3 didn't require much more than having and following a proven checklist, getting to stage 4 requires much more creativity, specific to your own goals and circumstances.

Second, you're dealing with a lot more people. If the framework not only indicated maturity levels but also visualized complexity, the gradients per stage would be clearer as the broad mass of users are now part of the analytical journey. The transition from the first to the second stage is very shallow, as the focus here is largely on data and infrastructure, which run mostly in the background. As people and processes as well as organizational changes come more into focus, the transition to the third stage becomes more ambitious and requires a more holistic and broader strategic approach. However, reaching the final stage is the biggest challenge, and bridging the gap requires new methods that have probably not yet been considered in the aforementioned approach.

To reach the last level of maturity, organizations need to find ways to enhance their entire decision-making process. It's critical to understand that this does *not* mean replacing self-service BI; rather, it's about *enhancing* self-service BI with another layer that leverages modern technology: *augmented analytics*, which we will explore further in the next chapter.

Conclusion

In this chapter, you learned about the importance of setting clear goals for your data-driven transformation and finding your analytics purpose. You should be able to locate your organization in one of the four stages of maturity and articulate what's needed to move to the next stage.

Augmented analytics, in particular, will be the key that unlocks stages 3 and 4, moving you closer to achieving mass analytics adoption and crossing the analytics chasm in your organization. It is the shift from data-driven to insight-driven decision making that you must make to finally reach the last level of analytics maturity. With that in mind, it's time to dive deeper into the concept of AA and see how it works in detail.

## CHAPTER 3

Understanding Augmented Analytics

We'll start this chapter by taking our definition of AA, as introduced in Chapter 1, and breaking it down into its key components. We'll then give you an in-depth introduction to the concept, with a special focus on empowering analytics users. You will learn what AA is, its benefits for business, its limitations, and how you can apply it to your workflows. You'll also discover how AA can address different types of bias. We'll finish by introducing you to some of the core technologies that make AA possible.

Don't skip this chapter! It lays the foundation for the rest of this book.

Definition

To recap, here's our definition of AA:

> Augmented analytics means adding value by providing *people* with access to *technology* that gives them the *analytical leverage* they need to accomplish the *business task* at hand in a *better way*.

Let's unpack the five key components:

People
> While most definitions of AA are technology-driven, we believe that AA is essentially about people. It makes people more successful by building on the inherent strengths that set human beings apart from any machine in the world: our unique experiences, creativity, and intelligence. A process where no human is involved can never, according to this definition, truly be an AA process.

Technology
> Although people are the driving force behind AA, technology is what makes it possible. We will talk about the different kinds of technology used in AA, which include (but are not limited to) artificial intelligence (AI) and automation.

Analytical leverage

AA helps people gain insights that would be difficult, if not impossible, for them to uncover from the data on their own. The leverage it provides is typically some combination of the following four levers:

- Improving your analytical thinking process
- Analyzing more data
- Analyzing data faster
- Making better predictions

AA's analytical leverage depends on the context, including the task at hand and the user's level of analytical maturity and data literacy. AA isn't a one-size-fits-all solution; it focuses on specific tasks, problems, or opportunities where it can provide value. The trick is to find just the right amount, the optimal "dose" of AA, to *enhance* the human decision-making process rather than replace or overwhelm it. We call this "finding the sweet spot": not too much, not too little, but just right. It's like choosing the right vehicle for a trip: some trips need a plane while a bicycle might be fine for others.

Business task

We look at AA from a business perspective. AA helps accomplish a *business task* in a given workflow—that is, a task that is value-driven and typically tries to answer a business question or help solve a business problem. This distinction is important because real-world business data is typically messy, contradictory, and hard to understand. AA treats these facts as the rule, not the exception.

Better way

The analytical leverage AA delivers must provide a better way for people to complete their business tasks. If there's no "better," there's no point in using AA. "Better" can mean many different things, but typically it boils down to completing the business task faster and/or with more reliable, less biased insights. We will further expand on both ideas later in this chapter. But we can't stress it enough: AA is *not* about replacing humans but rather *empowering* them to make better decisions with data.

"Technological overkill" is real. If you expose people with low analytical skills or low data literacy to heavily augmented AI technology, they may easily produce low-quality results. For example, say you have a salesperson who has never looked at a static report before. If you give them access to an overwhelming amount of customer sales data and the latest AutoML tool, they're likely to feel lost. If they produce results, they may do so on "autopilot," without doing the critical thinking needed to evaluate whether the prediction is actually valid and useful. What's more, research has shown (*https://oreil.ly/fzb9U*) that relying too much on technology in making decisions can decrease people's critical-thinking skills and overall intelligence.

Finding the right "sweet spot" of augmentation may be difficult in the beginning. One goal of this book is to help you find it.

The Five I's of Augmented Analytics

We believe there are five key traits that describe effective AA: it is insightful, integrated, invisible, indispensable, and inclusive. Let's find out what these traits mean:

Insightful

AA is *insightful*. It's not about presenting raw data but rather offering smart, actionable insights derived from that data. AA should be able to learn from past data, recognize patterns, and predict trends. This level of intelligence means that users don't just get information but also knowledge—knowledge that is actionable and can lead to better business outcomes. It's the difference between knowing how many people visit your website and understanding why they visit, when they're most likely to visit, and what you can do to increase those numbers.

Integrated

AA cannot exist in silos. To be genuinely effective, it needs to be *integrated* seamlessly into the business's existing workflows, tools, and business processes. An integrated system ensures that data is consistent and reliable and can be accessed easily across the company.

Consider the collaboration between marketing and sales teams, both of which rely heavily on analytics. Using an integrated analytics tool helps ensure that both teams are working off the same data, reducing discrepancies and enhancing their collaboration. This can decrease or eliminate the gap between analyzing data and taking action based on the insights derived from it.

Invisible

The best technologies are those that users don't even realize they're using. This is the essence of *invisibility* in AA. AA should be so deeply embedded into daily tasks and routines that users don't feel like they are using an external tool. This ensures smooth adoption and minimizes people's resistance to a new tool. Much like spell check automatically corrects errors while you type, making the process seamless, AA should work behind the scenes, providing insights and solutions without users needing to initiate or command it actively.

Indispensable

For a company to adopt any technology at scale, that technology has to be seen as *indispensable*. It should be so beneficial that users can't imagine going back to a time before it existed—much as people now rely on their smartphones every day. This means that AA needs to provide consistent value, in the form of time saved, better insights, or improved decision making. Over time, as users see AA's tangible benefits, it becomes an essential part of their daily routine.

Inclusive

Adopting AA transforms the whole organization and everyone in it, not just the data-savvy people. For the first time, everyone can participate in data analytics. We will dive deeper into this in the rest of the chapter.

Why are these traits so important? It's simple: practice has shown that if your organization doesn't nail at least three out of the five, you won't be able to reach organic mass adoption.

Overcoming the Limitations of Traditional Analytics Approaches

Decades ago, data analytics primarily meant dealing with descriptive BI solutions, which provided insights that were easy to understand. As technical capabilities matured, however, organizations needed much more sophisticated solutions to gain a competitive advantage. Simulations, classification algorithms, complex decision interdependencies, and predictive forecasting all promise to help us (and they do), but they are difficult to understand and accept.

Traditional approaches to analytics have inadvertently fostered a divide between data experts and everyone else, turning data analysis into an exclusive domain. This divide often leaves business professionals—who drive day-to-day operations and strategic decisions—at a disadvantage. Although they can use analytical tools to a certain extent, they can face barriers when delving into more sophisticated solutions. New analytical solutions offer deep insights, but the complexity of these tools requires active participation as well as a level of data literacy that often prevents business professionals from seamlessly integrating the tools into their regular workflows. As a result, business people are frequently left disconnected from the decision-making process.

Data literacy and employee empowerment address this to some extent, but the full effect is limited! Most people probably do not *want* to be actively data-driven, not because they don't like it in principle but because it means distraction, effort, and change.

This is where AA comes in. According to our definition, it's not just an extension of existing analytics capabilities: it's a paradigm shift in how we approach analytics across the organizational hierarchy. It embeds analytics into the tools and processes that business people use every day to make decisions, in subtle, intuitive, and unobtrusive ways. For data-driven action to become a habit, people need to be exposed to it; the idea is to make people implicitly data-driven by helping them make better and more informed decisions. To do this, we must "inject" analytics into their actions without them being explicitly aware of it, or at least without disturbing or distracting them.

This seamless integration means that analytics becomes a natural part of decision making in familiar environments rather than an external, often cumbersome add-on to daily tasks. It's about *augmenting*, not changing, workflows to make data insights accessible and actionable to everyone, regardless of their data literacy. Only when we connect the analytics, the people, and the workflows through augmentation can we achieve data fluency, the final stage of analytics maturity (Figure 3-1). Each individual maturity level requires focusing on a specific enabler in order to reach the next level. Augmenting workflows paves the way for the final stage.

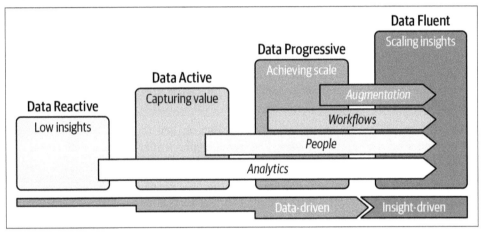

Figure 3-1. Enablers for each maturity stage

To meet business people where they are, AA needs to be deeply integrated into their everyday workflows. Chapter 5 will explain in greater detail how to do this. But as a quick preview, here's what we mean by *augmented workflows* and how they are made possible.

Augmented Workflows

An *augmented workflow* describes a business process that is enhanced using AA and that *meets the user where they are*. Very often, this augmentation is made possible by analytics, automation, and AI.

Let's give an example. Imagine a sales manager discussing a new sales strategy with some colleagues from marketing. The default process for this conversation might be a Microsoft Teams chat. Within that conversation, the sales manager realizes they need some data to make a better decision: for example, to know which sales campaign they should prioritize.

In a classic analytical setting, this question would require the sales manager to either ask the data team or pull data from a self-service BI system, depending on the organization's analytical maturity. In an augmented workflow, however, the sales manager could simply summon an AI-powered marketing KPI assistant into the Teams chat to help answer questions. There's no need to leave the current workflow because the necessary information is directly pulled in. This process is largely enabled by AI (in this case, generative AI), which handles the conversation, as well as by augmented frame engines, which deliver the actual data and insights for specific business objects.

Augmented Frames

Augmented frames is a concept that provides relevant information for a specific user persona in a specific workflow. It provides the right data in the right place at the right time. This concept is essential to enabling various types of augmentation of business workflows.

In this example, the company would define an extended frame (a list of campaign IDs) and send it to a *frame engine*. The frame engine would return a defined set of performance metrics for these campaigns as output to the workflow.

Augmented frames rely heavily on frame engines that process data based on defined frames. For example, a frame engine could formulate a comprehensive campaign description in natural language based on stored attributes of a particular campaign defined by passing a campaign ID. Generative AI may play a role, but this particular example of an augmented frame is primarily about automation: reliable data processing at scale. Thus, engines are mainly used to perform insights based on calculations on structured data, which we will explain in detail in Chapter 6.

The Benefits of Augmented Analytics

With augmented workflows, analytics users do not need to:

- Be aware of their information needs
- Know where to find this information
- Obtain the required information
- Process or analyze the information in depth
- Actively incorporate information into the workflow when required

The only requirement is knowing how to interpret the information to leverage it effectively, as shown in Figure 3-2.

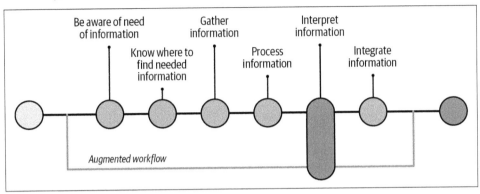

Figure 3-2. Augmented workflow efficiency

The benefits of AA-enriched workflows include:

Simplifying complex data analysis
Augmented workflows simplify the process of analyzing complex data and make the data accessible to users who do not have specialized data-analysis skills. This goes beyond descriptive insights or visualizations to include automated data processing, predictive analytics capabilities, and help interpreting complex interdependencies. The predictive insights these workflows provide can inform more strategic decisions.

Integrating analytics into daily workflows
Integrating analytics directly into the tools and systems that business users already use every day is the key capability. This seamless integration means that analytics users can leverage data insights without significantly changing the way they work. By making analytics more accessible, AA liberates data, allowing a broader range of employees to engage with and benefit from data-driven insights.

Improving decision making
AA tools enable customization to ensure that the insights provided are relevant to the specific needs and roles of different analytics users, increasing the practical value of analytics. This uncovers insights and patterns that may not be obvious, giving new perspectives and aiding in strategic planning. In addition, automating various aspects of data analysis reduces the risk of human error and bias, resulting in more reliable and accurate insights.

Improving time efficiency, increasing productivity, and standardizing
> Automating many aspects of data analysis saves time and increases business users' productivity. This allows them to focus on interpreting insights and making decisions rather than on gathering information and performing the mechanics of data analysis. Additionally, augmented workflows ensure that all knowledge workers have the same access to information, regardless of the effort they are willing to expend to make the best possible decision. This creates greater continuity in decision making, no matter who is involved.

Fostering data-driven culture and literacy
> Widespread use of AA fosters a data-driven culture by making data a central part of the decision-making process across levels and responsibilities. While AA does not require users to be data experts, its user-friendly nature helps the organization adopt new insights and improve overall data literacy by exposing more employees to data in a manageable way.

Encouraging business-level human–AI interaction
> This is a new dimension with a focus on human–AI interaction, which in the common definition of AA is limited to interactions between analytics professionals and AI for professional tasks. Here, however, the shift is about how AI in AA can interact with business users in ways that enhance their capabilities. Examples include conversational interfaces, intelligent recommendations, and adaptive learning systems that respond to user queries and behaviors.

Analytical leverage helps people generate insights that they may not have been able to generate themselves because of uncertainty, a lack of familiarity with data or information contexts, or a simple lack of time. Applying this analytical leverage can lead to several advantages for users. This section looks at some of them in detail.

AA Gives Nonexpert Users a Better Experience

AA tools with intuitive interfaces allow business users to obtain and understand insights effortlessly, even if they lack expertise in data analytics. Even traditional BI functions, such as descriptive and diagnostic analysis, don't require specialized knowledge (like SQL) anymore! The BI landscape is now dominated by overhauled dashboards that let even those with meager data literacy comprehend KPIs. However, this approach is no longer adequate: businesses require purpose-driven data analysis to convey their stories effectively. AA enhances those analytical capabilities.

This improved experience is not only limited to analytics users. Even more technical professionals can benefit from it. With the advent of new IDEs, developers, report designers, and data analysts can seamlessly incorporate domain-specific languages and models with intelligent features to help them manage and analyze information more efficiently.

Easily accessible cloud and database systems and no-code/low-code tools have revolutionized enhanced feasibility and help business professionals make informed decisions. These resources are even more user-friendly than professional analytics software that uses popular programming languages, such as R, Python, and Julia.

Automated Integration Provides More Complete Insights

AA can help businesses handle the growing volume and complexity of data by enabling them to process data from various sources, including databases, spreadsheets, and cloud systems. Variations in formats, structures, and metadata can make analyzing such data challenging.

Automated analytics tools can integrate these disparate data sources to create a unified view of the data and gain insights from all available sources. These tools often achieve this by intelligently interpreting *meta-attributes*: descriptive information about a data set's underlying structure and semantics. Automating this integration avoids manual intervention and expands the scope of the data.

With its ability to quickly process large and complex data sets, AA can help uncover hidden patterns or relationships that would be difficult or impossible to identify, especially for people who are not used to analyzing data. These insights can be critical in identifying new market opportunities or issues that may affect business operations.

AA Gives Faster, More Efficient Insights

If your company can make informed decisions quickly and efficiently, and it can receive, prepare, analyze, and act on data faster than your competitors can, you can close a proposal, project, or deal before they even have a chance to catch up. You may be surprised to learn that the large, externally visible use cases aren't always the ones where speed makes the difference. Optimizing internal processes with faster execution is really where you can significantly improve productivity and save costs.

About 80% of the tasks involved in gaining insights from data are repetitive. These tasks include importing, preparing, cleaning, and enriching data as well as identifying anomalies and imputing missing values. That means only 20% of tasks are dedicated to producing valuable insights. Although most enterprises acknowledge this issue, only around 10% believe they have effectively tackled it. Improving the efficiency of small internal processes, like streamlining workflows, automating tasks, and eliminating unnecessary delays, can have a significant cumulative effect (*https://oreil.ly/E0lFU*) on organizational efficiency.

Of course, speed alone doesn't make all the difference. According to a PwC study (*https://oreil.ly/TLLfQ*), applying AA is estimated to make an organization three times more likely to make a decision as intended and accelerates overall progress as much as fivefold.

Efficiency describes the ratio between effort and (in the best case, valuable) outcome. When a machine can do a task with less effort than a human, that's efficient. Processing very large data sets wouldn't just be inefficient for a human to do—it would be downright impossible.

The optimal analytics execution environment is often difficult to estimate and requires a lot of hands-on experience. Not all analysts can do it well, let alone business users. AA configures runtimes to be calculated or estimated from past experience, to ensure the best operational setting for the current analysis.

Standardization Reduces Human Errors and Bias for Better Insights

While a governance process can define rules for consistent manual execution, AA can apply exactly the same methods to each data set consistently. For example, the basic KPI of an insurance company is its combined ratio, or profit margin. This must be calculated and presented to all stakeholders using a consistent approach and method, with no room for misinterpretation or doubts about the origin, lineage, meaning, or accuracy of these key metrics. Individual parties may perceive the outcome differently, particularly when it comes to the details, so it is essential that the methodology remains consistent. AA, once implemented, tested, and deployed, will run the same way for all stakeholders.

AA tools can significantly reduce the risk of human error or bias, especially related to insufficient technical, statistical, or professional knowledge. By using ML algorithms and predictive models, AA helps businesses make more accurate predictions about future outcomes, such as customer behavior, market trends, or sales projections. On the micro level, you could, for example, analyze all customer transactions to predict the likelihood of a customer making another purchase or analyze the possibility of churn instead of just relying on aggregated measures. On the macro level, you can use AA to analyze time-series data or behavioral clusters for insights about market segmentations or industry trends. In addition, a standardized automated process can ensure that controlled changes in execution are binding, such as when a model is applied with changed parameters, and allows the system to expand its computing power automatically as needed.

Another example is dealing with insufficient data. Sometimes observations are incomplete, individual attributes are missing, or for some other reason the available data is insufficient. Analysts from different fields use different methodologies and analyze data for different purposes. They may be tempted to apply heuristics, assumptions, or imputations instead of using the available data unadjusted. This is appropriate in many use cases, but there is a risk that using varied methodologies will lead to different adjustments, ultimately generating findings that can no longer be traced back to the same starting point.

It is often advisable to enhance inadequate data quality in a centralized and automated manner so that subsequent analyses can rely on consistent fundamentals. However, automated data preparation and improvement processes can also be prone to errors and biases, which could lead to inaccurate conclusions. (We will discuss bias in more detail in "Overcoming Bias" on page 51.) Additionally, when teams have different analytical needs, centralizing data management can limit their creativity and innovation. Consider both centralized and decentralized approaches to cleansing data.

AA Tools Are Easier to Scale Up

As organizations collect more and more data over time, they need to analyze large data sets and perform more complex analysis to gain valuable insights. AA tools are designed to scale to meet these increasing demands without compromising performance. In addition, scalability lets you extend data analytics to make data-driven insights available across the organization.

AA Reaches Further Afield to Generate Unexpected Insights

Manual analysis needs a lot of planning and organization: otherwise, because of our limited resources, humans tend to perform the analyses with the most likely outcomes for our given tasks. The main advantage of using AA is to gain unexpected additional insights. AA can generate insights that a business would not even have considered or that wouldn't be feasible for manual analyses. A machine can try many more iterations and permutations in its analysis than a human can. If it doesn't deliver the insights or information you want, you can reject that and explore the next detail.

Sufficient skills and experience, and maybe even a good gut feeling, can help you focus on the best outcome, but there will always be a trade-off between reaching your result efficiently and performing the most comprehensive analysis. Overall, the business value of AA lies in its ability to help people make better, faster, and more informed business decisions by processing vast amounts of data quickly and accurately, uncovering insights that may not be immediately apparent.

Overcoming Bias

We all have cognitive biases that affect how we see the world, process information, and make decisions. When you're working with data, these biases (and additional methodical ones) can be intricate to navigate. For instance, users are often heavily stuck in the *solution space* of a problem—that is, they already have a solution in mind and perform their analyses without being open to other possibilities. Their biases and preconceived notions can lead them to overlook important insights or solutions.

Employing both human expertise and automation can help alleviate biases in data analysis. Throughout this book, we'll emphasize that an insight-driven approach that combines the two is crucial to harnessing the full potential of analytics.

In many cases, automated analyses that are running AA under the hood can help manage natural human biases and avoid errors. However, not all biases can be overcome through technological means.

We have established an index of how much expert support and automation can potentially improve results by overcoming biases, shown in Figure 3-3. Nearly all biases can be addressed by either human experts or automation, which is encouraging.

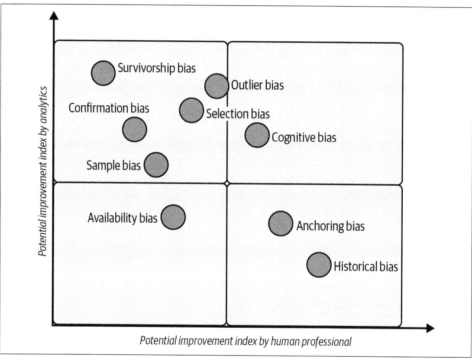

Figure 3-3. Improvability of various types of biases

Augmentation is particularly effective at addressing survivorship, selection, and confirmation biases. AA can calculate multiple data permutations and provide insights that researchers may overlook. This approach helps you explore less significant characteristics, which can uncover important trends. Utilizing a wider range of attributes also helps uncover unexpected observations without being affected by subjective beliefs or intuitions.

To avoid other biases, such as historical bias, you need a strong understanding of the problem and the data. Business professionals understand the intricacies and nuances of their specific domains.

To understand how automated analyses can mitigate bias, it is important to be aware of the different types of biases and to understand how they influence how people think about, consume, and process analyses in ways that can ultimately lead us to misinterpret important findings. Here is a brief overview of some of the most common types of biases:

Availability bias

Availability bias is our tendency to favor easily accessible information or data. While it's easy to just process what you can access, you could leave out information and thus give an inaccurate representation of the problem you are trying to solve. Awareness is the first step in controlling this methodological bias. Be transparent with stakeholders and explain how availability biases can affect results. Try to extend the scope of your data collection and explore alternative sources to ensure a comprehensive and objective data set. However, this approach also has potential limitations: for instance, the desired information could come at a high cost or lack sufficient quality. While there are established and sophisticated augmented techniques for dealing with availability bias, such as data imputation and enrichment, their effectiveness is limited in certain cases. Therefore, a balance between automation and human expertise is critical.

Confirmation bias

Confirmation bias is about how we subconsciously focus on, recall, or interpret information that supports our beliefs or hypotheses. This bias can endanger your reputation as an analyst. To prevent confirmation bias, reflect on your problem statement and the assumptions and convictions it conveys. Identify any personal beliefs that may affect your analysis and assess whether they have influenced your findings. Avoid jumping to conclusions too quickly; consider all available data, not just confirming evidence. Ask yourself whether contrary evidence could disprove your hypothesis.

Cognitive bias

Cognitive bias is the tendency to make decisions or draw conclusions based on unconscious thought processes, such as commonly held beliefs or prejudices, rather than based on objective reasoning. For instance, if you have been told that a certain segment of customers always performs poorly, this can influence your perception without your even realizing it. Cognitive bias and confirmation bias are closely linked. To avoid cognitive bias, strive for objectivity and carefully examine your benchmarks. Perhaps there is an exception within the underperforming customer group that deserves closer attention. Although the results may not meet expectations, they can still be positive.

Anchoring bias

    Anchoring bias is a form of cognitive bias that materializes when you depend too much on the first piece of information you come across while formulating decisions or drawing inferences—the original sticker price of a used car, for example. This primary chunk of data "anchors" your consequent decision making, even if it's irrelevant or erroneous. Deliberately setting anchors is a common sales tactic to influence decisions. Avoid this bias by being aware of your initial anchors. Seek out and consider all relevant information before making decisions. Question your assumptions, use objective criteria to evaluate your options, and set clear objectives and benchmarks before coming to a conclusion.

Selection bias

    Selection bias is closely related to, and often triggered by, confirmation bias. It describes our tendency to select data that supports our preexisting beliefs or hypotheses rather than considering a comprehensive set of data. We then direct our analysis toward finding correlations or evidence that confirm the desired result. These can be data sets, but sometimes they are single attributes or, worse, specific observations. This is not to be understood as fraud, but if you already know what factors will strongly influence the outcome, you may subconsciously reinforce the relevance of that information. Often this is an iterative process, where you add or remove other information again and again, reinforcing that initial tendency until you have clear "proof" of the hypothesis—that is, your analysis is influenced by so many exceptions and eventualities that it no longer shows the whole picture. As with confirmation bias, note your assumptions and hypotheses so that you can evaluate whether the end result fully addresses and describes the actual problem.

Historical bias

    Cultural, social, and economic norms and technical limitations from times gone by influence the accuracy and impartiality of our analyses and decision-making processes today. It's crucial to be aware of this bias, especially in economics and related fields, since the past data available for your analysis may be skewed or influenced by external factors. Historical bias also arises when you use historical data to make predictions, but fail to account for changes in circumstances that can drastically alter the outcomes, and when you base decisions or predictions on outdated or faulty data. If you're not fully informed, you are highly likely to make misguided decisions. Comprehensive business acumen is critical to avoiding historical bias.

Survivorship bias

    Survivorship bias is overly focusing on what "survived" a process without also considering what didn't. An example is looking only at graduates of a program rather than the entire cohort, including those who started the program but didn't finish. There are two problems with this: it can lead you to mistakenly believe that you have identified all of the necessary characteristics for success, and it could lead you to place too much emphasis on the qualities of the survivors, overlooking other important factors. To prevent survivorship bias, avoid exaggerating the traits of high-performing individuals. Instead, analyze candidates who share similar characteristics and closely examine any trends that arise. It can also be helpful to redefine success by creating multiple levels or categories based on class ranges or thresholds. This enables you to better understand trends and explore different classifications through clustering algorithms or supervised models. Be open-minded in revising your thresholds and explore alternative ways to define success.

Sampling bias

    Sampling bias occurs when you gather data from a sample that does not adequately represent the population or problem under study. Like availability bias, it can be linked to the limited availability of data. You can avoid sampling bias by expanding the sample size or using suitable statistical approaches to define the population clearly, such as stratified sampling techniques, oversampling, or random sampling.

Outlier bias

    Outlier bias is the tendency to overlook, exclude, or fail to exclude data points that don't fit a particular pattern. You need a good understanding of statistics as well as business acumen to determine how to handle outliers case by case. While you can identify them manually and decide to exclude them, in automated data-processing systems you'll need to apply technical methodologies, such as smoothing the accumulated results. This advice sounds simple, but implementing an appropriate statistical method to handle outlier bias is crucial to ensuring accurate and reliable results. This skill is rarely used, especially in business units.

Key Enablers of Augmented Analytics

There are two key enablers that make modern AA possible: the concept of augmented workflows and the concept of augmented frames. Both would be impossible without two core technologies: automation and AI.

Automation and AI

Automation is the main driver behind augmented frames, which are predominantly automated pipelines that generate insights either on demand or on a scheduled basis. There might be some AI involved here—for example, to calculate predictions inside a frame engine or add data annotations and explanations—but the main driver is automation.

At its core, *automation* in the AA context is about streamlining and optimizing repetitive tasks, ensuring data consistency, and enhancing efficiency. Think of it as setting up a series of dominoes: once the first one is tipped, the rest follow in a sequence without any additional intervention.

Automations play a critical role in many processes, including:

Data preparation
> One of the most time-consuming aspects of analytics is preparing your data. Automations can handle data cleaning, transformation, and integration, ensuring the data is ready for analysis.

Data retrieval
> With automation, users can schedule regular data retrievals, ensuring that the most up-to-date data is always available for analysis.

Reporting
> Instead of manually creating reports, users can set up templates and schedules, and automations can generate and distribute reports at specified intervals.

Alerts
> Automations can monitor data for specific conditions or thresholds and send alerts or notifications when those conditions are met.

Workflow integrations
> By connecting different tools and platforms, automations can ensure a seamless data flow, reducing manual transfers and data entry.

The beauty of automations is that once they're set up, they work behind the scenes, invisible to the end user but essential to the process. They are hard to maintain, though, so be wise about which processes you automate and which you keep manual. You will learn more about how to do this in the later chapters of this book.

Automations are a *deterministic* process: given the same input, you'll always get the same output. This seems logical, right? We stress this fact because it's what sets "regular" automations apart from AI automations. AI is the key enabler for augmented workflows. Generative AI, especially, allows business users to interact with augmented frames seamlessly. But there are more types of AI to consider for successful workflow augmentation. Let's explore the concept of AI next.

Artificial Intelligence: The Five Archetypes

Anytime something seems to work "magically," people tend to brand it as AI. But if you're building augmented systems, that definition of AI is not helpful.

That's why we'd like to introduce you to what we call the "five AI archetypes" (Figure 3-4). These archetypes group AI capabilities by the type of data they work with and the tasks they perform. While you probably wouldn't find this concept in a scientific journal, it cuts through the hype very effectively.

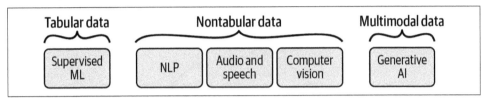

Figure 3-4. The five AI archetypes

In short, the five AI archetypes are:

Supervised machine learning
> Ideal for predicting small tabular data

Natural language processing (NLP)
> To make computers understand text

Audio and speech
> Often used to turn text to speech and vice versa

Computer vision
> To let computers "see" images

Generative AI
> To create completions given any data type

Understanding these archetypes will help you identify appropriate use cases for AI within your AA strategies. You'll most likely use them to augment a workflow (such as building a Q&A interface or analyzing a document), but in some cases, you could use AI to enrich an augmented frame (for example, to display a forecast given a time-series data set or to impute missing data).

Let's tackle the types one by one.

Supervised machine learning

Supervised ML is a powerful method for allowing computers to learn from existing data—typically in flat, tabular form—with the goal of predicting outcomes based on historical patterns. This approach is particularly effective when you know what you're trying to predict, whether it's a category (like "spam or not spam") or a numerical value (like the sales price of a house).

Figure 3-5 shows how this works. First, we collect a data set that contains various attributes (features) in addition to the outcomes we already know. In the house-pricing example, the data set would include details like size, location, and number of rooms as well as the sales price of each house. Supervised learning algorithms then analyze this data to identify the underlying patterns, or "rules," that link the features to the prices. Over time, the algorithm becomes able to predict the prices of houses it hasn't seen before based on the patterns it has learned.

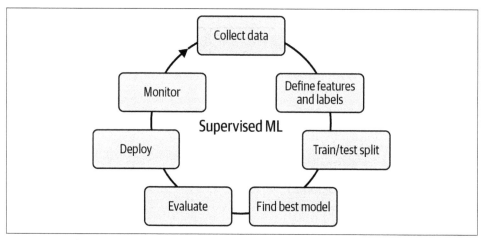

Figure 3-5. The supervised ML workflow

Deep learning, a subset of supervised learning, is often used for more complex types of data, such as images or text. It uses a layered approach to learning complicated patterns, making it powerful for handling sophisticated tasks. It's also the foundation for the other AI archetypes.

The supervised learning process can be further streamlined by a technique called *automated machine learning* (AutoML). This technique automates the search for the best model to fit the data, making it easier for those without deep technical expertise to apply ML. This democratization of the technology enables more people to use ML for various applications, from simple predictions to complex classifications, improving decision making across various workflows.

Let's dive into some examples:

Regression and time-series forecasting
Supervised ML can analyze historical data to predict trends with higher accuracy. This helps organizations optimize their resources and better manage inventory levels, staffing, sales, marketing efforts, and so on.

Classification

Supervised ML can efficiently group and categorize large amounts of data based on factors like customer demographics or product attributes. For example, a retail company might use automated classifications to analyze the purchasing behavior of different customer segments by age or income level.

Anomaly detection

Supervised ML can detect anomalies or outliers in large data sets, which can pinpoint potential instances of fraud in financial transactions or failures in industrial equipment. This helps organizations quickly identify issues and take corrective action before they escalate.

Recommendations

Supervised ML can make personalized recommendations based on customers' past behaviors and preferences. While this approach often powers recommendation engines in ecommerce stores, it can also be very useful in decision-support systems, such as by recommending similar cases.

Although supervised ML has the potential to revolutionize data analytics by speeding up time-consuming tasks and improving accuracy, there are limits to what it can do. For example, data quality and context are still critical for it to give accurate results, and human input is often necessary to ensure that its insights align with business objectives.

Natural language processing

Natural language processing (NLP) enables computers to analyze, interpret, and generate human language in the form of text data. It has a wide range of applications, such as sentiment analysis, entity recognition, key-phrase extraction, summarization, answer retrieval, and translation. It's particularly useful for understanding and processing textual data, such as reports, articles, emails, and social media posts. This makes it highly relevant to AA. It can help organizations gain valuable insights from vast amounts of unstructured textual data.

Here are some examples of how NLP can be used in AA:

Topic modeling

NLP can identify main topics or themes within large volumes of textual data, such as news articles or research papers. This enables organizations to quickly identify trends or emerging issues.

Automated text summarization

NLP technologies can summarize lengthy documents or articles, which enables people to understand the main ideas without having to read everything from cover to cover.

Natural language queries

Users can ask NLP tools questions about their data in natural language and receive answers in a similarly understandable format. This simplifies the process of querying data and makes it more accessible to users who do not have extensive technical knowledge.

Sentiment analysis

This is a very classic use case of NLP: automatically analyzing the sentiment of textual data, such as customer feedback, reviews, or social media comments. This helps organizations understand how customers perceive their products or services and make data-driven decisions to improve customer satisfaction.

Entity recognition

NLP can be used to identify and extract important information, such as dates, names, locations, and organizations, from large volumes of textual data. This capability allows analysts to quickly focus on the most relevant information.

Automated text annotation

A rather novel approach is to use NLP to generate annotations, descriptions, or keywords from charts or data, helping users quickly understand what the data is all about.

As with AutoML, the quality of the data and the context in which you use NLP are critical for accurate results, and human input is still necessary to ensure that its insights align with the business objectives and context.

Speech processing

Speech processing is an AI archetype that deals with audio files and overlaps significantly with NLP. It primarily focuses on two fields: *text-to-speech* (TTS) involves converting text into an audio stream that sounds like human speech while *speech-to-text* (STT) involves recognizing and understanding audio data (usually spoken language) and converting it to text. Many voice assistant applications, like Alexa, Google Home, Siri, and Cortana, combine TTS and STT technologies.

Speech processing can make AA more accessible and efficient by enabling users to interact with data and reports through voice commands. This can be particularly helpful for users with visual impairments or those who need hands-free access to data; it's also handy when you're on the go. (Haven't you ever wanted to interrogate your data while driving?)

Let's explore some typical examples:

Voice-controlled analytics dashboards
Integrating STT and TTS technologies can make analytics dashboards more accessible and easier to navigate. Users can issue voice commands to access specific data points, request visualizations, or apply filters without having to scroll through menus or use a mouse.

Voice-based data exploration
Speech processing enables users to ask questions about their data, allowing them to explore and analyze data verbally. For instance, a sales manager could say to their analytics system, "Show me this year's sales figures by region," and the system would respond with the relevant information. Speech recognition handles the inputs while NLP technologies interpret meaning and handle the conversation flow.

Audio report summaries
TTS technology can create audio summaries of reports, allowing users to consume information more efficiently.

Voice annotations and comments
Speech processing can help users add voice annotations or comments to their reports, making it easier to share insights and collaborate as well as helping to meet accessibility requirements for those with visual impairments.

Although speech processing can significantly improve user experience, it is essential to ensure that the technology accurately understands and responds to commands. This can become difficult when dealing with complex or technical jargon and when audio quality is poor, such as in noisy environments. Its effectiveness can also vary based on speakers' dialects or accents.

At its core, speech is one of AA's most direct ties to human interaction. Without humans in the loop, there's no speech analysis. At the same time, its universal interface allows more people to use analytics platforms efficiently, supporting the overall decision-making process.

Computer vision

Computer vision enables machines to "see" visual images or documents and analyze, recognize, or extract meaningful information from them. This AI archetype is particularly useful when processing large volumes of visual data, like identifying and extracting text from images, detecting objects or faces in photos, and analyzing medical scans.

In AA, computer vision extends the scope of analysis to include a wider range of data sources. Let's explore some examples:

Document analysis

Computer vision can extract and analyze text from scanned documents or images like invoices, receipts, or contracts, making it easier to process and include unstructured data in analytics workflows. It differs from optical character recognition (OCR) technology in that OCR recognizes text characters and outputs them as plain text whereas computer vision can also understand *context*, layout, and structure, like recognizing text from a multicolumn layout or extracting tables from documents.

Visual anomaly detection

Computer vision can detect anomalies or irregularities in visual data at scale. This is helpful in identifying manufacturing defects in products, unusual patterns in satellite imagery, and anomalies in medical scans. These insights can be used to improve quality control, track environmental changes, or identify medical issues earlier, leading to more effective treatment and better patient outcomes.

Data visualization enhancement

Computer vision can augment data visualizations with additional layers of information extracted from images or documents. For instance, you might enrich a geographical heatmap of sales data with information about the presence of competitors or the demographics of the surrounding areas.

Like other technologies, computer vision models have limitations. Their accuracy and effectiveness depend on the quality and context of the data. Training a computer vision model from scratch can also be costly, especially if you need to label large amounts of data (as in the case of visual anomaly detection). Human input thus remains necessary for training, using, and refining these models. You will learn more about strategies to integrate and deploy these systems later in this book.

Generative AI

Broadly speaking, the fifth archetype, *generative AI* (gen AI), refers to technology that generates text data or media files (image, video, or audio) using AI. That might sound trivial, but it's actually one of the greatest breakthroughs in modern AI. According to some experts, it's the biggest leap that humanity has made so far toward achieving artificial general intelligence.

While gen AI systems can theoretically span any possible medium, they are most popularly applied to text in the form of *large language models* (LLMs). The most prominent example of an LLM is OpenAI's GPT family of models (*https://oreil.ly/rjbRz*). This platform has generated significant buzz in the tech world and beyond because of its ability to generate humanlike language in a variety of contexts. The core concept is both simple and powerful: when prompted with some input text, the model can generate novel outputs that are relevant to the inputs and context aware.

Modern gen AI systems aim to be *multimodal,* meaning they can be trained on a combination of different data types. This results in more powerful models that allow users to input more than one type of data. While the results can be impressive, these models are still far from perfect and often produce errors or biased results. A significant challenge associated with generative AI, compared to other AI archetypes, is its nondeterministic nature. This means that requesting 10,000 predictions for the same input does not guarantee 10,000 identical responses, due to the inherent randomness and variability in the model's processing. This paradigm shift introduces substantial difficulties in scaling these systems.

Nevertheless, Gen AI services are applied to a large range of use cases, with more always being discovered. Let's take a more in-depth look at some of the most promising use cases for AA:

Natural language queries
You've seen this concept before, but this is a different approach. While traditional NLP techniques require users to formulate queries in a specific syntax, gen AI allows for natural-language inputs. This comes with a trade-off: it can generate incorrect or irrelevant results if the input is not precise enough or gives varying information. Handling an LLM like GPT-4 is not easy, especially in specialized domains, but it can make data analysis significantly more accessible by allowing users to ask questions and receive insights in a conversational manner.

Text-to-code
Gen AI can automate the process of writing code. For example, it can write SQL code to query databases from natural language prompts or generate Python, R, or JavaScript code to visualize data. This can allow users with beginner-level coding skills to analyze data and create visualizations, greatly reducing the barrier to entry for data analysis as well as decreasing developers' workloads.

Understanding data
Gen AI can help users understand their data better by providing context and insights beyond simple descriptive statistics. For example, an LLM can infer the schema of a data set based on just a few observations and explain how the data is related to other data sets or to a particular business problem.

Automated report generation
Gen AI can create comprehensive reports by analyzing data sets and generating narratives that highlight key insights, trends, and anomalies. This can save analysts valuable time and allow them to focus on more strategic tasks.

Data preparation

Gen AI can help to clean or structure data. For example, it can analyze a customer-support email to extract the customer's email address and information about the specific product they are inquiring about.

Analysis assistance

LLMs can guide and assist people without many data analysis skills. Imagine a business user sitting in front of a complex Excel spreadsheet, feeling so overwhelmed that even starting the data analysis feels difficult. LLMs can help turn a research goal or business question into a well-structured plan. They can help the user structure their data analysis around best practices, like crafting a good problem statement, breaking tasks down using issue trees, or choosing the right statistical methods for analyzing certain kinds of data.

We won't go as far as saying that the possibilities for gen AI are endless, but they're certainly vast, given its wide range of application areas and overlap with other AI techniques.

Learn More About AI

In this section, we've explored the five key AI archetypes and their high-level characteristics. While we could dive deeper into the intricacies of ChatGPT and company as well as emerging AI capabilities, the reality is that the frontier of AI is advancing so quickly that any detailed discussion would likely be outdated by the time you read this book.

Instead, we invite you to visit Tobias' blog (*https://blog.tobiaszwingmann.com*) where he regularly shares:

- In-depth explorations of current AI concepts
- Best practices for augmenting workflows with AI
- Use cases showcasing the impact of AI in various domains
- And much more!

The Limitations of Augmented Analytics

While we think that AA can revolutionize the way businesses understand and leverage their data, it is not without its limitations. It's crucial for businesses to be aware of these limitations to use the technology effectively and responsibly:

Overreliance on automated insights

AA can make data interpretation and insight generation much more straightforward. However, the danger lies in becoming overly reliant on these automated insights. Over time, businesses might lean too heavily on the analytics and miss out on the human intuition and gut feelings that have always been an essential part of decision making. For example, while predictive analysis might indicate a spike in sales next quarter based on historical data, a salesperson's on-the-ground experience may suggest potential market changes that could affect that outcome. With information so readily available, there's also a risk that teams might become passive, accepting data at face value without challenging or scrutinizing it.

Difficulty in handling ambiguity

Not all data is black and white. AA thrives on structured data but might stumble when faced with more ambiguous unstructured data. Parsing data like human emotions, cultural nuances, or open-ended feedback can be a challenge. Certain business situations are so multifaceted that they require human intervention to tease out the nuances and context. For example, consider a statement like "This product is sick." An automated customer-feedback analysis could easily misinterpret this statement if the system doesn't grasp the nuances of current slang.

Cost and resource implications

Implementing AA might require substantial capital, especially for enterprise-wide solutions, and system maintenance can be quite resource intensive. If your company does not realize the potential value of data yet, the estimated costs can quickly bury your whole AA initiative.

Interpretability issues

The "black box" nature of some AA can be a significant hindrance. Some systems use intricate algorithms, the workings of which can be hard to understand or explain, and these algorithms can obscure the origins of certain insights or predictions. For example, explaining the exact reasons behind an AI's recommendation to deny a loan application can be challenging. This can be problematic in actual business setups.

Implementation challenges

Introducing AA into an existing business framework often involves dealing with legacy systems that might resist integration with newer, more advanced technologies. As with every new technology, there's also a learning curve associated with these systems, and employees will need training.

Bias and inaccuracy

AA systems, like all systems, are only as good as the data they're trained on. Systems that are largely trained on historically biased data can perpetuate and even amplify those biases into the future. It's garbage in, garbage out: poor-quality input data will inevitably lead to poor-quality insights.

The Challenges of Augmented Analytics

Augmentation will be the enabler for data fluency, but it is a change that comes with challenges and pitfalls along the way. These include:

Resistance to change

People naturally tend to resist change, especially when it involves altering established workflows and processes. The introduction of AA may be perceived as a threat to the existing way of doing things or even to job security, especially if employees fear that automation may replace their roles. Start with a low-threshold introduction of augmentation, using only simple and accessible insights.

Information overload

If the rollout is too ambitious, AA runs the risk of overwhelming users with too much information. Employees may become frustrated or disengaged if they are bombarded with data and insights that are not immediately useful or relevant. This can lead to tool rejection, regardless of the potential benefits.

Confidence in the system and its quality

Building trust in the AA system is essential for success. If employees doubt the accuracy or relevance of the insights provided, they may be reluctant to rely on them for decision making. Building trust requires transparency about how the system works and the data and quality foundation it uses.

Analytics awareness requirements

While the goal of AA is to make data more accessible and to make deep data literacy irrelevant, a certain level of knowledge is still required to interpret and act on the insights provided. The general level of analytics awareness required may actually increase, at least that which is strongly related to business understanding, such as interpreting KPIs and understanding business interactions. People still need to comprehend not only what the data is telling them but also the data's context and limitations. Without this understanding, there's a risk of misinterpreting or misusing data or, in the case of gen AI, not questioning insights when in doubt.

Balancing automation with human judgment

While AI can greatly aid decision making, it's important to balance automated insights with human judgment. Employees may resist a system that seems to override their expertise or intuition. Emphasizing that AA is a tool to augment, not replace, human decision making can help gain buy-in.

Customization and relevance

AA systems must be customizable to meet the specific needs and contexts of different roles and personas within the organization. If the system is too generic, users may find it less useful, leading to resistance.

Ongoing training and support

Ongoing training and support are critical to successful adoption. In particular, analytics users need to feel confident with using the new tools and understanding the insights they provide to embrace the solution fully and become more data-driven. This includes not only initial training but also ongoing support and refresher sessions that are seen and accepted as a given.

For data-driven action to become a habit, people need to be exposed to it; the idea is to make people implicitly data-driven by helping them make better and more informed decisions. To do this, analytics should be "injected" into their actions: at best, without them being explicitly aware of it, or at least not being disturbed or distracted by it in their regular activities.

Conclusion

In this chapter, you've seen that AA is more than just a technological advancement; it's about bringing people to the forefront, leveraging their creativity, experiences, and intelligence. This human-centric approach is crucial in finding the "sweet spot" of AA: the optimal level of augmentation that enhances rather than overwhelms or replaces human judgment. In doing so, AA becomes a powerful ally in the business world, enabling us to accomplish tasks more efficiently and effectively, and often in better ways, than before.

The five key traits of effective AA (insightful, integrated, invisible, indispensable, and inclusive) underscore the importance of a holistic approach to analytics. They remind us that true effectiveness comes from integrating AA seamlessly into our workflows, making it an indispensable part of our daily routines, and ensuring it's accessible to all, regardless of technical expertise—and unlocking the final stage in your analytical maturity journey, Data Fluent.

As we transition to the next chapter, our focus shifts to ensuring that individuals and organizations are ready to harness the full potential of AA. We'll explore strategies for fostering a culture of data literacy, the importance of change management, and how to equip teams with the skills and mindset needed to thrive in an AA-enhanced environment. This preparation is crucial, as it lays the groundwork for successful AA implementation and ensures that your journey toward data-driven excellence is not just technologically sound but also deeply rooted in the human aspects of our organizations.

## CHAPTER 4

Preparing People and the Organization for Augmented Analytics

In this chapter, we share best practices for setting up your organization in a way that can support an effective implementation of AA. We'll focus on roles: business, technical, and in between. We also discuss why your organization needs an analytics center of excellence (CoE) to drive the analytics transformation.

In the context of an analytics transformation, we use the terms *role* and *persona* with specific meanings. *Role* refers to the overarching responsibilities and expectations associated with a broad function or position within the transformation. It captures the general scope and purpose of a particular category of responsibility. A *persona*, on the other hand, delves deeper and identifies a specific job or position within that broader role. Each persona has its own unique set of tasks, tools, and outcomes. It provides a detailed view of the people who perform the technical or business tasks associated with a role. For clarity, think of a *role* as a broad category of responsibility while a *persona* is a detailed, more nuanced representation of a specific position within that role.

This chapter focuses on how to successfully implement what you've learned so far about working with people and technical readiness to create the perfect foundation for adopting and using AA in your organization. To help people cope with the changes, it's essential that you empower and educate them. They need to understand the opportunities, the competitive advantages, and the responsibilities of each individual in this change. Technical readiness, on the other hand, includes the technical data infrastructure, processes, and advanced approaches to meet business demands.

Before we discuss how to raise the data literacy of the whole organization, though, we need to introduce a very effective framework for guiding change from a technical and human perspective: the influence model. Then we'll explore the fundamental role of data awareness in modern organizations, the art of data storytelling for effective communication, the strategic benefits of data-driven management, and the dynamics of leadership in the age of AI. We'll discuss the use-case approach, then finish with a plan for enabling, training, and motivating analytics leaders and translators.

Tailoring Augmented Analytics for Different Organizational Roles

This is a transformation made by people, for people. Therefore, you need to address the people in your organization and their roles. All roles are important to a successful transformation; they all have their own requirements, needs, and focus; and they are all interconnected. For example, you will need a variety of data scientists to apply analytics. But their actions are only relevant because the business users' needs and experiences shape the business and how it makes money.

The skills required to build a successful advanced analytics organization can be divided into three categories: business knowledge, analytical skills, and technical skills, as depicted in the Venn diagram in Figure 4-1. Depending on each role's orientation and position in the company, the way it combines these categories will vary greatly.

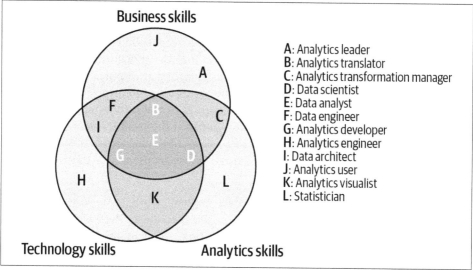

Figure 4-1. Analytics transformation personas in the three skill categories

Not all of these roles are necessary for your team; we just want to give you an overview of possible roles in the analytics transformation. The four top-level roles in the transformation are shown in Figure 4-2. First, leaders have a specific role in the transformation as *analytics leaders*. Then there are the people who stand between business and technology and perform business analysis. We address them specifically and give them a crucial new responsibility in the transformation: the *analytics translator*.

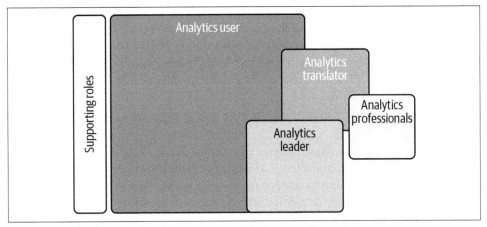

Figure 4-2. The four top-level roles in the analytics transformation

The *analytics user* uses data analytics to make better business decisions every day. This role could describe nearly everyone in your organization; from portfolio managers to marketing researchers, insurance underwriters to construction surveyors, machine operators to chefs, everyone needs to be able to work with analytical results and become more data-driven.

You can (and should) define these roles in great detail. For example, the fourth role, *analytics professional*, includes more specialized roles, such as data engineer, data scientist, data analyst, and software developer, as well as specialized support roles, such as transformation manager and data architect. For the moment, though, we'll focus on broader categories, so we'll refer to all the roles we just named as *data professionals*.

As your transformation reaches stage 2, the Data Active maturity level, we recommend focusing only on these four mandatory roles. Later, you can differentiate them more deeply. For now, let's explore them in detail, beginning at the top.

Analytics Leader

Analytics leaders are the role models who push data-driven transformation, drive the analytical mindset, and champion impactful use cases for business success.

"All good things come from above." This saying isn't always right, but there's a grain of truth to it: the impetus for change is naturally stronger when the leadership carries it forward. That's why it's crucial to categorize the organization's management and executive leaders into one dedicated role, with its own responsibilities and expectations.

Role and responsibilities

All leaders within an organization must embody the principles of analytics and cultivate a mindset centered on data-driven insights and innovative use cases that leverage business objectives. Analytics leaders play a pivotal role in driving the transformation. By setting an example for others, they underscore the significance of using analytics to achieve success in all aspects of the business.

Necessary skills

A well-rounded analytics leader should have sound business and technical knowledge, basic statistical skills, and a fundamental understanding of IT. It is critical that they be familiar with the whole enterprise's general KPIs, IT landscape, and current projects, and they should understand measures of central tendency and stochasticity. It is also important for them to understand how IT systems interoperate and how the company uses data to drive decision-making processes, enabling the organization to stay competitive and responsive to market changes.

Mindset

Leaders should be intrinsically motivated to contribute to the transformation. There will be leaders who, for some reason, will not be able to go along for the ride, but in most cases, empowering them will help get them on board.

The most important attitude an analytics leader should have is *openness* to the opportunities and changes this transformation will bring. They should be naturally curious to dig deeper and deeper into the data, question things, and find hidden insights. They must also think strategically about how to align those insights with broader business goals. A good degree of *skepticism* is just as essential, however, to ensure the quality and reliability of the data.

Adaptability is critical in data analytics, where new methods, approaches, tools, and techniques are constantly emerging; for the same reason, analytics leaders should also have a strong desire for *continuous learning*. *Collaboration* is essential, too: data analytics is often a cross-functional, cross-domain discipline that requires effective teamwork and breaking down silos.

Finally, *resilience* and *tenacity* are necessary to overcome the inevitable challenges and obstacles that arise in data projects. Many data projects fail. Leaders must learn to manage people's expectations and help them understand failed use cases for what they are: valuable insights into what works and what just doesn't.

Importance in driving transformation

Analytics leaders' vision and use-case ideas are the fuel for change. As role models, analytic leaders will make or break the transformation to a data-driven culture. As you learned in Chapter 3, the top-down approach is indispensable to the analytics transformation. Don't underestimate the influence of analytics leaders: without them, no transformation could succeed.

Analytics Translator

Analytics translators bridge the gap between business units' analytics needs and technical analytic expertise, and they translate the insights generated from data into real-world, large-scale impact on the organization.

This second role that we want to introduce is perhaps unexpected, a sort of ambassador who helps connect the business units more closely with analytics. The analytics translator is motivated to be part of the change—after all, this is a voluntary role.

In our experience, the question always comes up about who should fill this role, who is responsible for providing the skills and capabilities, whether these people are organized centrally in the CoE, and whether they are pulled away from their business units, creating an operational gap. Let's define the role very clearly.

Analytics translators ensure that the business gets real impact from its analytics initiatives. Much like linguistic translators, they communicate ideas and insights between the languages of business and analytics, demystifying buzzwords and interpreting complex algorithmic results in business terms. They foster information sharing, drive adoption among business users, and help ensure that a consensus emerges.

Translators are part of the business. Regardless of where in the organization they are located, they are critical to foster sharing that will improve analytic insights and drive adoption among business users. It is important to build a community to share best practices and lessons learned on a regular basis. Their willingness to collaborate is what breaks down silos.

Role and responsibilities

Analytics translators help analytics leaders brainstorm to identify and prioritize the business problems that will create the highest value when solved by an analytics initiative. These could be opportunities within a single line of business or cross-organizational improvements. Translators ensure that the solution delivers insights that the business can interpret and act on. They communicate the benefits of the solution across domains to drive adoption.

Necessary skills

Translators need excellent domain knowledge; look for experts in the business who have a strong overall understanding of processes across the company. They should be well-versed in the business's KPIs and other operational metrics and their impact on profit and loss.

In addition, analytics translators need a passion for quantitative statistics and structured problem solving. They are not necessarily dedicated analytics professionals, and they don't need deep technical expertise in programming or modeling, but they do need to know what models or analytical methods are available and can best be applied to solve a problem.

Translators must also understand the effects of potential model errors that can introduce bias, such as overfitting and outliers. In short, communication is the critical skill in this role. Translators ensure the transfer of results, findings, insights, and knowledge from analytics to business and management.

Mindset

Analytics translators need an innovative, open, and entrepreneurial mindset. Their enthusiasm, commitment, and business acumen help the organization navigate technical, political, and organizational obstacles. Analytics translators also need a tolerance for frustration; they should understand that failure is part of the process.

The most important skill that a successful analytics translator has is in-depth business knowledge. Thus, the best way to fill this role is to train motivated internal colleagues. Building the statistical and technical skills of someone with years of experience is more likely to succeed than trying to impart all that knowledge to new external hires.

There are currently no certifications or degrees for analytics translators. Some companies create their own business-specific analytics translator academies, using business, methodological, and technical immersion. This allows them to adapt their training frequently and respond to the data-maturity level of each individual translator.

Importance in driving transformation

Organized in a community to share experiences of the best practices and lessons learned, analytics translators will be a key factor in the success of individual business units undergoing transformation. This role is indispensable to the team. Establishing this role early and building organizational competence in it will generate strong benefits in the medium term as you move to become a Data Progressive company.

Analytics User

Analytics users are people who consume analytics and use the results to gain and interpret insights, make decisions, and create value.

Role and responsibilities

This role is a more passive one that represents most people in the organization—easily 80%. They are deeply involved in the business and, for the most part, have no direct involvement in data analysis. The whole transformation is done mainly for them.

This is the key group to win over to achieve broad analytics adoption. Your biggest leverage in achieving data fluency is to help these people overcome barriers and be more data-driven in their daily workflows.

Necessary skills

Analytics users' skills are mainly business related; some may have a slight statistical orientation, which really helps to support problem-solving skills. They must have appropriate analytics awareness.

The challenge is that, because this role is so broadly defined, it is very diverse. You'll have people whose work is deeply business related and who rarely touch analytics. Others will be directly affected by analytics results—for example, because they directly use dashboards or knowledge repositories. Their levels of maturity in technology and analytics-related skills will be very different.

Mindset

Approaching this role as a unified group will not lead to success. Individual analytics users need different approaches to help them embark on the analytics journey. Unlike analytics leaders and analytics translators—who tend to have intrinsic motivation to contribute, understand the need, and see the change through—most analytics users are likely to be motivated by a sense of compulsion. They are expected to take part in the transformation as part of their jobs. In the beginning, they probably don't realize how important their active contribution to the transformation is.

Honestly, that's fine. They just want to do their jobs. A sales manager wants to be a sales manager, an underwriter wants to be an underwriter, and an accountant wants to be an accountant. For them, data analytics is not an end in itself. They mostly don't care whether their workflows are supported by analytics or digitized. What's more important is to involve them in the transformation in an appropriate way to increase value contribution, and this will have to go beyond conventional skills training and awareness raising.

It is therefore difficult to say what skills are generally required for this role; the answer is: it depends. But an open mind is a desirable quality in all transformation and change processes, and everyone should have that.

Personas

If you are very early in the Data Active step—for example, providing domain-specific solutions in reporting or BI dashboarding—you'll need to define your user personas much earlier. By the time your organization reaches the transition from Data Progressive to Data Fluent, you should have a clear picture of how to differentiate the user role in terms of the value streams in your organization and their activities. While you can always proceed without a specific definition, having one will give your work and actions more structure and focus and will make users feel recognized. Each job has a unique perspective as well as a specific set of concerns and potential barriers related to the transformation.

Let's look at some examples of job personas for analytics users:

Sales manager

> Responsible for achieving sales goals and motivating the team, the sales manager relies on analytics to gauge strategy effectiveness, predict trends, and assess team performance. Understanding key metrics, such as lead-conversion rates and regional sales patterns, is critical to achieving targets.

Marketing specialist

> The marketing specialist wears many hats, from orchestrating compelling campaigns to understanding customer behavior. Analytics is like a compass for them, showing them what resonates with their audience. Knowing which campaigns deliver the best ROI or how a demographic engages with content can refine their marketing approach.

Accountant

> Accountants ensure that the company remains fiscally sound and forward-looking. Analytics provides the foundation for forecasting and strategizing. Looking into detailed financial reports allows accountants to optimize budgeting, understand the nuances of profitability, and make data-driven fiscal decisions.

Supply chain manager

> Supply chain managers ensure that products flow seamlessly from warehouses to customers and choreograph the intricate dance of supply and demand. Analytics is their early warning system, alerting them to potential supply chain disruptions, inventory mismatches, or supplier hiccups. A clear snapshot of demand forecasts or supplier performance can streamline operations and prevent costly missteps.

HR manager

> Beyond hiring, HR managers are the stewards of company culture and employee growth, ensuring that the organization remains a thriving environment for talent. Using analytics, they can gain insight into the heartbeat of the organization: understanding employee satisfaction, identifying hiring bottlenecks, and charting talent trajectories.

Customer service representative

> Key to customer satisfaction, customer service representatives use analytics to evaluate service performance, identify common issues, and improve service quality. Metrics on resolution time and customer feedback guide service enhancements.

Product manager

Product managers drive product development from concept to launch, utilizing analytics to understand customer interactions, feature popularity, and areas for improvement. Insights into user behavior inform innovation and product competitiveness.

The right personas will depend on your organization and its business model. When designing them, try to define different responsibilities and analytics needs. Ask questions like:

- How does this person deliver to the value chain?
- What are they responsible for?
- What are their analytical needs?
- What challenges do they face?
- What sets them apart? Do they require individualized handling in your transformation?

For instance, an accountant has different analytics needs than a risk engineer. The accountant is primarily concerned with standard BI descriptive analytics whereas the risk engineer requires assessment instruments, such as potential as-if analysis, and might even use gen AI to summarize complex third-party risk surveys.

Try to answer these questions for the personas of analytics users in your organization. (See the sidebar "Example User Persona: Insurance Underwriter" on page 85 for an example.) If you identify a specific need for analytics, handle each persona individually.

Data Analytics Maturity and Personas

Consider distinguishing the data analytics maturity levels of individual personas, not just the organization as a whole. Here's a breakdown of how this can benefit employees and the transformation:

Customized training and support

Not everyone will have the same level of comfort and proficiency with analytics. By segmenting based on data maturity, you can personalize training and ensure that each individual receives the support they need to perform optimally in their role.

Resource allocation

Understanding maturity levels can help the organization, and especially the CoE, allocate resources more efficiently to create tailored solutions and focus attention where it's most needed. Roles at a higher maturity level may need more advanced tools while beginners may require basic training.

Change management and progress measurement
> Understanding where each persona is in their analytics journey can help change-management teams address the fears, challenges, and sources of resistance specific to each maturity level and set appropriate goals and benchmarks. A baseline understanding of each persona's analytics maturity allows you to measure progress and growth over time.
>
> Go about this thoughtfully. For some organizations, especially smaller ones, introducing too many segments or levels can overcomplicate the process. A unified approach may be more practical. Consider finding personas at a certain maturity level that can be treated similarly to save effort and resources, support collaboration, and break down silos.
>
> The risk of losing employees during the transformation increases, especially if there is a tendency to overengineer the process and employees perceive that the people taking action have little understanding of the needs of the business. If resources are limited, you might focus on increasing analytics capabilities overall rather than implementing fine-grained, personalized approaches.
>
> Consider culture, too. In some organizations, segmenting employees by maturity can unintentionally create a hierarchical culture. This can be counterproductive and even divisive. We recommend a supportive and appreciative framing: segmentation helps people leverage their talents in the most appropriate way.

Importance in driving the transformation

Analytics users are critical to an organization's analytics transformation as they represent the majority of those who use data insights and apply them to decision making, embodying the shift to an insight-driven culture. Their diverse backgrounds require customized analytics solutions that meet different needs and drive broad adoption and continuous improvement through valuable feedback. Crucially, their role goes beyond technology, and they drive a mindset shift across the organization by demonstrating the benefits of analytics in their daily workflows. The engagement of this group is critical, making them key players in integrating analytics into the company DNA and ensuring the success of the transformation process.

Analytics Professional

Now let's look at the last of the four roles, the people who implement the transformation: analytics professionals. *Analytics professionals* are professionally trained in advanced data analysis, statistics, ML, handling data, and/or programming.

Role and responsibilities

Outsiders often imagine this role to be a unified group with unified skills, but of course that's not the case. Certainly, most of them have strong technical skills, but each individual specialization has its raison d'être and is critical to developing the analytics maturity of the organization. We'll look more closely at individual personas for these specializations in a moment.

Necessary skills

Despite their differences, analytics professionals tend to be on the technical side of the skill spectrum. Coding, computer science, and programming skills are crucial for them since they translate business requirements into machine-executable forms. Mathematical and statistical skills are also important but are critical only for specific roles. In general, it is important that they have a good understanding of the business.

Mindset

Critical to the success of an analytics professional is a relentless curiosity, a willingness to experiment and push the boundaries of what is possible to uncover hidden insights. They also need to be collaborative and ensure the seamless integration of data insights and business functions. Agile thinking and continuous personal development enable them to adapt quickly to the ever-changing data landscape while their tenacity in problem solving helps them overcome technical and conceptual obstacles.

A great data professional not only looks for the best solution but also has a strong business acumen that ensures their efforts are aligned with the strategic goals and vision of the organization. In doing so, they take responsibility for the value of the solution and actively drive adoption.

Importance in driving transformation

Analytics professionals are key catalysts in an organization's technical analytics transformation. They are tasked with the dual responsibility of understanding complex business objectives and translating them into meaningful analytical solutions. They meticulously build, refine, and optimize models to ensure that the insights that are extracted from the data are both accurate and actionable. A hallmark of their expertise is their commitment to data integrity, ensuring that data is reliable, usable, and ready for analysis.

However, their role goes beyond technical tasks. They are storytellers who work with the analytics translator to translate complex data results into clear, understandable insights that drive business strategies. In an ever-evolving data landscape, they are also at the forefront of constantly adapting and staying current with the latest methods and tools.

Technical specialist personas

Let's look at some specialist analytics professionals and their roles on the path to analytics. They are all different, and they are not all equally important at each maturity level. They are also interdependent. To differentiate and structure the professional roles a bit more, we'll divide them into two groups: technical roles and supporting roles. The technical roles are the ones most laypeople imagine—data analysts, statisticians, data scientists, and data engineers, among others:

Data scientist

Develops advanced models and algorithms to extract insights and predictions from data. Data scientists are more on the mathematical and statistical side of the skill spectrum. They tend to have limited programming skills compared to analytics developers and data analysts but are great with ML and statistical analysis.

Data analyst

Derives insights by querying data, performing statistical descriptive and diagnostic analysis, reporting, and visualizing data. Data analysts often use tools such as SQL, Excel, and BI platforms as well as analytical programming languages like Python and R. They typically have an intermediate level of business understanding and are a good intersection between business translators and technology.

Data engineer

One of the most underrated technical specialist roles, the data engineer prepares "big data" for analytical or operational use, enabling the work of data analysts and data scientists. Data engineers manage and optimize data lakes and databases so that data can be stored, queried, and piped effectively, and they ensure the accuracy and availability of the data. They build, maintain, and optimize the data pipelines and architecture.

Analytics developer

This role develops, implements, tests, and integrates analytics solutions and applications, web applications, and API web services. Analytics developers work closely with analysts and scientists and translate analytical insights into programmatic packages, engines, and software.

Analytics engineer

Ensures that ML models and analytics solutions are seamlessly deployed, scaled, and maintained. DevOps is the analytics engineer's field of action. They are typically required at a later stage in the analytics value chain and are critical during the late stages of the transformation.

Analytics visualist

Specializes in representing data and insights visually, often using tools such as Tableau, Power BI, and Markdown reports. Analytics visualists specialize in explaining, rather than exploring, data. They have a flair for design and storytelling, so communication is a big part of their skillset. They often design dashboards and user interfaces for analytics applications.

Support specialist personas

There are also some supporting roles that are critical to the transformation. Please keep in mind that this list is by no means complete:

Data architect
Responsible for designing and implementing the data infrastructure, ensuring scalability and accessibility. Data architects design the new future-proof technology stack and define operational environments for analytics solutions. They don't have to be based in the CoE but should be closely aligned with their counterparts on the IT side.

Data governance officer
This role ensures data quality, privacy, and regulatory compliance and acts as the guardian of quality. It focuses on ensuring that analytics insights are based on a reliable foundation. Data governance during transformation is a complicated task. Data governance officers must participate in inspiring people and fostering the creative mindset that a transformation requires but balance this with compliance, regulations, and policies—responsibilities and tasks that are not much fun. They will need support to fulfill this critical role.

Change management specialist
This role helps the organization adapt to the new data-driven culture, addressing resistance and facilitating training. Change managers are critical to any change in an organization, especially when their methodology is applied to the analytics journey. Many people will struggle with the changes of becoming data-driven. Helping people find their place in the change is essential to the new culture you want to establish.

Business analyst (BA)
This role often works closely with analytics translators to define business problems that analytics can solve. Analytics translators are mainly taking over this position in the analytics transformation, but BAs are often established in an organization for IT requirements. As mentioned previously, BAs can even become analytics translators if they are located in the business rather than in specialized capability units.

Subject matter experts (SMEs)
Specialists in specific business areas. SMEs provide context and expertise to ensure that analytics solutions are relevant and actionable, working alongside BAs and primarily supporting analytics translators. SMEs typically come from the business units; they don't necessarily have close contact with the CoE and aren't really involved in analytics. They are excellent candidates for the analytics translator role.

Analytics transformation manager

The most critical supporting role and the driving force behind the transformation, located within the CoE. If you have a good transformation manager and a supportive transformation team, you're already halfway to a successful transformation. In fact, this role is so important that we're going to give it its own section.

Analytics Transformation Manager

Analytics transformation managers play a pivotal role in driving the strategic vision and ensuring that the organization successfully evolves into a data-driven entity.

You might have one transformation manager or a few. Figure 4-3 illustrates just how broad their field of action is. Finding the right person will be challenging but well worth it.

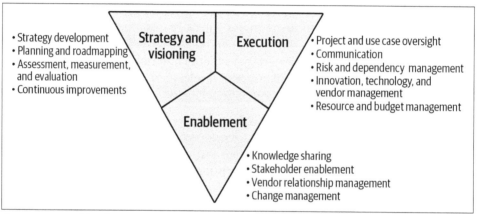

Figure 4-3. Fields of action for the analytics transformation manager

Role and responsibilities

Analytics transformation managers orchestrate and enable change. They work closely with stakeholders, organize awareness initiatives, and act as the first point of contact and spokesperson for the CoE. In later stages of the transformation, their responsibilities expand to include managing resources, mitigating risk, and ensuring profitability. Whereas the change manager role focuses on mitigating the impact of a change in progress, the transformation manager actively shapes the strategic vision.

Strategy

This role works with senior leadership to define the strategic goals of the analytics transformation and align them with overall business objectives. Transformation managers plan how to achieve those goals by creating a comprehensive roadmap that outlines milestones, timelines, and resource allocation.

Measurement

Transformation managers define, track, and monitor KPIs and other metrics of the transformation's success and impact. After the initial transformation, they evaluate its ongoing impact, identify areas for further improvement, and ensure its sustainability.

Execution

Transformation managers must monitor the progress of analytics projects and initiatives to keep them on track and within scope. They determine how the transformation is communicated internally and externally. They identify potential risks, dependencies, and other challenges and develop strategies to mitigate them. They manage the transformation budget, allocating human and technology resources and ensuring that they are used efficiently and effectively. They seek out and integrate innovative tools, methodologies, and approaches to enhance the journey of the analytics transformation and manage vendor relationships. They also advocate for the responsible use of data, ensuring that the transformation respects both legal boundaries and ethical considerations.

Enablement

Transformation managers develop and implement change management strategies, engage with stakeholders across the organization to build support, and facilitate knowledge sharing and collaboration across teams and departments. They establish mechanisms for regular employee, stakeholder, and even customer feedback and use the feedback to guide and assess the transformation process.

Necessary skills

Transformation managers need a wide range of management and cultural skills, in addition to their technical and strategic competencies. These "soft skills" include leadership, communication, collaboration, problem solving, and adaptability. The transformation manager doesn't have to be a technical expert but should have enough of a foundation in the latest analytics innovations, technologies, methodologies, and best practices to make informed decisions.

Successful transformation managers need a visionary outlook; they must anticipate trends and prepare the organization for what's coming. Because not everyone in the organization may understand analytics or what it can do, the transformation leader must also have the skills of an educator and coach, helping people at all levels understand the value of the transformation and how to get involved.

Mindset

Transformation leaders need a mindset of continuous improvement. They must champion the cultural shift and even become the face of change, embodying the values and behaviors that the organization is trying to instill. They must embrace challenges and drive change with passion and ownership. And since the journey of transformation is fraught with many challenges, they should be resilient, able to overcome setbacks and keep the momentum going.

Importance in driving transformation

On the ambitious journey of analytics transformation, the analytics transformation manager becomes the linchpin of success. This role goes far beyond mere project management—it's about designing a data-driven future and paving the way to get there.

The manager's expertise lies not only in strategy formulation but also in orchestrating all implementation activities. Transformation managers bring together stakeholders from the C-suite to the frontline to ensure collective buy-in by bridging communication gaps. They demystify analytics, transforming it from an intimidating concept into an accessible, valuable tool for everyone through targeted awareness efforts. To do this, they organize professional development initiatives to ensure that the workforce is ready for the new data-centric landscape and to create a broad understanding of the value of analytics to the business.

Without analytics transformation managers, an organization's journey to analytics maturity will remain essentially unorganized and disjointed. They are the face of the transformation, and their passion for the transformation serves as a model for many others who are adapting it for themselves. Finding the right person will be challenging but well worth it; a good transformation manager and a supportive transformation team will be halfway to a successful transformation.

Summary of Key Roles

Table 4-1 summarizes the four key roles of analytical transformations. Remember that all of these roles are required for success.

Table 4-1. Summary of the four key roles in the analytics transformation

Analytics leader	Analytics translator
Role and responsibilities: Drives an analytics mindset, aligns with business goals, and formulates ideas for their specific business area.	*Role and responsibilities:* Connects technical and business teams, extracts insights from data, and collaborates across organizational centers of excellence.
Necessary skills: Profound business acumen, basic statistics knowledge, IT understanding, and awareness of IT system interdependencies.	*Necessary skills:* Solid business acumen, proficiency in mathematics and statistics, and foundational computer science skills.
Importance in driving transformation: Leads analytics projects and sets direction for business unit transformation. Essential for fostering a data-driven organizational culture.	*Importance in driving transformation:* Bridges the gap, aligning analytics with business objectives and translating complex data into actionable business insights.

Analytics professional	Analytics user
Role and responsibilities: Key players in analytics transformation, including data engineering, analysis, and science.	*Role and responsibilities:* Making data-informed decisions in their daily roles, even if not directly involved in the analytics process.
Necessary skills: Proficient in computer science, math, and statistics; understanding of business for effective stakeholder communication.	*Necessary skills:* Business domain knowledge; basic IT and statistics understanding can improve their ability to interpret analytics outcomes.
Importance in driving transformation: Essential for executing complex data tasks, they develop and oversee data-driven decision systems.	*Importance in driving transformation:* Applying data insights to business challenges; driving the success of analytics in decision making.

The analytics user group, easily the majority, is the key group to win over for broad analytics adoption. Helping these people overcome typical barriers to becoming more data-driven in their daily workflows is a major source of leverage.

Example User Persona: Insurance Underwriter

Description: The insurance underwriter is the key risk manager of an insurance company. Underwriters use guidelines, personal judgment, and advanced predictive analytics to determine terms and conditions of insurance policies and decide which risks to cover and at what price. Their decisions directly affect profitability.

Primary responsibilities
- Evaluate the risk level of insurance applications
- Determine policy terms, coverage limits, and premiums
- Collaborate and negotiate with insurance agents and brokers
- Stay up-to-date on market developments, industry regulations, standards, emerging risks, and new risk assessment models, tools, and techniques

Analytical needs
- Advanced risk assessment software tools; depending on the type of insurance, these systems could be factor based or utilize simulation analytics
- Market trend analytics that provide a detailed view of emerging trends in the insurance market to influence underwriting decisions
- Regulatory and compliance reports
- Claim analytics to help develop effective methods for mitigating risks

Challenges
- Minimizing the potential for loss while balancing the need to attract new customers
- Keeping pace with the dynamically changing aspects of the risk environment, such as cybersecurity, nascent markets, and climate change

- Adapting to the technologies and predictive models that are revolutionizing traditional underwriting methods

Why this role needs dedicated handling in the transformation
- Underwriters operate at the intersection of profitability and risks. Their decisions, if supported by strong and precise analytics, can significantly enhance the bottom line.
- The nature of risks is evolving with technological advancements, climate changes, and socioeconomic shifts. Analytics can equip underwriters with the foresight to anticipate and understand changes.
- As the insurance industry shifts toward increased automation, underwriters should be well versed in the latest analytical techniques to combine conventional underwriting knowledge with modern data insights.

The Center of Excellence

A CoE is, in short, a unit dedicated to organizing the analytics transformation. During the Data Active maturity phase, it collects and connects all the loose threads of analytics activities that emerge.

Creating a Center of Excellence

Your transformation will need a CoE. Without it, you will not reach the Data Progressive stage.

CoEs are often built from the sophisticated analytical capabilities of established business units. We recommend identifying these areas and units early on. The CoE is usually initiated by the chief information officer or chief operating officer, with the commitment of board members who understand the relevance of analytics to the business.

The CoE should not necessarily bundle all data and analytics functions together. In fact, we recommend separating responsibility for data analytics from responsibility for data management, data governance, and data infrastructure. There is no question that these units, departments, and responsibilities need to work very closely together, but as Julius Caesar once said, "Divide et impera": divide and conquer. The overall transformation is so large that one unit will rarely have all the necessary skills; in attempting to handle everything, such a unit quickly loses focus and connection to the business.

A good division, as mentioned previously, is between data management, BI with standard reporting, and analytics skills with data science. The CoE comes into play at a later stage of maturity, as we mentioned, especially in the transition from the Data Active stage to the Data Progressive stage, which involves intense transformational tasks.

For this reason, the CoE's staff rarely comes from IT. In fact, we strongly recommend developing the CoE from within the business rather than from within IT. If you don't have dedicated and easily data-ready business units capable of driving the transformation, then you should look to IT to handle the responsibility. But remember that the whole transformation is about supporting the business and breaking down silos. Ideally, you want a dedicated CoE team to emerge from the most data-savvy and analytics-savvy departments so that the team fully understands the problems and needs of the business units.

There's an adage in computer science called Conway's Law that states: "Any organization that designs a system (defined broadly…) will produce a design whose structure is a copy of the organization's communication structure."[1] In this context, this means that setting up a CoE on the IT side keeps the skills and responsibility on the IT side. If you really want to break down silos, though, you need to bring the responsibility of becoming data-driven close to the business by setting up your CoE on the business side.

However, this raises a fundamental problem. We've established that the CoE does not handle *all* analytics issues and challenges; depending on how you divide the work, data management (and possibly other functions) will be handled in a different department or business unit. When you initially staff the CoE, you draw experts away from those business units. This weakens them for a time, but the division managers of those units must remember that this is an investment in achieving the overall goals of the company.

At HDI Global in 2019, for example, we decided to take this approach. The company was setting up a completely new CoE team, on the business side and closely linked to the business units, and drew its initial staff from its data-based areas: Natural Catastrophes, Underwriting, Controlling, Consulting, and Risk Management.

If you don't have the appropriate analytical and technical skills on the business side, bring in some people from IT, but you should still give more weight and focus to the business side, as shown in Figure 4-4. People from the business units will always have a stronger connection to, and thus stronger credibility with, future stakeholders there.

---

1 For our purposes, "designing a system" means defining the structure of an approach to an analytics transformation. See Melvin Conway, "How Do Committees Invent?" (*https://oreil.ly/KmeFO*), *Datamation*, April 1968; and Martin Fowler, "Conway's Law" (*https://oreil.ly/cHznn*), MartinFowler.com, October 20, 2022.

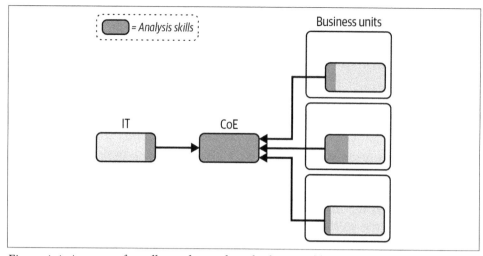

Figure 4-4. A center of excellence drawn from both IT and business units

Your next challenge, then, is convincing the business units to give up their best data experts to staff a new CoE. Here, communication is king. Connect your request to your common understanding of the company's mission. The manager certainly won't be happy, but they will understand the necessity.

Look for people in the company who have a good reputation outside their fields and who are respected for their expertise. If you can persuade them to participate in the CoE, or perhaps support it personally, others will follow their lead. Again, don't underestimate the importance of role models in the overall transition.

Above all, though, convince the people you want to recruit. Some people may feel insecure about leaving their comfort zones, where they have the strongest expertise. They may have reservations about whether the company will be able to sustain its cultural change in the long term.

Your new team will need to establish a dynamic together as a team, and that takes time. We recommend that you emphasize their previous successes in their current domains and let them know how important their skills and abilities are to the company's success in this important step in the transformation. These people will make the difference. Make sure they realize that this is an opportunity to shape the future success of the company.

Defuse any possible fears of not being strong enough to really take the next step here. Show them that the mindset has changed and that the company is ready for the transformation.

Approaches to Organizing a CoE

To help you understand how the CoE fits into the organization, this section looks at centralized and decentralized approaches and which work best, especially in the Data Progressive maturity stage (stage 3).

The decentralized approach

Usually, in a Data Reactive (stage 1) organization, one at the beginning of its analytics journey, you will find centralized capabilities for data and reporting on the IT side and some of these capabilities in the business units—some of which have advanced data savvy, some of which do not. While the non-data-savvy business units are totally dependent on IT solutions, the more sophisticated business units approach data and insights in their own way. They are agile in responding to their own domain's needs, innovating, and coming up with new ways of doing things. This can result in disconnected and unaligned domains, but it also provides the highest degree of independence.

The decentralized approach can be very tempting, but its disadvantages for the organization outweigh the advantages. Domains' development capabilities and design know-how for sustainable analytics infrastructures and processes may be insufficient, which can lead to operational inefficiencies.

For example, risk management departments are often staffed with mathematicians: well-trained analytical thinkers with strong problem-solving skills. It is not uncommon for them to start optimizing what they do with the skills they have at hand, usually Excel and VBA. In the best cases, they may use a functional programming language like Scala, R, Python, or SQL. They tend to produce semi-automated solutions for calculations, data transformations, and so on that solve their current problem. However, the solution often can't be scaled because they've never learned how to design an analytical solution with interdependencies on other domains or on organization-wide processes and systems.

Business units operate independently when it comes to data and analytics, with a strong focus on addressing specific business needs. There is often weak governance and unclear ownership as well as few opportunities for other units to benefit from these solutions. Collaboration and support among units are weak due to the lack of a unified strategy. The risk of creating significant silos within the organization increases as a result of this disjointed approach. These shortcomings need to be addressed, or they will become an obstacle to transformation.

Maybe you're a little confused now, because we mentioned that decentralizing analytics is one of the most important enablers to becoming data-driven. It is, but in a different, more organized, and more collaborative way: a federated approach.

The centralized approach

But first, the other extreme is a completely centralized approach to analytics owner-ship. This approach is most common in smaller companies, and it can be a perfectly valid business model for them. This approach is often taken where there is little or no technical or analysis capability in the business units, either because they are highly involved in repetitive, simple, manual work or because there are just a few experts who are highly focused on a specific issue that offers little automation potential and usually has little to do with analysis. It is common to have a tightly centralized CoE that handles all the core functions, including standard reporting.

The biggest advantage is clear: well-trained developers can design the best, most efficient infrastructure and data-handling processes. However, they lack business knowledge and insight into customer needs. To successfully apply this operating model, the guiding principles should be close cooperation, a manageable number of people on both sides, a strong commitment to working together, and giving the same amount of attention, priority, and effort to all issues, major and minor. The latter is one of the biggest challenges because a centralized unit will always be a bottleneck.

A centralized CoE must prioritize its efforts to manage its limited capacity. It may lag in emerging changes in the organization and struggle to act quickly on them. Cen-tralization rarely translates to shared responsibility and ownership of data delivery across the business. Often, IT lacks insight into business interdependencies and the specifics of the CoE's solutions, leading them to resist taking full ownership beyond the technical part of the solution.

The federated approach

We'll now introduce you to the federated model, an approach that falls between the two extremes—a model we believe is the only way to successfully combine ownership, technical sophistication, and collaboration. This model will ultimately take you to a higher cultural level and gain value for the business.

There's no single definition of a federated system, and it manifests differently in dif-ferent organizations depending on whether the central CoE or the decentralized units are more pronounced and how far along the organization is in its transformation.

In short, though, a *federated model* is one in which the CoE drives the transformation centrally at the beginning, but then the organization shifts toward a stronger decen-tralized federated model as its data maturity grows.

At the outset, many tasks are unclear. The technology is not fully ready, collaboration models are undefined, and a common analytics governance model is not yet in place. The CoE can address this by demonstrating how to tackle use cases and initiating programs to improve data literacy or at least analytics awareness. We thus recommend starting the CoE with a more centralized approach, then moving toward decentralization as you assign roles within the business units and as you establish appropriate data literacy within the business units.

This shift also lays the groundwork for transferring more responsibility to the business units, which helps to democratize data: with stronger analytical capabilities, business units can become data providers, not just consumers. This is the idea behind the *data mesh*, a data architecture concept defined by Zhamak Dehghani in her book *Data Mesh* (O'Reilly). Dehghani describes data mesh as shared responsibility for data products across business domains. Treating data and insights as assets that deserve proper ownership, she argues, leads organizations to a higher level of data culture.

But let's take a step back. Why is it so important to decentralize analytics at a higher level of maturity, as pictured in Figure 4-5?

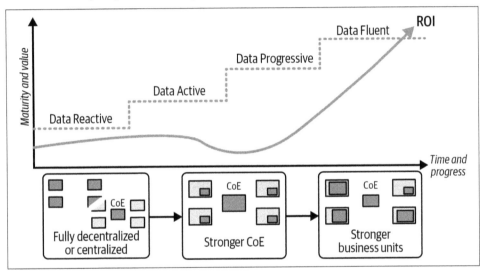

Figure 4-5. Types of federated models by maturity level

First, as awareness of analytics has increased, organizations have gained a greater understanding of the opportunities to leverage analytics for their business and are keen to become data-driven. This leads them to generate more ideas for insights they want and more requests (and demands) for analytics solutions. Ultimately, if they're operating from a centralized position, they can't meet these demands. They end up evaluating, prioritizing, and weeding out ideas because of a lack of capacity.

The advantage of a federated model is that if you empower the business units to handle most of their needs, you increase their sense of ownership of their problems and their ability to create value for the whole organization. This is a good feeling, and it's important for establishing a new culture.

In addition, business units mostly do common descriptive and diagnostic analytics tasks. In a federated structure, the CoE doesn't need to deal with these simpler tasks. It can focus on the really challenging issues and on supporting weaker business domains. The business units, meanwhile, are better able to combine their new analytics knowledge with their understanding of the business and its needs. It saves a lot of time and effort to do the thinking yourself rather than spending hours explaining it to a third party.

Be aware, though, that increasing federation requires stronger governance, or at least guidance and a commitment to a common framework of regulations and the limitations of what each unit can do.

It's up to you how you design your federated approach. We recommend a distributed, decentralized approach such as federation collaboration, which fosters efficiency, ownership, and a strong sense of togetherness. However, there is a spectrum of federated models. Look for the sweet spot that fits your organization's size, business model, staffing, strategic vision, and maturity. Find out what you need and where you stand: is your CoE the transformation driver you still need to kick-start the transformation and get everything rolling, or is it now a supporter, helping business units become excellent on their individual analytics journeys?

The first is characterized by the fact that, as the lead unit driving the analytics transformation, the CoE plays a pivotal role. Business units have begun to nurture and develop their analytics capabilities and expertise under the strong guidance of the CoE. While these units manage foundational tasks, the responsibility for the execution, implementation, and application of analytics, data, and relevant use cases remains firmly within the purview of the CoE.

The second is defined by the fact that the CoE operates as a compact, specialized unit. Its primary focus is to provide guidance. Acting as a facilitator, the CoE spearheads key initiatives, such as centralized learning, ensuring technical readiness, and conducting technology research. While capabilities are shared between the CoE and the business units, the CoE holds the overarching responsibility for ensuring that the transformation succeeds. However, the business units are responsible for use cases and analytics specific to the business domain.

Figure 4-6 explores the different levels of federation. The next section will help you better understand their pros and cons as well as how your approach might change over time as your analytics journey matures.

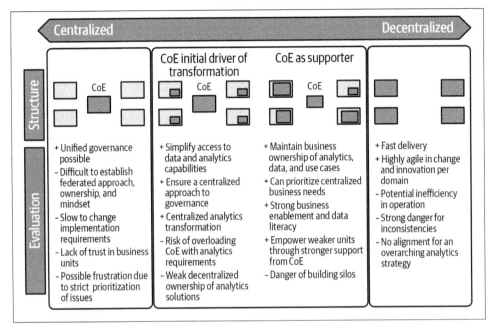

Figure 4-6. Federated business models throughout the analytics transformation

To drive a common analytics strategy, you *need* a CoE. This is critical. Its existence is a strong indicator of a more mature analytics transformation. A completely decentralized or fully centralized solution, on the other hand, is a strong indicator that a company is operating at stage 1, the Data Reactive maturity framework.

If your organization's goal is to become Data Progressive (stage 3), choose a model somewhere in the middle. We don't recommend starting with a fully (or almost fully) centralized approach. If the business units are strongly disconnected from analytics, you might have little choice but to centralize. But even then, always try to involve the business units in the CoE's activities as soon as possible. Gaining the business units' commitment, awareness, and curiosity will be critical. Therefore, try to quickly shift the initial full responsibility for use cases and their implementation from the CoE to a combination of both models, and at least transfer ownership of analytical use cases to the business units.

The more shared responsibility you can give the business units, the easier it will be to build people's interest in data skills and leverage the analytics transformation for business success. But this will be a marathon and not a sprint; you will need a lot of perseverance and patience.

The CoE's main role is to drive analytic transformation across the enterprise. Its tasks include:

- Ensuring data liberalization
- Creating analytics awareness and a bring-along data competency
- Building a "lighthouse" use-case execution pipeline to get the organization thinking analytically
- Collecting analytics opportunities that offer quick wins and low-hanging fruit to create momentum
- Working closely with the business units and data management and connecting their strategies
- Creating an analytics culture in the company
- Convincing the most ambitious and passionate people in the company to take ownership of the transformation

In summary, you absolutely need a CoE to reach the Data Progressive stage of maturity. We recommend a federated approach, starting with a strong CoE at the beginning, then decentralizing more and more once the business units are fully involved.

Driving Transformational Change with the Influence Model

An analytics transformation is a serious, often difficult organizational change. Many transformation initiatives fail, often due to human factors. Employees—the backbone of any organization—must understand and fully embrace the change for it to take root and succeed.

This is where the *Influence Model* comes in: a strategic framework based on sound academic research, first introduced by McKinsey in 2003 (*https://oreil.ly/Hk-CE*). The Influence Model addresses the core of successful organizational change: the human element. It's not just about having a plan or implementing a new software system; it's about influencing mindsets, shaping behaviors, creating cohesive understanding, and helping people believe in the organization's direction. This model focuses on four key areas (*https://oreil.ly/hSTt4*), shown in Table 4-2:

- Fostering understanding and conviction
- Reinforcing change through formal mechanisms
- Developing talent and skills
- Role modeling

Table 4-2. Quoted from McKinsey's Influence Model (https://oreil.ly/hSTt4)

"I will change my mindset and behavior if…"	Principle
"…I understand what is being asked of me, and it makes sense."	Fostering understanding and conviction
"…I see that our structures, processes, and systems support the changes I am being asked to make."	Reinforcement with formal mechanisms
"…I have the skills and opportunities to behave in the new way."	Developing talent and skills
"…I see my leaders, colleagues, and staff behaving differently."	Role modeling

Each of these key areas addresses the psychological and behavioral aspects of a change to ensure not only that the change is implemented but that employees internalize it.

At its core, this model is about understanding the "why" behind change and managing that change effectively. The Influence Model provides the tools to help you do this. For each initiative or change process you undertake, carefully consider the four "building blocks" outlined in the next sections.

Fostering Understanding and Conviction

Humans naturally seek consistency between their beliefs and their actions. A common challenge in change is assuming that everyone already knows why the change is happening. Two notable psychological tendencies contribute to this: the false consensus effect (*https://oreil.ly/4k5EN*), where people overestimate the extent to which others share their own attitudes, beliefs, and opinions; and the curse of knowledge (*https://oreil.ly/td4Cl*), where people find it difficult to imagine that others don't know something they know.

So what's the solution? Leaders must create a compelling change story and establish feedback loops to ensure that everyone understands it. Digital platforms and awareness-raising initiatives can help engage employees in these changes and make them feel that they're a part of the journey. If everyone isn't convinced about the transformation, the change will be over before it has really started.

Reinforcing with Formal Mechanisms

Our behaviors are generally the result of reinforcement and conditioning. But employers often go about this in the wrong way, without aligning rewards and desired behaviors. For example, rewarding employees financially may work up to a point, but money is probably not the ultimate motivator; other factors, like purpose and collaboration, may have a greater impact. How you use these rewards matters, too: they can be less effective if they're too predictable. It's best to make rewards fair, varied, and truly purposeful.

Moreover, the organization must improve the working environment in which employees operate, which encompasses working conditions, restrictions, and culture. If the "new" environment offers the same old structures and processes, you can't expect behavioral change.

Developing Talent and Skills

Humans are capable of learning and adapting throughout life. But a few things can get in the way of that process:

Inherent bias
> Many of us are unaware of our knowledge gaps because we are inherently biased. We don't know what we don't know.

Perceived solvability[2]
> People often assume that complex problems can be solved somehow, without actually tackling them and testing the approaches. This is particularly true in the AI environment, where the underlying technology accomplishes wonderful things in vaguely understood ways. It's important that people understand how problem solving actually works, because finding a solution usually involves a lot of hard work.

Learned helplessness
> Repeated mistakes or negative experiences can lead individuals to believe that they cannot change, creating a state of "learned helplessness." Organizations must instill the belief that effort can lead to improvement. With the advent of analytics, there are more opportunities than ever to demonstrate this in action.

Role Modeling

People naturally imitate others, both unconsciously (such as mirroring others' speech patterns) and consciously (such as deliberately adopting a particular behavior). While many think of role models in terms of historical figures or celebrities, influence within organizations can come from unexpected sources. In our digital age, people often value the opinions of crowds, such as when we trust Yelp reviews or read posts by LinkedIn users with large followings.

What this means for transformation is: don't underestimate the role of people with large "circles of influence." Convince these people early on of the transformation's purpose and the opportunities it brings. Their advocacy will help to embed the transformation more quickly and sustainably in the minds of others, and thus drive

---

2 Defined by Professor Michael Löwe, 2007 FHDW Hannover, in a direct conversation with his students in preparation for an exam.

it forward. This is why analytics leaders are so important; they lead by example. How they behave will be how the organization behaves.

It is surprising how often these critical elements are overlooked during major organizational change, even though the fundamentals of the influence model are rooted in human nature. For successful change, all of these elements should be addressed holistically. They may seem like common sense, but in the chaos of change, even the basics can be easily forgotten.

Any time you introduce a new initiative, solution, or change, we recommend asking yourself if all four elements are being adequately addressed. For example, when introducing a new use case, you might ask:

- Have I made the purpose of this use case clear?
- Can people use the results of this use case properly?
- Does embedding these processes ensure easier access to insights?
- How do I "reward" the early adopters?
- Do I have the support of people with influence?

This sort of cross-checking helps you to test your own actions and course correct if necessary. Use this framework. It really is very powerful.

The Influence Model is critical to supporting analytic transformation in organizations. It focuses comprehensively on the human element that is key to the success of such initiatives. By addressing the psychological and behavioral aspects of change, the Influence Model ensures that employees not only adopt new technologies and processes but also internalize these changes. This creates a more receptive environment for change by addressing key causes of restructuring failure. It aligns employees' behaviors and attitudes with business and transformational goals, overcomes resistance, and improves overall business performance. Changing the environment in which you operate is only half the battle.

Cultivating a Data-Literate Culture

We divide the big topic of data literacy into four subtopics (Figure 4-7): data awareness, data storytelling, the strategic benefits of data-driven management, and the dynamics of leadership in the age of AI. Each of these topics equips analytics leaders and translators with the skills they'll need to lead their organizations through the transformative power of data. This educational journey is about creating a data-centric culture that thrives on informed decision making and continuous innovation.

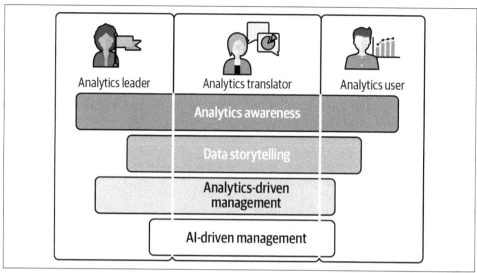

Figure 4-7. Four key aspects of data literacy

You may be wondering: how is data literacy even necessary if AA is just being integrated into your business workflows? The answer is simple: you need a high level of data literacy—especially among your analytics translators—to be able to find and develop the use cases that should augment critical business workflows in the sense of AA. On the other hand, analytics users—the masses—don't need a high level of data literacy to benefit from these workflows. But they need something called "analytics awareness," a concept that we'll explain in the next section.

That's why each role requires different training. Analytics leaders should focus (at the least) on analytics awareness and data-driven management while analytics translators need the full range of this training. For analytics practitioners, awareness and story-telling provide a solid foundation for analytics adoption, although the skills required will vary by position and role, as you can see in Figure 4-7. Let's take a closer look.

Cultivating Analytics Awareness

The evolution to data-driven decision making requires people who aren't analytics professionals to understand the full spectrum of data technologies and analytics processes, so they can communicate effectively with analytics professionals and use data to gain strategic advantages. The primary goal of data awareness is to ensure that they recognize the value of high-quality structured data.

At the heart of data awareness is understanding the data analytics process: a complex journey from data collection to analytical insights. As you, as a business professional, immerse yourself in this area, you'll become adept at ensuring the integrity and maximizing the quality of data.

Immersing yourself in the world of data also means becoming familiar with how to visualize it. Analytics leaders, translators, and users can study best practices to learn to transform complex data sets into clear and compelling visual narratives. Each visualization serves as a critical link between data and decision making.

The data-awareness journey continues with the concepts of AI, ML, and deep learning. Understanding these terms and their applications allows nonanalytics professionals to critically assess the capabilities and limitations of AI, foster constructive dialogue with data scientists, and formulate realistic expectations for AI projects. This includes treating responsible and realistic use of gen AI tools, especially LLMs like GPT, as a core competency, given that they are now part of business professionals' everyday toolbox.

As the digital and physical worlds merge through IoT, sensors and smart devices are contributing to the data explosion, with unprecedented opportunities to improve processes and create value.

Storytelling with Data

In an era of data saturation, the ability to tell a compelling story is paramount. Data storytelling bridges the gap between raw numbers and effective communication by balancing statistical rationality with narrative clarity. This skill is essential for professionals who need to present complex data findings to different audiences within the organization.

Again, it helps to first understand the purpose, the "why," behind data storytelling. It's a preparation for a deeper dive into the "how": the methods and techniques that turn data into compelling stories tailored to the needs of the audience and the goals of the presentation. Business professionals must learn to communicate with data in a way that is appropriate for their audience, mastering the subtleties of tone, context, and character to deliver presentations that resonate with and influence their audiences.

As they hone their storytelling skills, professionals also become curators of data narratives. They distill vast amounts of information into cohesive stories, using techniques such as storyboarding. This structured approach ensures that key messages are conveyed accurately and that audiences remain engaged and informed.

Mastering visual tools is another essential part of data storytelling. Charts and visual formats all have their strengths and applications. Choosing the right visualization is a strategic decision that can significantly improve how well your audience understands and absorbs information.

Decluttering, or removing the unnecessary to focus on the essential, isn't just a design principle; it's also a critical communication strategy. By learning to declutter visualizations, professionals ensure that data presentations are not only aesthetically pleasing but also psychologically compelling, focusing the audience's attention on what really matters.

Data visualization is certainly less a science than an art, but it is an important part of the data literacy skillset of people working in the analytical environment and should not be neglected.

Embracing Data-Driven Management

Becoming a data-driven organization is more than a technology upgrade: it's a fundamental change in decision-making culture. For managers, this shift requires a deep understanding of data's intrinsic value and the practical know-how to use it for strategic purposes.

From the outset, managers must learn the benefits of data-driven decision making and recognize the central role of the analytical value chain in refining raw data into strategic insights. This understanding is critical to recognizing how data can go beyond locally scoped operational support to become a core business asset and even pave the way for optimized processes and innovative data products. A central part of this transformation is committing to an analytics strategy. Once managers commit to and begin implementing the strategy, they can gain insight into common pitfalls and learn how to overcome challenges with strategic vision and operational acumen. They will also be empowered to optimally align their efforts with the individual business strategy.

Data integrity is critical. Managers have a special role as the guardians of data quality. They must understand how the integrity of a business's data affects its health and work proactively to maintain that integrity.

Managers are also concerned with the human factor: building and maintaining data ownership, addressing capability gaps, and promoting a culture of continuous learning and improvement.

Leading in the Age of AI

As the final competency, *data thinking* encompasses the strategic mindset required to integrate data into the DNA of the organization. Leaders explore the synergy between design thinking and data analytics, using tools such as the Analytics Use Case Canvas to generate ideas and align data initiatives with business goals and user needs to shape a data-aware organization.

AI, once a distant concept, is now an integral part of the business conversation. As AI reshapes industries, managers and executives in particular need to move from mere awareness to active engagement and understand AI's potential to drive innovation and profitability. This educational journey begins with demystifying AI and its complexities. From there, leaders can learn to identify and nurture AI opportunities, anticipate the challenges associated with AI initiatives, and create an environment in which AI can thrive. This foundational knowledge sets the stage for leaders to build an AI strategy as an extension of analytics strategy and project management, ensuring that AI investments translate into tangible business results.

The project-based learning competencies give managers the methods to manage the lifecycle of AI projects from idea to implementation. It is a practical roadmap, a use-case approach to AI project success that covers use-case development, proof of concept, and the intricacies of AI engineering and operations.

The culmination of this journey is *business integration*. Executives should tap into the wisdom of AI thought leaders by integrating best practices into a cohesive AI and business strategy that can guide the organization through the complexity of AI adoption, providing the necessary capabilities, technology stack, and management practices to leverage the transformational power of AI. By understanding and communicating this to your leaders, you will lay the foundation for a successful AA implementation.

Although many of the upskillings describe skills very much focused on new management competencies, these should be opened up for all analytics roles. Acknowledging how leaders act and why will help them adapt and strengthen them as role models. Through these learning focuses, analytics leaders and translators will not only be educated but also empowered to drive analytics transformation, foster data literacy, develop a data-centric culture, and lead their organization into a future where data and AI are an integral part of success. They are the ones who ultimately must identify, evaluate, and drive the value of use cases for the organization, and it is absolutely essential that they are fully prepared.

The Enablement Program

Data literacy alone is not an enabler. You need to embed it in an enablement program. This section describes different programs geared specifically toward analytics leaders and translators, who need to be treated differently. For leaders, the focus is on analytical thinking, data-driven management, understanding the analytics strategy, and serving as a role model. For translators, the focus is on their bridging role and how to tackle analytical challenges independently while driving a collaborative approach.

Training Formats for Analytics Leaders

Leaders need a starting point for their journey, with frequent follow-up delivered in formats that help them grow in their roles. That starting point is an initial engagement workshop or camp to get everyone on the same page. We recommend holding this workshop after the analysis strategy has been finalized.

These programs are time-consuming and expensive. They last for one or two days, and taking executives away from their work for that amount of time is a big deal. Once you find the right place and time, invest heavily in creating value-added content in a coherent format that doesn't waste their time. This workshop doesn't directly contribute to company ROI—it's an investment in awareness—so it has to be clear to leaders that they will get something out of their time commitment.

Combine your content with fresh and exciting elements, and create an environment that gives leaders time to share and exchange ideas, build relationships, and network. We recommend no more than 20 people per workshop, ideally a truly diverse mix of leaders from different domains. Depending on the size of the organization, you may need to hold several events.

Initial workshop

The initial one- to two-day workshop (or "camp") will be where you make a first impression on all of the organization's leaders, so be aware that first impressions last. This is your chance to establish a common language, to make them aware of the change and the opportunities it will bring, and to introduce the skills and roles required. Your goal is to enlist the support and commitment of senior management and to gain a better understanding of how to shape further change.

It's essential to give the workshop a memorable sequence. Here's the structure we recommend:

Step 1: Explain the purpose
> Start with a detailed explanation of the purpose of and strategic approach to the transformation. Lay out the status quo, the company's insight-driven ambitions, and your roadmap.

Step 2: Demystify the buzzwords
> Explain *data analytics* and other key terms and concepts, such as *data science, descriptive and predictive analytics, artificial intelligence*, and *generative AI*. Help everyone to understand data analytics at the highest level and show how analytics fits into strategic decision making.

> Give concrete examples that are memorable enough for everyone to follow. For example, use a case that perfectly describes the path of analytics from descriptive to prescriptive, with house prices or the Iris data set or whatever (it's best to ask your data scientists; they'll provide lots of content).

Step 3: Give examples
> Give examples by presenting your first internal use cases or, if you don't have any yet, using external examples from your industry or from other industries. Explain them and, if possible, demonstrate them live.

Step 4: Introduce the use-case approach

Next, explain analytics-driven management. In particular, focus on ideation and use-case implementation. Show how your use-case pipeline will work and what your end-to-end approach is. In Chapter 5, you will find an example of a possible implementation of a use-case approach.

Step 5: Brainstorm

Have participants brainstorm their own use-case ideas. Divide them into groups and guide them through a design-thinking process, which supports the audience with a well-structured approach: start with a well-defined problem statement of the case, then discuss the business value and required data, and draw a possible future solution. Let them present their ideas and challenge one another. You will find that this is a win-win situation for everyone involved as it encourages analytical thinking and can generate good use cases for your backlog.

Step 6: Put their ideas through the use-case process

Next, show the leaders how their ideas fit into the use-case process as a starting point. Point out how ideas are evaluated for feasibility and business value and considered for possible pilot projects. You may even be able to demonstrate how a prototype is created. Pick a small, less complex case and show live how ML can provide initial insights. You can use no-code tools to do this, which are great for demonstrating a workflow and giving executives a sense of feasibility when they realize that not everything needs to be coded.

Step 7: Introduce roles and responsibilities

Each manager and leader needs to know what their role is and what their responsibilities will be in the transformation as well as the roles and responsibilities of the people they'll be managing. They need to understand the changes the transformation will bring and what the new roles are. Help them understand how to integrate the analytics translator role within their teams. They also need to get an initial idea of how to approach the integration of analytics for strategic decision making.

Step 8: Establish the status quo

To gauge the transformation, you need a clear sense of the organization's current maturity. Prepare a survey to ask participants how they view the use and relevance of analytics and how they perceive their own readiness, the readiness of their teams, and the readiness of the organization as a whole. These insights will help you determine further focus areas for the transformation and give leaders a sense of ownership.

Step 9: Get buy-in

During the month following the workshop, get buy-in from participants. Ask each person what they want to do to fulfill their role as an analytics leader and what they need from the CoE to be successful.

The ideas you'll get during this workshop will be pure gold—use them to guide your upcoming actions. So think of this "leadership camp" as a great opportunity for all participants, both as leaders and for the development of the CoE.

The initial camp is your first appearance in all leaders' perception; always be aware that first impressions last. It is the chance to establish a common language, to make them aware of the opportunities and the change as well as the skills and roles required for the transformation. You can gain the support and commitment of your senior management and better understand how to shape further change.

Follow-up programs

The initial workshop is just the beginning. You're creating a long-term leadership engagement program around analytics transformation, and that's not a one-time thing. Your approach should be educational, experiential, and culturally integrated. Table 4-3 details how we suggest structuring such a program.

Table 4-3. Example structure for an ongoing leadership enablement program

Event	Frequency	Purpose	Description
Executive roundtables	Every two months	Ongoing conversation about their experiences with analytics	Regularly scheduled sessions cover rotating content on specific analytics topics, such as new technologies or use cases within or outside the industry, and encourage leaders to share their challenges and best practices. This ongoing exchange ensures that empowerment is not a one-time event but an integral part of leaders' professional routines.
Quarterly skills enhancement practical workshops	Every four months	Strengthening the role and consolidating soft skills	Quarterly workshops help managers deepen their roles and responsibilities in the transformation. The focus is less on the technical aspects of the transformation and more on consolidating soft skills, with practice and repetition.
Analytics ThinkLabs	Every six months	Collaborative problem solving	ThinkLabs bring leaders together to apply their analytical skills to real business challenges with cross-functional teamwork, a problem-solving mindset, and outside-the-box thinking. External speakers inspire innovation and provide fresh perspectives on specific topics—for example, ideation for gen AI use cases or design thinking for integrating certain algorithms into dedicated workflows. These events also help keep the backlog of use cases current.
Leadership summit	Once a year	Reflecting on and celebrating progress	This annual summit is the culmination of the engagement program and provides a forum to reflect on the year's progress in transforming analytics. It is also an opportunity to celebrate successes and recognize the contributions of individuals and teams. This event plays a critical role in maintaining momentum and setting the agenda for the year ahead.

In addition, fully leverage and consolidate other supporting activities. Consider adding mentoring from analytics experts to your internal leadership development program to personalize the learning experience and provide direct support. Give leaders access to online learning resources so that they can enhance their skills on their own.

As a more formal reinforcement mechanism, dashboards can help leaders track their personal contribution to the transformation by monitoring KPIs. You might also consider community networks, but with caution. Platforms such as Microsoft Teams can overwhelm managers, who sometimes perceive their content as undesirable. It's better to stick to regular structured formats to avoid information overload.

Training Formats for Analytics Translators

Developing a long-term program for analytic translators requires an approach that evolves with their unique role as the bridge between technical analytics teams and business stakeholders.

Initial workshop

Begin with an intensive workshop, "Kick-off Workshop: Introduction to the Translator Role," that sets the framework for the analytics translator's journey. Its content should include the overarching goals of the analytics transformation, the importance of their role as translators, and how to align technical capabilities with business strategies. Address the individuals' expectations, what their goals are, and how they want to develop. This workshop is essential for familiarizing participants with their roles and providing them with the basic knowledge they need to excel.

Follow-up programs

Table 4-4 provides an example of programming that can serve as follow-up to this workshop.

Table 4-4. Example structure for an ongoing leadership enablement program

Event	Frequency	Purpose	Description
Deep-dive sessions	Every month	Honing technical and business acumen	On a monthly basis, analytics translators should attend sessions that provide a deep dive into specific analytics tools, methodologies, and use cases. This ongoing series ensures that translators are fluent in both the language of data and the language of business. Each session should end with actionable takeaways that translators can apply directly to ongoing projects.
Analytics ThinkLabs	Every four months	Facilitating cross-disciplinary collaboration	Analytics translators should also take part in the ThinkLabs described in Table 4-3. Translators can ensure that teams within the lab maintain a balance between technical feasibility and business viability. They facilitate communication among data scientists, engineers, and business leaders. As champions of the analytics and business perspective, translators can encourage the adoption of insights derived from data to inform the ideation and prototyping processes within the lab. They can lead the discussion in ideation sessions and guide the development of concepts with their experience from other use cases.

Event	Frequency	Purpose	Description
Analytics leadership summit	Once a year	Reflecting on and celebrating progress	Translators should also participate in the annual leadership summit, for presenting use cases and success stories that showcase how analytics has driven business results, providing evidence of the value of data-driven decision making. They can advise and participate in active presentations, giving insight into how data and analytics can help shape the strategic direction of the organization. The summits provide a platform for translators to build relationships with senior executives, raising the visibility and importance of analytics on the executive agenda. As the voice of technical interoperability, translators can articulate what is technologically possible.

To complement these key events, we recommend the following supporting activities:

Active involvement in use-case implementation

One of the most important levers for translators to fulfill their role is their active involvement in the use-case implementation process. Not only are they responsible for communicating the progress of the implementation, but they should also become more and more involved in active development. Feedback loops and peer coding sessions with the analysts will help improve translators' analytical skills and enable them to implement more of their own ideas in the future, serving the federated approach.

Mentoring and shadowing programs

Analytics translators are matched with leaders from other business areas and experienced analytics professionals to foster a deeper interdisciplinary understanding and provide insight into different business areas and analytical processes. Translators spend time with their mentors in their day-to-day work environment, which allows them to gain practical experience and identify potential parallels in the area of analytical solutions. This direct collaboration creates valuable synergies, helping translators solidify and expand their role as facilitators between the worlds of data and business strategy.

Ongoing certification courses

Continuous learning and professional development courses offer certificates in the latest analytics methodologies, emerging technologies, and advanced lateral leadership skills. These courses are designed to deepen translators' skills and equip them with the latest trends and tools for effective data analysis and interpretation.

Project presentations

Regular project presentations let analytics translators demonstrate how to apply analytics to gain tangible business results. Translators explain their ideas, visualize their successes, share best practices, and learn new approaches. These events are critical to recognizing translators within the organization and building their confidence.

Feedback loops

By establishing structured mechanisms to give translators constructive feedback from stakeholders, feedback loops are essential for continuous improvement. They provide valuable insight into the effectiveness of translators' work and allow them to fine-tune their methods and approaches. Regular feedback ensures that translators can grow in their role and continuously adapt to the changing needs of the organization.

Data Literacy Training

Good content alone is not enough to ensure success. Even when participants recognize the need for training, time is always a limiting factor. Analytics translators might do well with a dedicated, long-term training program that is part of their agreed-upon role and can thus be built into their schedules. For managers' schedules, however, a long course is unlikely to be suitable. Some employees may also lack the motivation and endurance to complete long courses, which is why a motivational approach is important. For example, not everyone is able to organize their own training.

Companies have begun to recognize this problem. StackFuel (*https://oreil.ly/lvfZf*), for example, offers an upskilling program that combines organized and self-paced training within a certain time frame. This provides structure and helps participants track their overall progress and data literacy. This approach ensures that everyone is on the same page and no one is rushing ahead. So determine the right formats for leaders and translators, then combine them with events and programs designed to engage the community of analytics translators.

Technical Training

We've discussed data literacy for the business roles, but it's also essential to have a proper technical development program for the analytics professionals. It's hard to make any generic recommendations here: the training they need will depend a lot on the company's technical orientation and analytics ecosystem. For instance, if the company depends heavily on vendor solutions, people will need specific training on those solutions.

What we *can* recommend is to focus on general analytics skills, such as basic statistics, data processing, and open source programming languages. SQL, Python, and R are crucial foundations for coding skills.

In addition to new skills, professionals need to improve their technical and methodological skills continuously. In our experience, analytics professionals usually know their needs best and often want to use specific sources to improve their knowledge. Specialized providers such as DataCamp, Udacity, Udemy, and LinkedIn Learning offer a wide range of online training. Look for engaging and motivating resources.

Analytics professionals certainly don't need a fully guided approach, but rewards and a structured approach will help them be more successful. In our opinion, DataCamp has current content and a strong motivational approach.

In addition, there are a lot of other concepts that can be helpful to retrain people to become data professionals. Reading books is always a good approach. You might also consider attending special programs like Springboard or StackFuel Reskills.

Conclusion

The critical takeaway from this chapter is the importance of the four key analytical roles to the business. Each of these roles has expectations; some produce content, and others consume it. The leaders, who are expected to drive the entire transformation by example, and the analytics translators, who bridge the two worlds of business and analytics, have particularly important functions. The transformation manager actively shapes and guides the transformation and actively accompanies the change. Each role requires a certain mindset and skillset, and can be further subdivided into different personas with their own individual functions, depending on the business model.

Without these roles, you will not be able to implement your transformation to the point of achieving stage 3, Data Progressive status. You will also need to create a CoE to kick-start the transformation and to lead and organize all change initiatives. This unit is the one most capable of understanding business needs and implementing analytics solutions.

As your organization matures in its AA transformation, it's important to shift your approach to applying analytics. Serving increasing demand from a centralized unit will inevitably lead to limitations, so at a certain point, you will need to distribute responsibility for using analytics. We recommend adopting a federalized approach that empowers decentralized units while ensuring coordination and guidance from an accompanying CoE.

In the next chapter, we will discuss how use cases can help move the organization forward in data maturity. You will also understand how AA will be essential to achieving the final stage of data fluency. We will discuss the key aspects of the need for adoption and technical integration, their benefits, and their challenges.

## CHAPTER 5

Augmented Workflows

You've learned a lot so far about the fundamentals of employee empowerment and the organizational environment required to implement AA successfully. Without executive ownership, ideas from analytics translators across the organization, a CoE driving the transformation, and an effective infrastructure to translate the ideas into use cases, there would be nothing to augment business users' processes and workflows.

The whole transformation is an iterative approach, and AA is now becoming a key driver for the final phase. It's a two-way relationship, as Figure 5-1 shows: there can be no AA without the right level of maturity in analytical transformation, and there can be no ultimate excellence without AA.

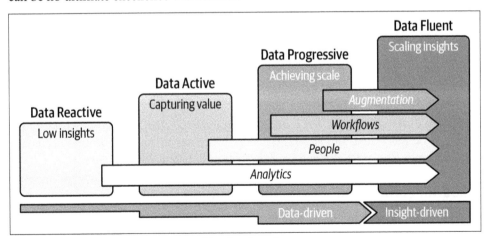

Figure 5-1. Augmentation as an enabler for data fluency

The final phase must now focus on enabling the majority of employees, the analytics users, to effectively participate in the benefits of analytics through the technical integration of analytics into their workflows. That's what we'll explain in more detail in this chapter.

Types of Workflow Augmentation

As Figure 5-2 shows, new workflows need to follow a rubric often called *TRICUS*: they should be timely, relevant, insightful, credible, unobtrusive, and specific.

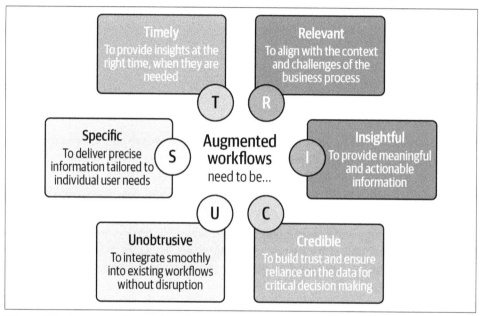

Figure 5-2. Augmented workflow characteristics

Each type of workflow augmentation serves a different purpose and is suitable for different kinds of tasks and decision-making processes. They show how versatile and adaptable AA tools can be across various business contexts and workflows.

There are different types of AA workflow augmentation for knowledge workers, and they can be integrated into several business processes to support diverse needs and requirements. The most obvious are fixed-rule and insight enrichments.

Fixed-Rule, High-Confidence Augmentation

In *fixed-rule augmentation*, the system automatically makes decisions or takes actions when certain predetermined criteria are met, without the need for human intervention. This type of augmentation is called *high-confidence* because reliable data quality and proven, definitive AI models allow organizations to operate with a high level of confidence. It is common in process automation, where it's often used to optimize operational costs and ensure consistency in delivery standards. It's very reliable for routine, well-defined tasks but less flexible when dealing with complex, nuanced situations.

Typical use cases for fixed-rule, high-confidence augmentation include integrating customer segmentation in a customer relationship management (CRM) system, routing insurance claims to handlers, and navigating or prepopulating entries in inventory systems.

Idea and Insight Enrichment

Idea and insight enrichment is about augmenting the human decision-making process with additional data-driven descriptive and predictive insights and visualizations to enrich users' understanding and decision making. Humans are in the loop and making the decisions. This could include highlighting trends, predicting future scenarios, or providing visual representations of data to uncover hidden patterns. It's particularly useful for strategic planning, where it acts as a "copilot," giving recommendations and surfacing previously undiscovered insights.

Enrichment doesn't necessarily (and often can't) provide a clear recommendation, but the information it offers helps analytics users choose a comprehensive solution. One example of enrichment would be to benchmark comparable past cases in the early stages of a sales proposal. A second example comes from commercial insurance, where enrichment might involve assisting underwriters by benchmarking new risks, evaluating the profitability of the client's industry segment, or comparing the structures of reinsurance assigned to previous comparable risks.

Conversational Augmentation

Conversational augmentation uses gen AI and LLMs to interact with users in a conversational way. This often takes the form of an AI assistant, which can answer questions, make suggestions, proofread drafts, generate ideas, provide explanations, or even suggest improvements. This type of augmentation is highly interactive and user-friendly enough to be accessible to those with limited technical expertise.

The most striking examples of such augmentation come from IT: coding-assistance tools, such as GitHub Copilot, which help developers write code, create documentation, and design interfaces. McKinsey (*https://oreil.ly/tvkKT*) estimates that these tools can make developers' coding workflows significantly more productive. More generally, another McKinsey study (*https://oreil.ly/k5Set*) found that automation could improve the workflow productivity of knowledge workers with higher education by 25%, since they deal disproportionately with unstructured data (in the form of text and documents).

One example is recruitment. By integrating a conversation engine into the HR system, recruiters can use an AI to challenge their own opinions on job vacancies in direct comparison with the position on offer. Current LLMs, such as the GPT models, can compare offers with job descriptions, augmenting the decision making and workflow for recruiters. Another example, from the commercial insurance industry, is processing large texts, such as contracts, claims reports, and site-risk survey analyses. Users can have the model summarize these documents, then discuss the findings with it to gain a better understanding. With effective training and skillful preprompting, you really can use gen AI to leverage insights for augmentation.

Contextual Augmentation

Contextual augmentation, also called *adaptive augmentation*, is less common but valuable. This refers to AI systems that adapt to the user's context, learning from their interactions and preferences to provide more personalized and relevant information. The system adjusts its interactions and the level of detail and type of data it presents, based on the user's role, expertise, or current task.

Contextual augmentation is common in consumer recommendation systems and personalized social media feeds. In a business context, this tool can formulate predefined responses as emails that mimic the user's language and tone.

Collaborative Augmentation

A less common type, *collaborative augmentation,* is about enhancing teamwork and cross-functional collaboration among team members by providing shared dashboards, real-time data updates, knowledge repositories, and other tools that help people collaborate as they analyze and interpret data.

A typical user could be an analytics translator who uses collaborative knowledge repositories to gain insight into the progress of use cases and model results. Another example is adding an Azure chatbot agent to Microsoft Teams to add support and advice to each team's conversations based on a solid knowledge base, such as internal work instructions or compliance documents.

Each type of workflow extension serves a different purpose and is suitable for different kinds of tasks and decision-making processes. The workflow extensions define how AA can be integrated into business workflows. You can see the versatility and adaptability of these tools in various business contexts.

The Analytics Use-Case Approach: Finding Workflows to Augment

With hundreds, thousands, or even hundreds of thousands of existing workflows and business processes in your organization, how do you actually find the ones to augment? Where do you start? And how do you take an idea into effective execution?

This is where the *analytics use-case approach* helps you out. In essence, it's an operational framework that transforms untapped potential (in the form of ideas) into a robust analytical product, ensuring sustainable business excellence and fostering innovative thinking.

The use-case approach helps you develop and maintain a *use-case pipeline* that allows you to respond very quickly to analytical business needs and move cases from idea to finished product, including providing the appropriate infrastructure, resources, and capabilities. This step-by-step approach gives a clear, structured path from concept to operationalization. It makes the innovation process less risky, since each stage serves as a checkpoint to validate your assumptions, refine your goals, and sharpen your business focus.

For companies with mature analytics, this methodology is not just a procedural advantage but also a strategic enabler of operational excellence. Its process of validation and iterative refinement helps you ensure that the organization's analytics investments are both prudent and targeted. It also bolsters agility, helping the business adapt quickly to new opportunities and challenges in iterative steps, challenging ideas aligned closely with the business objectives and market dynamics. In essence, it is an operational framework that transforms untapped potential in the form of ideas into a robust analytical product, ensuring sustainable business excellence and fostering innovative thinking.

Figure 5-3 illustrates the use-case approach over time. The following sections will dive into each of its six phases.

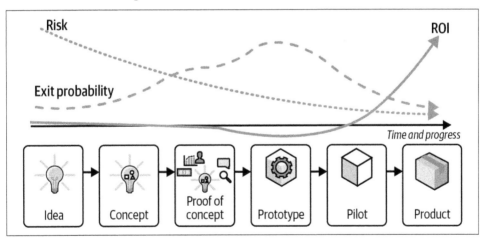

Figure 5-3. The use-case approach

Phase 1. Idea: The Initial Spark

Like many journeys, that of a use case begins with an idea. An idea can be defined as a conceptual spark that identifies an opportunity or problem that potentially could be solved through data analysis.

The germ of an idea is recognizing a challenge or opportunity within the organization that could be addressed through improved data analysis and its application. The idea forms a *hypothesis* (or proposed explanation) about how to use data analytics to solve a problem, improve a process, or capitalize on an opportunity. It also represents the seed of innovation by proposing a novel way to use data analytics to achieve business goals. It assumes that the challenge has an analytical solution, one not yet fully developed or validated.

Deliverables

Ultimately, the deliverable of this first phase, which is typically created outside of the process somewhere in the business, is a concise description of a problem in the business environment and a draft of the solution to which it is intended to add value.

Risk and ROI

The risk of leaving the "use case" at this point is very high, as at this moment it is not a real case but a rough idea that someone has in mind and, in the best case, has written down to convey it to an audience. Ideas arise quickly but can also be quickly discarded. However, it is the beginning of a possible transformation use case.

The return on investment (ROI) here is basically zero, as no real work has yet gone into the case. Only the formulation of the idea can be described as an investment, but we would generally neglect that at this point.

Project maturity

Project maturity is also close to zero because the only thing that exists is an idea for a use case, a workflow, or the improvement of a process. In our experience, many idea generators have a very well-formulated idea that leads in a clear direction. From this perspective, you can say that it may be a very mature idea, but the overall process of bringing the idea to life is at the lowest level.

Phase 2. Concept: Structuring the Idea

The problem with good ideas is that they *remain* ideas unless you formulate, structure, and communicate them.

The *concept* phase is when you examine a new idea within the fundamental framework of the company's strategic direction, technical infrastructure, and available data. It is primarily about identifying a challenge, evaluating the benefits of overcoming it, and proposing a solution. It is a phase of exploration and brainstorming, during which the idea is still malleable and the project's direction has not yet been determined.

People often base their ideas on a desired solution but find, upon closer look, that they haven't sufficiently examined the underlying problem. At the very least, it's important to examine the origin of the data early on when designing a solution. Our experience has shown that if you skip this stage, you risk coming up with abstruse, unrealistic ideas. Examining related data sources also helps people distinguish better between analytical use cases and operationalization (or purely technical) cases.

The starting point of the concept phase is a *problem statement*. For example:

> We need to be able to simulate and analyze the development of certain insurance portfolios because of changing conditions or external triggers, such as a change in strategy, new market opportunities, or necessary adjustments, to measure the potential impact and ultimately steer a portfolio in a certain direction.

The final step is to define the potential solution. This is not a detailed list of requirements—it's more about challenging expectations and getting the idea provider to think about integration and interoperability.

Assessing a use case's dimensions

You can use four basic dimensions to help articulate the concept: the problem, the value involved, the data environment, and the solution. Some examples of questions you might ask about each dimension include:

Problem dimension
- What challenge facing our organization are we currently addressing?
- How does this issue hinder our operational efficiency or profitability?
- To which key business objective does this challenge relate?
- What goals do we hope to achieve by addressing this use case?
- Who is affected by this challenge, and how?

Value dimension
- What type of value creation are we anticipating?
- Who stands to benefit from resolving this issue?
- How would resolving this issue benefit stakeholders?
- What kind of return or advantage would this bring to the business, its workforce, and/or its customers?
- Could the solution to this problem create a competitive advantage?
- Could addressing this problem lead to innovation or significant process improvements?

Data environment dimension
- What data should we consider pertinent?
- Do we have access to all the necessary data?
- What new data sources could we explore to gain better insights?
- Does this use case require real-time data analytics?
- How should we integrate external data sources?
- How can we evaluate and improve the quality of our data?

Solution dimension
- What does the proposed solution encompass?
- What specific goals or performance indicators will signal success for this project?
- Which analytical techniques or processes should we consider?
- How might we leverage emerging technologies to address this problem?
- Are there opportunities for automation within the proposed solution?
- How do we ensure the sustainability of the solution over time?

Consider posing these questions in a workshop to get the discussion going and start generating ideas.

Deliverables

The most important result of this phase is a *use-case canvas*, shown in Figure 5-4. It is critical that this canvas is both comprehensive and concise, capturing the essence of the project's goals.

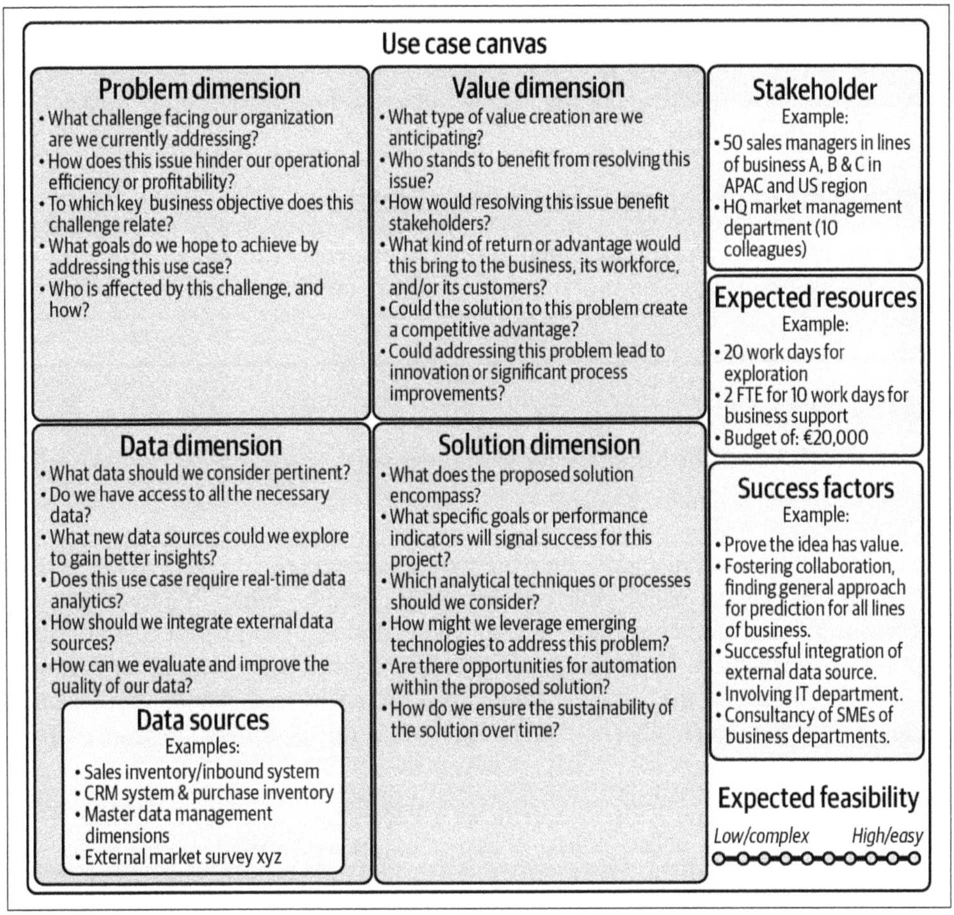

Use case canvas

Problem dimension
- What challenge facing our organization are we currently addressing?
- How does this issue hinder our operational efficiency or profitability?
- To which key business objective does this challenge relate?
- What goals do we hope to achieve by addressing this use case?
- Who is affected by this challenge, and how?

Value dimension
- What type of value creation are we anticipating?
- Who stands to benefit from resolving this issue?
- How would resolving this issue benefit stakeholders?
- What kind of return or advantage would this bring to the business, its workforce, and/or its customers?
- Could the solution to this problem create a competitive advantage?
- Could addressing this problem lead to innovation or significant process improvements?

Stakeholder
Example:
- 50 sales managers in lines of business A, B & C in APAC and US region
- HQ market management department (10 colleagues)

Expected resources
Example:
- 20 work days for exploration
- 2 FTE for 10 work days for business support
- Budget of: €20,000

Data dimension
- What data should we consider pertinent?
- Do we have access to all the necessary data?
- What new data sources could we explore to gain better insights?
- Does this use case require real-time data analytics?
- How should we integrate external data sources?
- How can we evaluate and improve the quality of our data?

Solution dimension
- What does the proposed solution encompass?
- What specific goals or performance indicators will signal success for this project?
- Which analytical techniques or processes should we consider?
- How might we leverage emerging technologies to address this problem?
- Are there opportunities for automation within the proposed solution?
- How do we ensure the sustainability of the solution over time?

Success factors
Example:
- Prove the idea has value.
- Fostering collaboration, finding general approach for prediction for all lines of business.
- Successful integration of external data source.
- Involving IT department.
- Consultancy of SMEs of business departments.

Data sources
Examples:
- Sales inventory/inbound system
- CRM system & purchase inventory
- Master data management dimensions
- External market survey xyz

Expected feasibility
Low/complex   High/easy
○─○─○─○─○─○─○─○─○

Figure 5-4. A use-case canvas

Risk and ROI

The risk of abandoning a project at this stage is somewhat higher than in the idea phase. You might find, upon closer examination, that the case isn't an analytics case. Maybe it's not even a real problem. But if the problem is valid, you can create the use-case canvas and move to the next phase.

Of course, project risks are still very high at this stage. The idea is untested, data availability is not yet assured, and the concept must still be aligned with the business objectives. Conversely, ROI is speculative: it's all about potential and predictions, with no tangible return in sight.

Project maturity

Maturity is only just emerging at this stage. It is a phase of exploration and brain-storming during which the idea is still malleable and the direction of the project has not yet been determined.

Phase 3. Proof of Concept: Testing the Waters

The *proof of concept* phase is designed to test the analytical feasibility of the idea and assess its business value. Can the concept be implemented? If so, how?

Assessing business value

To prove a use case, there are two important considerations:

- What value does the use case have to the company?
- How feasible is it to implement?

On the business-value side (definitely the most challenging), you need to know what value this use case drives for your business. This could be something like improved processes, increased revenue, more profitable portfolios, or improved customer perception or satisfaction. Is the proposed solution a short-term or long-term way to achieve this value? Is the use case imperative, driven by compliance or regulatory issues, or is it fundamentally about enabling innovation? Is it linked to your business strategy?

If you have appropriate KPIs, use them as a benchmark to compare different use cases on metrics such as portfolio size or the number of affected tasks, customers, or employees. This will help you compare cases, identify "low-hanging fruit" or easy wins, and prioritize use cases.

To guide the discussion, questions to ask include:

- What opportunities exist to streamline workflow and achieve cost efficiency?
- How does this project align with our overarching business goals, vision, and strategy?
- When can we expect to see economic gains from this initiative, and what are the projections? Does it achieve value over the long term or the short term?
- How can this enhance our customers' perceptions and satisfaction levels?
- In what ways will this improve customer engagement and loyalty?
- How will this project contribute to competitive differentiation and market leadership?

- What drives our business value: improved processes, increased revenue, more profitable portfolios, improved customer satisfaction? What else?
- Is this project imperative, driven by compliance or regulatory issues, or does it fundamentally enable innovation?

We believe that the best approach is establishing an objective supervisory committee of business experts to listen to use-case pitches. The CoE should assist in this task, but the final decision should rest with the business professionals. This gets them involved in shaping the analytics transformation, and it's the perfect forum to spread the word about ideas and give visibility to the people behind those ideas.

If you have suitable KPIs, you can also use them as a benchmark to compare different cases, based on metrics such as the size of the portfolio or the number of tasks, customers, or employees involved. We know that setting uniform evaluation criteria for all cases is the most difficult part. Because of the diversity of the cases, different KPIs are required. One case might be about improving staffing levels in the company so that, for example, the working days saved are appropriate. In another case, the aim could be to increase the company's revenue or achieve significant savings, which would require financial KPIs.

Furthermore, in many cases these are fictitious, hypothetical values, as it is often not clear whether the case will be successful or not. So be realistic and modest when it comes to the expected improvements. Also emphasize what individual cases can do to enable value. Often, piloting new approaches and technologies does not bring direct benefits but lays the groundwork for future cases that do. We recommend agreeing with other IT and innovation projects on how to measure value using KPIs, which rules apply, and which dimensions to use. This will help others to understand your measurement and create a certain degree of uniformity within the company.

Assessing feasibility

How you define feasibility also depends on your business model, ecosystem, and industry. Feasibility is no easier to evaluate than business value, but the framework for doing so is much better defined. Dimensions to consider include:

Data availability and quality
　　Is there enough data for a model? Is its quality high?

Modeling and data-engineering complexity
　　How complex is the challenge in terms of data science and engineering? Is the data set especially large?

Complexity of integrating workflows
　　How difficult is it to integrate the proposed solution into the workflow? What systems do we need to touch?

IT infrastructure and modeling platform(s)
What modeling and operational platform(s) should we use?

Dependencies
Are there any external dependencies or legal considerations to consider? Are there business constraints on how or when to roll this out (such as other large projects)?

Transformation and adoption
Do end users on the business side support adopting this solution? How much effort will be required to roll it out?

In most cases, analytics professionals should assess feasibility, ideally with the support of an analytics translator. Hold a "feasibility check" session that brings together data engineers, analysts, data scientists, SMEs, and analytics translators with diverse skillsets to discuss the task. In addition, initial prototyping and technical coding can be done in parallel by data professionals in the CoE or in decentralized domains to gain more accurate insights.

Deliverables

The result of the business-value and feasibility checks should be:

- Feasibility studies
- Initial analytical tests to demonstrate the value of the use case
- An evaluation KPI that helps to position each case within a two-dimensional value matrix

This will help you compare cases, identify "low-hanging fruit" or easy cases, and decide on priority when executing cases. As we mentioned, this is just one possible type of evaluation; it depends on your individual needs to take into account more measures.

Risk and ROI

The risk in this phase is still high because you're testing the concept in the real world. The proof of concept serves as a reality check that can either strengthen confidence in the project or highlight insurmountable challenges. Of course, this also increases the likelihood that the use case will be stopped. The ROI is not yet tangible at this stage but may improve slightly with a successful proof of concept.

Project maturity

The project is not yet mature. The idea is no longer just a concept on paper but is undergoing its first practical tests, bringing it one step closer to realization.

Phase 4. Prototyping: Shaping the Concept

If the proof-of-concept result is positive, the next step is to create a prototype. The goal is to implement the analytical concept in an operational prototype, test its technical and methodological feasibility, and increase analytical maturity. The prototype could be, for instance, a first data exploration on a relational database, a complex data preparation from different data sources, an initial analysis pipeline to create a first workflow, or preliminary model tests to see if the data contains a required information gain and if the initial hypotheses are likely to be confirmed.

This process is about exploring the analytical challenge and testing its feasibility but is *not* yet about tackling things like technical integration or software engineering. When programmatic skills for initial analytics workflows or explorations are not yet available, try using low-code or no-code engines. They can help you to perform descriptive analyses of the data quickly and roughly test initial ML experiments. A very accessible tool for this is Orange (*https://oreil.ly/ahpjc*). Although it uses only the processing power of a local computer system (a severe limitation), it helps you get a quick overview of the data's structure and first algorithmic approaches in case of doubt. Figure 5-5 shows an example of this kind of exploration in Orange.

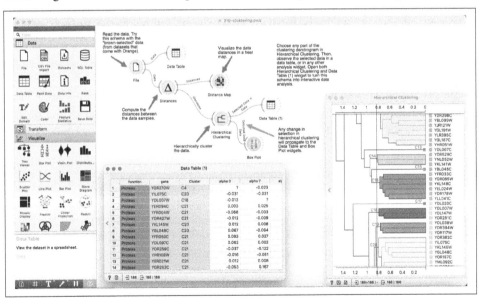

Figure 5-5. An example workflow prototype in Orange

The workflow described in the example is a method data scientists use to gain a quick and thorough understanding of the Baker's Yeast Brown gene data set, a popular data set in the field of explaining ML. First, Orange examines the distances between each

---

instance by creating a *distance matrix* that quantifies the similarity or dissimilarity between pairs of data instances.

Next, Orange applies *hierarchical clustering*, a special type of clustering algorithm that builds a treelike structure called a *dendrogram* that visually represents the arrangement of the clusters. The dendrogram is an important tool for data scientists. It shows how the clusters are formed and enables interactive analysis. You can select different parts, or branches, of the dendrogram to isolate specific data clusters and examine them in more detail to identify patterns, similarities, or anomalies. In this example, you could very quickly and effectively perform exploratory data analysis (also in a visual format) using pattern recognition to extract insights that are not immediately apparent from the raw data.

In the prototype phase, the aim is to understand the data, its structure, and its systematics so that you can decide quickly and reliably whether the algorithms are expedient and whether your hypothesis can be supported (at least for the time being). Low-code tools can help to prototype quickly but are not a must. Our recommendation would always be to go in the direction of coding, as this skill cannot be compensated for by such tools and is obligatory in the next phase at the latest. But if low-code tools are helpful in accelerating your first analytics insights, use them. This can be seen as an early form of AA, which is directed to supporting data professionals.

Deliverables

If the prototype works, the result is a functional first technical implementation. This may be code that works to a limited extent or even only in a subset of the data to demonstrate the potential of the use case.

Risk and ROI

The risk of abandonment begins to decrease as the prototype makes a theoretical concept more concrete. Technical implementation and integration challenges may arise, but these are often more manageable than conceptual uncertainties. Nevertheless, this is where the likelihood of an exit is highest, as only here does it become clear whether the hoped-for value can actually be realized.

ROI is not yet achieved at this stage, although successfully demonstrating a prototype can facilitate stakeholder buy-in and potentially unlock further investment. In fact, from this point on, ROI starts to become negative, as more and more effort and costs go into exploring the use case.

Project maturity

Maturity improves significantly during the prototyping phase, as the use case begins to take shape and prepare for real-world deployment.

Phase 5. Pilot: The Test Run

Entering the pilot phase means testing the prototype under real operating conditions. The goal is twofold: to use the prototype to realize its initial potential and to refine it through direct feedback on its feasibility in daily operations. This is where you truly determine its viability.

Imagine your team has developed a classification model for customer segmentation, with extremely good prediction results. You've connected this model to a website on the backend to customize the user experience and make specific offers. Unfortunately, the classification process takes too long—longer than would be appropriate for real-time analysis. If this can't be corrected, the use case might not achieve the desired value, and you may have to discard it. In this case, there is certainly room for optimization, but it must be clear that the case is not yet in safe harbor.

Deliverables

The main deliverable is an improved version of the code. This is accompanied by comprehensive documentation of the pilot phase, including operational logs, monitoring procedures, evaluation results, user training, and feedback surveys.

Risk and ROI

Risk is further reduced as the project proves its viability in a controlled, real-world environment. The more successful the prototype and the more positive the feedback, the lower the risk. Exit risk decreases dramatically at this point but is still present. A failed test in a production-like environment can still cause the case to fail.

ROI is now at its lowest point, and exiting the project at this stage would incur the highest effort to date before the business can actually realize the value.

Project maturity

Maturity reaches a critical point during the pilot phase. The project is no longer an internal prototype but an operational tool, undergoing rigorous testing and optimization.

Phase 6. Product: Full Deployment

After a successful pilot, the use case is ready to mature into a full product. The goal of this phase is to make the solution available in production across various workflows.

Deliverables

Deliverables include:

- A robust rollout plan
- An operational plan for software that is widely used and integrated into work processes
- Sophisticated governance structures
- Release management processes
- Comprehensive code documentation
- Defined service-level agreements (SLAs)

Risk and ROI

Risk is lowest at this stage because the product has been extensively tested and is ready for use. Concerns now shift to operational risks and maintaining service quality as well as to adopting the new solution consistently. Your transformation-management and change-management skills come into play here to ensure successful usage of the solution.

ROI expectations are at their peak, as the product is now delivering the promised benefits and starting to generate returns that will (ideally) exceed the initial investment.

Project maturity

The project is at peak maturity. A polished product is ready to deliver value and drive change within the organization.

Making the Make-or-Buy Decision

Perhaps the use-case approach sounds overwhelming to you. How on earth should you be able to handle more than one of these concurrently? We have good news: you don't have to do it all by yourself. In fact, many use cases shouldn't be done by you at all but should be outsourced to an external vendor or partner.

To shed light on this approach, let's quickly explore the options for building use cases.

It's not a binary choice

The decision to make or buy an augmented-workflow solution isn't simply black or white. Instead, picture it as a continuum, with "fully developed in-house" on one end and "fully purchased solution" on the other, as shown in Figure 5-6. Between these two endpoints lies a vast landscape of options.

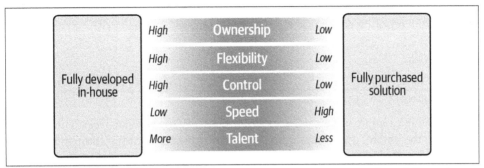

Figure 5-6. Factors in deciding whether to make or buy an augmented-workflow solution

Here are some examples of workflows enhanced with chat capabilities:

Fully developed in-house solution
> You build a custom chatbot from scratch so employees can chat using Microsoft SharePoint.

Mostly developed in-house solution
> You integrate a generic "chat with my documents" chatbot platform into Share-Point.

Mostly purchased solution
> You use a fully managed chatbot platform, like Microsoft Copilot Studio, and add some customization.

Fully purchased solution
> You buy a Microsoft Copilot license so that employees can chat using SharePoint.

In most cases, you'll likely mix prebuilt components or models from vendors with developing specific parts of the application in-house. This hybrid approach allows for more flexibility and control. Of course, this requires in-house talent, which you should have in abundance if you're in the Data Active or Data Progressive stage.

To determine the right balance, consider the following key factors.

Use-case stage

As mentioned before, proofs of concept and prototypes are all about quickly testing feasibility and potential impact. The goal is to learn fast and fail fast. Prototypes are typically not integrated with your IT environment, which typically makes this stage a great candidate for off-the-shelf or vendor solutions.

On the contrary, pilots and production use cases are typically tightly integrated into your system environment. This is where you need more control, governance, and reliability. It's critical here to reassess whether the off-the-shelf solution still makes sense. Sometimes it's better to tailor-make the integration once the use case has survived the proof-of-concept and prototyping phases.

Strategic value

Strategic value is how important and impactful the solution is to your overarching business goals.

Consider the example of autonomous driving for a company like Tesla. This use case alone has the potential to make or break the entire existence of the company, so it has an exceptionally high strategic value. On the other hand, a document-text-extraction use case for an insurance company might be valuable, but the business will survive without it.

The importance of a use case can change over time. Something initially seen as very important may become less important as the market changes; other projects that started small can become very valuable, as chatbots have in their evolution from simple customer-service tools to essential components of the customer experience.

External solution performance

No off-the-shelf solution will be a perfect fit. But how *close* does it come to meeting your needs? Remember that the "good enough" threshold can vary.

Take, for example, an augmented workflow that categorizes customer-support tickets with a 75% accuracy rate. That may not seem impressive at first glance. However, if your manual process only achieved 60% accuracy before, then the augmented solution represents a significant improvement. For some applications, even a small improvement in accuracy can lead to significant operational benefits or enhancements to customer satisfaction.

Internal resources

Internal resources refer to the technical resources available within the organization, such as data, infrastructure, and skilled teams. It's not just about whether you *have* the resources you need but how effectively and efficiently you can *use* them to build the solutions you want. (You may have a room full of developers, but if they're all working on other projects, that won't get you very far.)

Decision Scenarios

While the factors we just discussed are the most critical ones in the make-or-buy decision, there are many more to consider, especially for larger enterprises. Factors like organizational readiness, cultural fit, regulatory compliance, and ethics can play huge roles in adopting and implementing augmented workflows. But for now, let's concentrate on our smaller subset and learn how to decide between "making or buying" in different scenarios. The flowchart in Figure 5-7 helps you visualize this process.

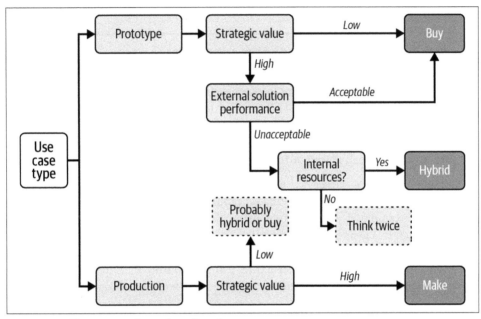

Figure 5-7. Use-case make-or-buy flowchart

Scenario 1: Prototyping a use case with low strategic value

Here, the decision is simple: go with an off-the-shelf solution. Even if you have available internal resources, they are better spent on use cases with high strategic value. Remember, your main goal in the prototype phase is to quickly test and validate ideas, not to reinvent the wheel.

Recommendation: buy

Scenario 2: Prototyping a use case with high strategic value

For high-strategic-value prototypes, first check if an off-the-shelf solution meets your needs. If so, use it to test feasibility and user feedback quickly.

Recommendation: buy

But what if none of the vendor solutions are good enough? Check if you have the resources to build a hybrid solution internally. For instance, you could build the main ML model in-house and use third-party components for the rest or vice versa.

Recommendation: hybrid

If there are no internal resources, building a prototype is a tough call. If the use case has very high strategic value, you might consider investing in infrastructure or data or in hiring (temporary) staff. However, these things are complex. Gauge the potential ROI critically before making such a commitment.

Recommendation: think twice

Scenario 3: Productionizing a use case with low strategic value

If you've successfully prototyped a "quick win" use case with a vendor solution that meets your needs, it makes sense to keep using it or to build on it for production. For instance, if you have created an AI prototype to automate manual data entry using ready-made software, and it fulfills your needs and can smoothly be added to your current systems, it will likely be cheaper and faster to keep using the vendor solution for production. You can always switch to building it yourself later.

Remember that every AI service needs ongoing maintenance and support. Even if you need customization, you can still just rebuild parts of the workflow and adapt as needed. For example, if you prototype using a chatbot service from a US vendor but want to switch to European for production, you could check if you can consume the core component (the AI model) as a service hosted in Europe, then build the rest of the application on your own infrastructure, using open source or no-code tools.

Recommendation: hybrid or buy

Scenario 4: Productionizing a use case with high strategic value

First of all, if you've managed to move a use case with high strategic value from prototype to production, congratulations! You've already crossed a major hurdle. If the use case is really paramount to your business, it almost always makes sense to allocate some dedicated resources to building it yourself. After all, this is what will differentiate you from your competitors and add significant long-term value to your business.

Recommendation: make

From our scenarios, it's clear that the "make" option is usually not the best choice. Your initial efforts will likely produce only a few strong use cases that are crucial for your competitiveness. It's OK to build those internally with a dedicated team. But for most use cases, don't get too caught up in the details. A company in the Data Fluent stage doesn't have a handful of analytics use cases in production; it has *thousands*. Most of them are small and low impact, but their value adds up.

Especially if your organization is in an early stage of analytical maturity or is a nontechnical small or medium-sized business, handle most of your augmented use cases with off-the-shelf or hybrid solutions. This allows you to focus on the core aspects of your business. It's best to start small and seek expert help at the beginning. The more you try, the more you learn.

Overarching Success Factors

Several overarching factors play a critical role in successfully implementing use cases. They include:

Transparency
> You can achieve transparency in how your organization develops use cases by using an interactive use-case library (see "The Use-Case Library" on page 133 later in this chapter). Buy-in from senior management is critical, as is a fee model that clearly delineates responsibility for funding.

Standardized monitoring
> Regular monitoring to measure the use case's success against predefined metrics helps keep projects on track and productive. Defining operationalization criteria and regularly evaluating use cases against them are also important for avoiding the sunk cost fallacy (*https://oreil.ly/0DNU5*).

Agile methods
> Agile methods have proven to be very effective for developing and operating data-driven use cases. Incorporating DevOps and MLOps concepts from the outset can streamline the path from concept to product. Fostering a data analytics community, especially one that involves analytics translators, can drive innovation and collaboration.

The approach we describe here emphasizes a structured yet flexible transition from idea to deployable product. This path requires careful planning, a consistent focus on deliverables, and a flexible response to feedback and changing conditions. This mix of strategic overview and tactical agility is the keystone of successful analytic transformation.

In addition to following these structured phases and strategies, it's important to stay abreast of the evolving data landscape and technological advancements. Even as you focus on the current state of your organization's data and your analytics capabilities, keep an eye on emerging trends that could affect use cases. Integrating new technologies, adapting to regulatory changes, and scaling your use cases to keep pace with business growth are all critical considerations that can impact the long-term success and sustainability of your analytics transformation.

Balancing Automation and Integration

Many augmented workflows fail because they rely too heavily on automation and integration at the beginning. To be clear, highly integrated and highly automated augmented workflows have the highest leverage for your business (because they do most of the heavy lifting for the user), but they are also the hardest to build. In most cases, it's better to design your use cases to augment the workflow with relatively low degrees of automation and integration. Once you gain more experience, you can scale them up.

How does this work? Take a look at the simple matrix in Figure 5-8, which we call the *integration-automation framework*.

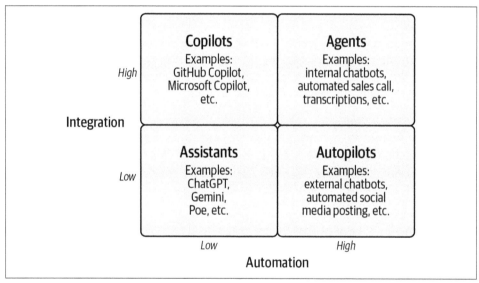

Figure 5-8. Integration-automation framework

This framework is based on a simple principle. It classifies use cases based on two criteria: how integrated and how automated they are. *Integration* refers to how deeply the use case is embedded into your existing system landscape. *Automation* refers to how much of its work the use case will perform with minimal human intervention.

Think about this for a second. Most people would assume that integration drives automation and vice versa. But that isn't necessarily true. For instance, you can create a use case that includes some automation but is not fully integrated into your system environment. To help you understand the difference, here are four types of use cases and where they fall along this matrix:

Assistants

The lowest level of use case is what we call *assistants*. Typically, employees work with an external application that requires them to handle inputs and outputs manually (like copying and pasting text or uploading and downloading files). The degree of integration is low, and so is the degree of automation. ChatGPT is a classic example. Make no mistake, these apps can be powerful. As of this writing, ChatGPT is probably the most capable external AI assistant you'll encounter. Other examples include Poe, Google's Gemini, Microsoft's AI-powered Bing search, and any other AI tools where you upload and download files manually (like the standard version of Midjourney, for example).

Copilots

Similar to assistants, copilots require users to do the heavy lifting (that is, their degree of automation is low), but they are heavily integrated into your system landscape or business workflow. This is currently one of the most promising fields in AI: every major software company is evaluating whether to include these "copilot" features in its products. GitHub Copilot, Microsoft Copilot, Einstein Copilot in Tableau, Duet AI in Google Workspace, and the AI features in Slack and Notion are all examples.

Copilots are great because they know what you're doing *at the moment.* For instance, if you use Outlook Copilot to reply to an email, it will already know the previous conversation history from that email thread. No copy-paste necessary. It also eliminates the friction of signing up for a new app. However—and this is the biggest difference compared to the next use-case type—with copilots, the AI-generated suggestions cannot be implemented without approval. So employees can (and must) review and correct the AI's outputs as needed. This use-case type is popular because it offers great value, even if the AI models aren't 100% perfect.

Autopilots

Autopilots have a high degree of automation but a low degree of integration. Imagine you train an AI-powered chatbot on your website and internal documents to answer first-level customer-support queries. Once deployed, this chatbot runs fully automatically, answering customer questions 24-7 without manual intervention.

Yet this chatbot isn't really integrated. Its integration usually boils down to putting a small HTML or JavaScript snippet on a website. (We recently implemented one on our website for this book!) If you tell that chatbot, "I want to buy the book," it will return an Amazon link. However, it can't take your order and put it into a booking system. If you wanted to do that (which *is* technically feasible), you'd need to increase the degree of integration (see the next type, the Agent, for that).

Other examples of autopilot use cases might include:

- A social media tool that does automated content moderation
- An automated surveillance system that sends email notifications
- A robotic vacuum cleaner in your house that cleans on a schedule

Agents

Agents are the holy grail of AI and augmented workflows. Everyone wants them. Imagine having an internal chatbot that can answer common questions *and* perform tasks like resetting passwords, giving refunds, and taking book orders. To be clear, these use cases do exist, but they are the hardest nuts to crack. They need a robust, battle-tested infrastructure (which we'll introduce in Chapter 6). At this stage, you're not only dealing with the challenges inherent to AI (like inaccuracies, hallucinations, and performance issues) but also the good old-fashioned IT issues involved in integrating a bunch of legacy applications. Further examples of agent use cases include:

- Automatically processing and forwarding incoming documents
- Serving personalized recommendations on your website
- Flagging quality issues in a manufacturing line

We're big fans of these use cases, and our goal is to empower you to get there as quickly as possible. But they are *not* the best way to get started.

When you start to augment your workflows with enhanced AI capabilities, there are two ways to proceed. You can go from left to right (low automation to high automation) and increase the complexity of use cases by automating them more. Or you can go from bottom to top (low integration to high integration), where the main challenge is to integrate what you have even further into your systems or workflows. It's typically not a good idea to do both at the same time—that is, moving diagonally and increasing the level of integration and automation at once. Don't jump right from assistants to agents.

Our experience working with different AI projects across multiple domains has taught us that the best approach generally is to tackle use cases in the order in which we just introduced them:

> assistants → copilots → autopilots → agents

The key is really to start with use cases that keep a human right in the loop (assistants and copilots). This way, you'll be able to control the AI outputs, ensure quality results, and learn more about the workflows over time. The beauty of these use cases is that they are generally the least complex, which makes them great candidates for early prototypes and proofs of concept.

The Use-Case Library

A *use-case library* is a strategic asset of significant value: a central catalog of and repository for the organization's analytical efforts—past, present, and future. Ideally, it is an interactive library that captures each use case's maturation journey, from idea to fully functional analytics tool. The library is an essential component of the use-case approach. In the ideation phase, it gives reference points for what can be considered or tried. In the proof-of-concept and prototyping phases, it provides valuable data points for feasibility and comparative analysis. As projects move into the pilot and maturity phases, the library serves as a record of the journey.

More than just a repository for analytics projects, a use-case library is a strategic tool that captures the learning, growth, and innovation of an organization's analytics capabilities. It is a cornerstone to building an analytics-centric culture. Its benefits include:

Promoting transparency across the organization
> Documenting the goals, methods, progress, and results of each use case facilitates decision making and encourages cross-functional collaboration, since stakeholders from different areas can see which analytics initiatives are being addressed across the board.

Enabling monitoring
> A use-case library enables management and teams to monitor each case's progress, assess its impact, and make informed adjustments as needed.

Incubating innovation
> By providing a detailed view of current and completed projects, the library can inspire teams to build on and refine existing work and ideas and develop new ones. Sharing knowledge and experience can accelerate the innovation cycle and reduce duplication of effort.

Motivating the organizational culture
> A use-case library can create a fear of missing out among teams and departments that have not yet engaged in analytics initiatives. This can motivate them to explore their data-driven opportunities.

Making stakeholders visible
> The library showcases those involved in each use case, recognizing their efforts and creating internal benchmarks for expertise and execution. This visibility can lead to career advancement for individuals and help the organization identify and nurture its analytics talent.

Figure 5-9 shows an example implementation of a use-case library using Casebase (*https://oreil.ly/pkOe_*), a library-inventory tool specifically designed for analytical use cases that follows the six-step approach from idea to final product.

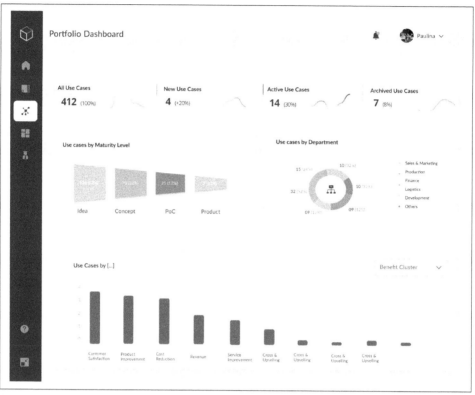

Figure 5-9. Casebase portfolio overview

The library's most important feature is providing an overview of all use cases from *all* domains that have been collected across the company. Since use cases from other domains, like innovation management or IT, are included, you may be able to adapt them to your own domain using meta-configurations. This advantage is extremely important for augmentations because having a common input funnel for a wide variety of use cases creates more visibility into other domains and allows IT and analytics to work much more closely later on in augmented workflows. Thus, the library's cross-domain overview and requirements management are very helpful.

Evaluating cases for their feasibility and business value (see Figures 5-10 and 5-11) is important to ensure that you allocate optimal resources to the most promising cases. If you are focused on running use cases regularly, it's imperative to have a tool that offers transparent communication about the results and even the ability to evaluate and assess within the tool. Proofs of concept are a frequent and continuous part of the use-case process.

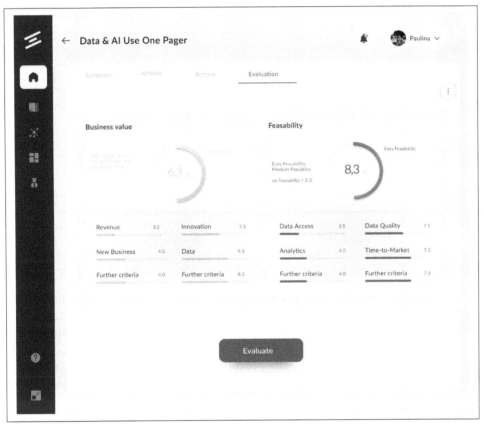

Figure 5-10. Casebase evaluation of business value and feasibility

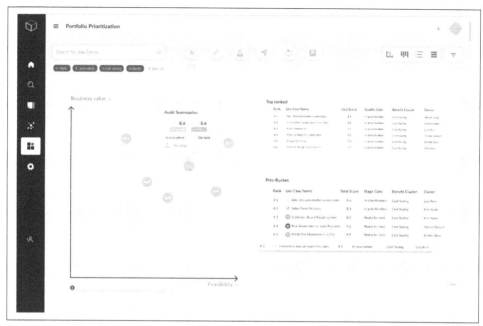

Figure 5-11. Casebase overview about evaluating business value and feasibility

Knowing the use cases in detail, including the status of ongoing work, is important for everyone involved to gain a comprehensive understanding of the overall process.

A Kanban board (Figure 5-12) is also useful for communicating the detailed execution of individual initiatives. It helps not only the analytics professionals but also the stakeholders to understand the expected execution time, resource planning, and allocation of each key resource. A Kanban is usually more detailed in its planning than the headings of the overarching process, such as the idea, concept, or proof of concept. It allows specific subtasks to be defined for each use case and dependencies to be documented.

Figure 5-12. Kanban execution of use cases in different stages

We recommend that you take a closer look at your specific working environment. In most cases, companies have a dedicated resource-planning solution for Agile development. There are dozens of possible solutions, and even Microsoft Teams offers a way to document activities in a task board. Interdependencies between technical resources and the capacities of the people required can perhaps be documented more easily there.

The charm of integrating Kanban into your use-case library is that it ensures full transparency for all stakeholders, including those not involved in the wider Agile development initiatives. This may matter more for the application than feasibility.

An even more important function of the use-case library than the process overview is providing details about individual use cases: a detailed description of the problem, the desired benefit, and the intended solution (see Figures 5-13 and 5-14). This can increase people's understanding of and conviction about implementing the use cases. Keeping people informed about current findings, initial results, and progress also gives them the opportunity to participate. For comprehensive documentation, we recommend including links to additional knowledge sources, such as knowledge repositories, product pages, and Git repositories.

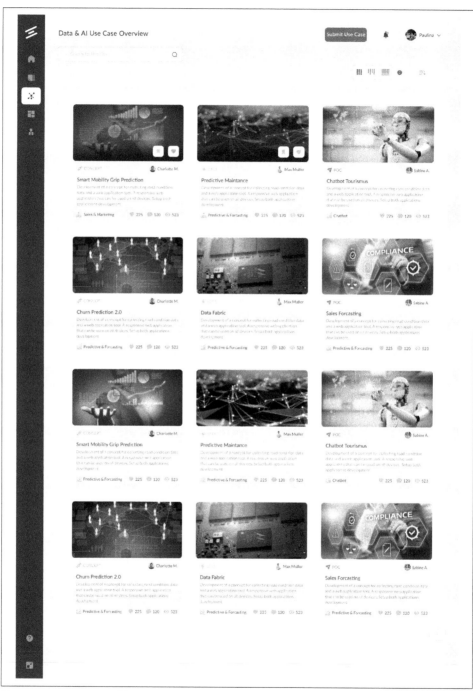

Figure 5-13. Use-case library overview

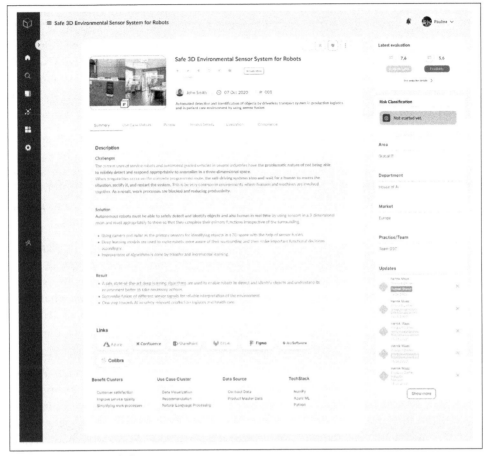

Figure 5-14. A detailed use-case overview

Technical Requirements for Implementing AA

In Chapter 3, we talked about the challenges and limitations of AA from a business and people-centric perspective. To conclude this chapter, we'll now discuss the *technical* challenges of implementing AA in your organizational environment. Then, in Chapter 6, we'll present a concept that will serve as a basis for actually implementing AA solutions.

One of the biggest challenges is fundamental to AA: the need to integrate analytics solutions *into workflows*. Delivering traditional data and analytics solutions is simple: you deploy a product in an appropriate environment, and that's where it ends. Of course, that's not without effort: you still must account for factors like a suitable runtime environment, authorization management, training, and ML/DevOps. But when you produce a deliverable, like a dashboard, report, or tool, you've fulfilled the last step in the use-case approach, and you can start using the solution.

In AA, however, you have to consider different ways of delivering solutions, and the corresponding workflows still need an adoption step. Here, the effort can be extreme. You have to involve other players and teams and plan activities, and sometimes do all this in established systems and tools that have completely different technical runtimes or are technically difficult to expand. While delivery is the end of the conventional process chain, in AA that chain must extend to include integration activities.

At first glance, this seems much more complex, since further technical implementations now must be carried out. Remember, though, that AA eliminates the need for adaptation-support activities, simplifying the product phase. And since driving adoption and active acceptance of new solutions is one of the biggest challenges of the approach we've shown you so far, don't overestimate the effort of technical integration.

Your use case will only be successful once you've successfully integrated the analytical solution into the workflows. Of course, how you assess success (through ROI or individual exit risk, for instance) depends on the individual solution. For example, for a solution designed as a standalone tool like a dashboard, you can achieve a high ROI earlier, and implementing a specific workflow might be optional. We are convinced that for most solutions, though, you'll only achieve a high ROI through successful technical integration.

Figure 5-15 expands the use-case approach we showed you in Figure 5-3 to include a further integration step: *augment*. In the next section, we'll consider the most important aspects of this step and discuss how best to tackle them.

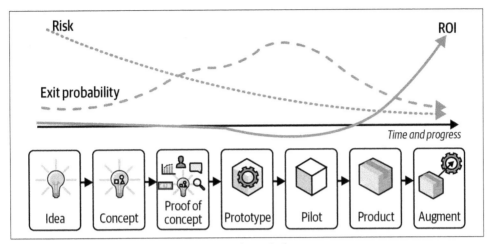

Figure 5-15. The updated use-case approach, including a new step: augment

Infrastructure Setup Challenges

While you can design the technical implementation of AA in very different ways, the implementation must be adapted to the overall infrastructure. The most obvious providers of analytical insights here are microservice infrastructures. We recommend relying on REST APIs, which are established, well supported by analytical programming languages, lightweight, modular, secure, and reusable. They can be integrated into almost all systems and create independence from vendor solutions, which is always recommended. A good overview of microservice infrastructures can be found in this guide by Martin Fowler (*https://oreil.ly/JSVIO*).

SAP and Microsoft offer corresponding solutions, such as integrating business objects into SAP or Power BI into Microsoft Tools and Office. We don't touch on these solutions here, though, because they depend heavily on vendors and do not offer the same lightness and independence.

Your augmentation should be technology agnostic. Whatever your legacy infrastructure and its runtime, your analytics should be autonomous and independent. Cloud providers, such as Microsoft Azure and Amazon Web Services (AWS), offer ways to provide analytics as web APIs. Python and R provide easy-to-use web-service endpoints to make analytics and data available. In addition, both programming languages offer a variety of connectors for a wide range of data sources. They should be your first choice for implementing analytics as code. Example 5-1 illustrates one such option: R Plumber. This very simple example API provides detailed contract information for a specific `contract_id`.

Example 5-1. An example of an R Plumber data-provisioning service

```
# file:api.R library(plumber) library(dplyr)

# Imaginative sample data frame
  contracts <- data.frame(
    id = 101:110, name = c("Customer A", "Customer B", "Customer A", "Customer A",
        "Customer C", "Customer V", "Customer Z", "Customer G", "Customer A",
        "Customer Z"),
    date = as.Date(c("2023-01-01", "2023-01-05", "2023-01-10", "2023-01-15",
        "2023-01-20", "2023-01-25", "2023-01-30", "2023-02-04", "2023-02-09",
        "2023-02-14")),
    product = c("Product 1", "Product 2", "Product 1", "Product 1", "Product 2",
        "Product 1", "Product 5", "Product 2", "Product 2", "Product 1"),
    premium = c(120, 150, 180, 210, 240, 270, 300, 330, 360, 390) )

#* @apiTitle Contract Filter API
#* @apiDescription API to filter contracts by contract number

#* Filter contracts by contract number
#* @param contract_id The contract ID to
# filter by
#* @get /filterContracts
function(contract_id) {
    filtered <- contracts %>%
        filter(id == as.numeric(contract_id))

    if (nrow(filtered) == 0)
        return(list(message = "No contract found with the given number"))

    return(filtered)
}

plumber::plumb(file='api.R')$run()
```

In addition, R Plumber automatically creates a Swagger API endpoint to inspect and access the new web services. Swagger is an open source software framework supported by a large ecosystem of tools that helps developers design, build, document, and consume RESTful web services. It provides a web-based user interface (shown in Figure 5-16) that enables easy testing and interaction with APIs as well as tools to automatically generate client libraries, server stubs, and API documentation. This framework is widely used because of its simplicity and scope in managing the entire lifecycle of an API, from design and documentation to testing and deployment, and it is supported by R Plumber.

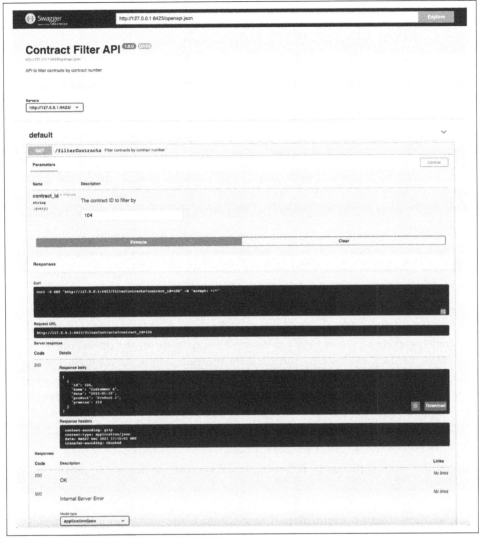

Figure 5-16. Example Swagger API Interface for an R data-provisioning service

Here is the result we get by directly requesting the API via the terminal:

```
curl http://127.0.0.1:6423/filterContracts?contract_id=104

[{"id":104,"name":"Customer A","date":"2023-01-15","product":"Product 1",
    "premium":210}]
```

In general, it is important to think early on about an internal analytical infrastructure that deals with developing and providing solutions. Algorithms, for instance, must be built as software artifacts to make them available as packages, analytical engines, or web services. Build up employees' skills in analytical programming languages at this point, if you haven't already done so during earlier transformation iterations. They can also largely use these skills for full-stack development.

In addition to the IDEs, you'll need to create appropriate runtimes for deploying and executing these languages. Descriptive reporting engines, no- and low-code options, and Excel solutions will not be completely sufficient for extensions, so we again recommend relying on Python or R at the early stages. Both languages have extensive repertoires of functionalities that allow full-stack development and offer the best capabilities for analytical operations like data pipelining and ML or extensive extensions for all analytical challenges.

In R, it is very easy to create package structures that encapsulate analytical functions and can be used in different contexts. Packages can be embedded in other applications, deployed as service endpoints, or integrated into user interface frontends.

One beneficial approach is implementing R packages as executable engines. These packages are structured somewhat differently in their use than are pure function packages, which contain a collection of functions of a uniform domain (such as dplyr, which contains various data-wrangling functions).

Engines are executable artifacts that are given environment variables at runtime and executed via defined function endpoints. For example, an engine that performs the internal aggregate of a customer's sales must encapsulate all the operations required to obtain the data, evaluate it, and perform the calculation. At runtime, the engine receives all the environment variables it needs (such as the path to the data) as either parameters or environment settings. It performs the corresponding operations by calling the execute function and passing the relevant customer identifier. These engines are ideal for establishing company-wide standardized workflows since they combine functionality with interoperability.

However, if your entire setup is heavily based on SAP or Microsoft, and it is easier for both the analytics team and IT to deploy and integrate solutions within those universes, then take advantage of those opportunities. Better to have a highly dependent solution than no augmentation at all because the initial jump to independent solutions is too great.

The code in the following examples creates a customer engine to analyze purchases. Start by implementing the execution function in Example 5-2.

Example 5-2. Customer-purchase analysis engine

```
#' Execute Customer Purchase Summary
#'
#' This function retrieves customer and purchase data based on environment
#' variable paths, filters them based on a specified customer ID, and returns a
#' summary of their purchase history along with their personal information.
#'
```

```
#' The function reads customer data and purchase data from RDS files, whose
#' paths are specified by environment variables. It then filters this data
#' for a given customer ID, summarizes purchase information (number of purchases,
#' total and average purchase amount), and joins it with customer information.
#'
#' @param customer_id A numeric or character value representing the unique
#' customer ID.
#'
#' @return A data frame containing customer's personal information (customer_id,
#' name, age, city) and their purchase summary (num_purchase, sum_amount,
#' avg_amount). If no customer is found, it returns a message indicating
#' that no customer was found for the given ID.
#'
#' @examples
#' execute(1234) # Replace 1234 with a valid customer ID
#'
#' @import dplyr
#'
#' @note The function relies on two environment variables: 'CUSTOMER_DATA_PATH'
#' and 'PURCHASES_DATA_PATH' to locate the RDS files. Ensure these are set
#' in your R environment.
#'
#' @export
#'
execute <- function(customer_id){

  # Use environment variables for file paths
    customer_data_path <- Sys.getenv("CUSTOMER_DATA_PATH")
    purchases_data_path <- Sys.getenv("PURCHASES_DATA_PATH")

  # Reading data from the paths specified in the environment variables
  customers <- readRDS(customer_data_path)
  purchases <- readRDS(purchases_data_path)

  filtered_customers <- customers %>%
    dplyr::filter(customer_id %in% !!customer_id)

  if (nrow(filtered_customers) == 0) {
    return(list(message = "No customer found!"), result = filtered_customers)
  }

  filtered_purchases <- purchases %>%
    dplyr::filter(customer_id %in% !!customer_id) %>%
    dplyr::group_by(customer_id) %>%
    dplyr::summarize(
      num_purchase = n(),
      sum_amount = sum(purchase_amount),
      avg_amount = round(mean(purchase_amount), 2)
    )

  result <- filtered_customers %>%
  dplyr::inner_join(filtered_purchases, by = "customer_id")

  return(list(result = result, message = "Success!"))

}
```

Here is the corresponding package description file:

```
Package: customer.engine
Type: Package
Title: Customer Data Analysis and Purchase Summary Engine Version: 0.1.0
Author: [Your Name or Your Team's Name]
Maintainer: The package maintainer <yourself@somewhere.net>
Description: This package provides tools for analyzing customer data and
    summarizing their purchase history. It includes functions for reading
    customer and purchase data from RDS files, filtering based on customer ID,
    and calculating key statistics such as total and average purchase amounts.
    Designed for use in retail and e-commerce data analysis, it offers a
    streamlined approach for customer data handling and insights generation.
License: [Specify License, e.g., GPL-3]
Encoding: UTF-8
LazyData: true RoxygenNote: 7.2.3
```

Here is the final execution of the encapsulated purchase function:

```
Sys.setenv(CUSTOMER_DATA_PATH = "data/customer.rds")
Sys.setenv(PURCHASES_DATA_PATH = "data/purchases.rds")

customer.engine::execute(c(1500, 9552))
```

Finally, the output:

```
  customer_id   name  age     city  num_purchase   sum_amount   avg_amount
1        1500  Alice   40  Phoenix            107     49353.34       461.25
2        9552  David   26  Houston             89     38878.83       436.84
```

Are SQL interfaces also an augmentation solution? Yes and no.

Of course, the most obvious solution is to use classic SQL interfaces to transfer data to your own system. Integration is usually not very complex: every developer has at least basic SQL knowledge, and there are connectors and drivers for every database in every programming language. However, the disadvantages outweigh the advantages in terms of effective augmentation.

SQL requires access management on the database. Of course, database access is a common standard, but it brings more challenges than benefits when it comes to effectively augmenting existing workflows. Access is usually to tables and views, so you have to know each one's meaning, relationships, and constraints. In addition, databases are directly connected, which can have serious implications for the company's access infrastructure—especially if different databases are running in different cloud instances or even through different providers.

Databases can also be difficult to replace or move to a different runtime. The more systems there are that have direct access to a database, the more complex it becomes to migrate that database from Oracle to Postgres, for example. All these dependencies have to be resolved, which means a lot of organizational effort.

Finally, it is important to remember that the governance of the insights derived from common data provisioning, as described previously, cannot be guaranteed. Direct access to the data can lead to different implementations and interpretations, as each consuming system must do to some extent. The implementation of the insights then takes place somehow governed in the respective system, regardless of whether the respective runtime is even suitable for such processing. We have seen countless implementations push the capabilities of a language like Java or C# to their limits to process large amounts of data internally.

In addition to the API DIY approach and SQL interfaces, many purchased and open source solutions provide an *abstraction layer* (also called the *data access layer* or DAL) on top of databases, or even file access or other kinds of data storage. However, they always create a dependency on the solution and usually do not solve the insight governance problem. A guiding principle that has always held true is that today's vendor solution is tomorrow's legacy technology.

Our recommendation is to offer analytics for augmentation as web APIs implemented in analytical programming languages, with organized access by an API hub, as shown in Figure 5-17. Open source frameworks like Kong (*https://oreil.ly/y3ixK*) can support you with this. The most effective analytics will be customized for the business and will require individual implementation, so adopt analytical programming early and train staff in the required skills if necessary.

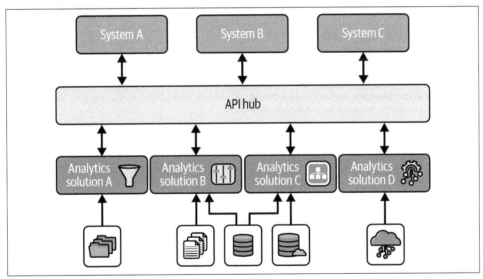

Figure 5-17. API access to analytics solutions

In addition to conventional infrastructures for structured data and analytics, it's increasingly important to have a corresponding infrastructure for unstructured data. This will provide the basis for carrying out augmentations based on context-relevant documents. As with integrations in conventional infrastructures, you should create and offer programmatic access as an API.

The capabilities of gen AI and LLMs in particular offer completely new possibilities for augmentation and make it essential to think about appropriate document management. Imagine you are in the inventory systems for individual contracts, and you choose a contract. An augmentation by a service returns a summary of all the specific conditions for this contract.

The infrastructure for this is far less complex than you might think. The service has access to the contract documents. It sends a series of complicated prompts to an LLM to summarize the specifics of the document. This can be as complex as you like, especially if there are dozens of documents that need to be analyzed. Then, indexing and embedding services or even vector databases are required for document management. We don't want to drift off into detail: the important thing is that programmatic implementations are essential if the augmentations are to support the business in a targeted manner. Python is particularly suitable here for implementing such functionalities with open source libraries like LlamaIndex and LangChain, for example, and providing them as services, as shown in Example 5-3.

Example 5-3. Example LangChain workflow

```python
# Import necessary libraries
import os
from langchain.llms import OpenAI
from langchain.chains import LLMChain

# Function to extract exclusion clauses from a contract
def extract_exclusion_clauses(api_key, contract_file):
    # Initialize the language model with GPT-4
    llm = OpenAI(api_key=api_key, model="gpt-4")

    # Load the contract document
    with open(contract_file, "r") as file:
        contract_text = file.read()

    # Define the prompt for extraction
    prompt = "Extract all clauses related to exclusions from the following contract:"

    # Initialize a langchain chain with the LLM and custom prompt
    extraction_chain = LLMChain(llm=llm, prompt=prompt)

    # Process the document and extract the clauses
    extracted_clauses = extraction_chain.run(input_text=contract_text)

    # Return the extracted clauses
    return extracted_clauses

# Load API key
api_key = os.getenv('YOUR_API_KEY_ENV_VARIABLE')
contract_file = "contract.txt"  # Replace with the path to your contract file

# Extract and print the exclusion clauses
exclusion_clauses = extract_exclusion_clauses(api_key, contract_file)
print(exclusion_clauses)
```

IT System Integration Challenges

Integrating AA into a company's IT infrastructure is a multifaceted challenge that goes beyond simply setting up the necessary infrastructure. The successful integration of AA into the existing IT landscape is crucial to realizing its full potential. This integration must fit seamlessly into users' workflows and ranges from adapting to legacy systems on the one hand to embedding the integration into newly developed systems on the other. AA has a profound impact on an organization and affects the IT department's ongoing projects and plans. This section addresses these integration challenges, examines the hurdles and opportunities that arise, and offers insights into navigating this complex terrain effectively.

Dealing with legacy systems

Many companies work with older IT systems that are not easily made compatible with modern AA tools. For this reason, certain prerequisites are essential: for instance, the technology stack must be API or web API enabled. You won't be able to adequately augment any applications still running on environments that do not allow connection to conventional web API infrastructures. Changes often require retrofitting or upgrading these systems, which can be complex and costly.

To be fair, such a situation is unlikely; it's hard to imagine a company offering modern AA delivery structures but still running workflows on infrastructures that cannot use them.

The much more likely situation is that the legacy tech is "stuck": it's based on adequate infrastructures, but the implementations are so old (or not implemented in a comprehensible way, or implemented by people who haven't been with the company for long) that companies usually decide to keep them running as long as necessary but not extend their use past that point. This makes integration much more difficult. Think carefully about whether it is worth extending such a system. Once you reach a point where you're only doing maintenance, you aren't far from decommissioning the system and replacing it with a new solution.

The best approach is to think about how to integrate analytics when renewing these systems. That decision certainly isn't driven by augmentation capabilities alone: the effort to provide additional analytics solutions in API infrastructures wouldn't be justified up front, because no one would consume them. That's why the best opportunity is to do both at the same time.

Today, there are no runtime environments that *can't* consume web APIs, so all we can recommend is to rely on coding tools, not generation tools.

Project dependencies

Whether you're integrating analytics into new or existing systems, planning is important. The integration will cost resources and time, so your feasibility checks and use-case planning must account for that. It's important to present this transparently in external communications with stakeholders and clients.

Do your analytics planning in coordination with IT. IT projects usually have their own roadmaps and objectives, so their first priority is rarely the third-party influences that AA integration adds. Draw up a joint roadmap with IT to align the objectives and ensure effective resource planning on both sides. Joint objectives and key results (OKRs) or program increment planning (PIP) can help you find consensus.

Augmentations can quickly be deprioritized if they are not promoted accordingly, so it's important to raise awareness. IT projects are often driven not by the desire to offer a new and even better user experience but by the desire to adhere to an ambitious decommissioning roadmap. Analytics leaders can use these opportunities to directly improve the renewal of the system with suitable augmentations. Their role gives them a say in IT projects, and they can steer intentions and priorities. Just be sure to carefully weigh what's more important: a quick launch or a holistic approach that includes the augmented workflows. Our experience shows that subsequent integrations work well, but a well-planned holistic implementation ultimately demands less effort.

In addition to the analytics leaders, other roles must now be involved.

IT decision makers are responsible for the organization's technological direction and face the complex task of integrating AA into existing IT infrastructures. Their responsibility goes beyond mere implementation; they must actively chart a future in which analytics solutions not only coexist but also *synergize* with existing systems to ensure seamless functionality, experience, and system scalability. The challenge is not only technical; it's also about transferring the analytics transformation's cultural shift from the business domains to IT. IT decision makers own and shape the IT roadmaps. Involve them early and help them understand the value of analytics and its relevance to business users so that they can factor that into their planning.

In addition, you'll need business analysts. They are the process architects who shape the workflows, so prepare them ahead of time to think about augmentation. They take on a similar role as the analytics translator, linking the worlds of business and IT and translating AA insights into actionable strategies. Their awareness of AA's potential will change how people across departments perceive and use analytics as they define core system workflows.

At the end of the Data Progressive phase, bring the analytics translator(s) and business analysts together in joint initiatives. Their interaction will be important during the final phase: one defines the solution while the other ensures its effective integration into the workflow.

Governance Challenges

AA solutions need a solid technical foundation, especially in terms of runtimes and scalability, but also in security, compliance, and maintenance. Scalability is critical: regardless of the type of consumption, applications must be highly available and stable. However, they are run somewhat differently in AA.

While many people are used to using analytics directly through tools and dashboards, AA applications run in the background. As part of an overall processing chain, they're often invisible to the end user. Indeed, the end user might not even know that they're currently using a complex, fully assembled workflow.

Systems and components must be properly coordinated since errors in individual components can cause the entire workflow to break down. This is nothing unusual, but the problem here is that the workflow's components can be highly distributed and are often provided by different responsible parties (data or analytics owners). Ensure a high level of reliability here to guarantee the interaction of all components. System integration testing of individual components is essential. We also strongly recommend that you establish minimum standards for test coverage, runtimes, and availability.

In addition, integration into workflows means a completely different way of implementing individual analytical services, which must be able to deal with higher frequencies of use and stateless transactions. Algorithms that are not part of dedicated tooling will need intelligent strategies to deal with sessions and efficient data access. Transactions will be much shorter but more frequent.

When parts of an entire assembled workflow process sensitive data, it's crucial to clarify everyone's responsibilities. At first glance, it might seem obvious to place this responsibility with those providing the granular functionality. But how can they ensure appropriate use in different workflows when in doubt?

Consider the following example: a company introduces an augmentation to its CRM system that directly shows sales managers information about a customer's purchase history, return rate, and credit score, all provided by different analytics services. This gives them a 360-degree view of the customer. Some of this information is very sensitive, particularly credit scores. The system should deny customer-service employees access to the sensitive parts of customers' information. The responsibility to control this can hardly be done by the analytics component owner of the credit-score information. Although the owner adheres to all compliance requirements as much as possible, they have little influence over how consuming workflows use the information and whether they treat it confidentially. Thus, the implemented workflow itself must ensure access control and the necessary multiclient capability.

We align with a widespread recommendation here: introducing *contracts* for users of individual functionalities in augmented workflows. This concept is already established for data products, where it is called *data contracts*. In her book *Data Mesh*, Zhamak Dehghani describes how to establish distributed responsibility for data products and ensure a standard level of compliance. In an additional article, "How to Move Beyond a Monolithic Data Lake to a Distributed Data Mesh" (*https://oreil.ly/pxd8K*), Dehghani defines six paradigms to address when providing data as a product: discoverable, addressable, trustworthy and truthful (with defined and monitored service-level objectives), self-describing, interoperable (governed by open standards), and secure and governed.

We build on these paradigms and extend them. Analytics products should be:

Discoverable

Analytics products must be easy to find. You can improve discoverability by providing a centralized platform or catalog with detailed information about each analytics product, such as the types of analytics it supports, the questions it can answer, and user guides.

Addressable

Each analytics product should have a unique identifier or address so that it is easy to find and reference. This is especially important for APIs that provide analytics services. The addresses should be intuitive and consistent across the organization to facilitate access and integration with other tools and platforms.

Trustworthy

Analytics products must provide trustworthy insights and predictions based on high-quality, clean data. This includes transparent documentation of data sources, analysis methods, and any assumptions or limitations. Regular validations and updates are necessary to ensure the integrity of these products.

Self-describing

Analytics products should be user-friendly and self-explanatory. This means they should have clear documentation, easy-to-understand interfaces, and perhaps even interactive elements that guide the user in interpreting results. This increases the usage of an analytics product in augmented workflows by augmented workflow developers. To reduce dependency on IT or data-science teams, the results' *semantics* (meaning and interpretation) and *syntax* (how the data is structured and queried) should be clear to the user.

Interoperable

Analytics products should comply with established industry standards and should be able to interact with different runtime environments for integration into business workflows.

Secure

Ensuring secure access to analytics products is essential. This includes implementing strict access controls to protect sensitive data and analytical insights, such as role-based access control, authentication protocols, and encryption. These measures should align with the organization's broader IT security policies as well as with global standards for data security, privacy, and ethics.

We add one more paradigm that defines analytical products' use more narrowly:

Responsibly used

The boundaries and guidelines for the analytical product's appropriate, legal, and ethical use should be defined. Outline the specific use cases for which the product is designed; highlight restrictions on applications that are unsupported or explicitly prohibited. This should include compliance with data-governance policies, relevant data-protection laws, and ethical standards for data processing and analysis.

This paradigm addresses user responsibility and emphasizes the importance of avoiding bias, misinterpretation, and misuse. It regulates how the information can be disseminated and how to maintain confidentiality. It also regulates what the information should be used for to avoid misinterpretation and mandates providing information about every product's limitations. The point is to ensure that the analysis product is used responsibly, lawfully, and meaningfully and that the interests of all parties involved are protected.

Here are the possible elements of an analytics contract, defined according to the paradigms:

Product description and purpose

- Overview of the analytics product, its features, and its intended use
- What types of analytics, reports, and data visualization does it offer?
- What kind of augmentation can be achieved with it (for example, fixed-rule, high-confidence augmentation)?

Findability

- How users can find and access the product
- Location of the central catalog or platform where the product is listed

Addressability

- Unique identifier or address for the product
- Metadata about the product, including version, release date, and summary of features

- Instructions for accessing the product, including any API endpoints, dashboard URLs, and the like
- Notes on integration with other systems or platforms

Trustworthiness and truthfulness
- Statement on the data quality and accuracy standards to which the product adheres
- Description of data sources and methods used
- Transparency about constraints, assumptions, and conditions under which the product performs optimally

Self-describing semantics and syntax
- Detailed documentation on how to use the product, including user guides, FAQs, and sample analyses
- Definitions of terms and metrics used in the product
- Explanation of data structure, formats, and query methods

Interoperability and global standards
- Guidelines for data integration and harmonization with other data sets or tools
- Listing of company-wide standards for dimensions and identifiers used in the product

Security and access control
- Details of security measures to protect data and insights
- Description of access control mechanisms, such as role-based access

Support and maintenance
- Information about support channels and resources available to users
- Schedule for regular updates and maintenance
- Procedure for reporting problems and requesting improvements
- Contact channels
- Response times for support requests and problem resolution

Performance and SLAs
- Expected performance metrics and service availability

User responsibilities
- User responsibilities in terms of ethical use, data handling, and compliance with legal standards
- Consequences of violating the conditions for permitted use
- Recommended use of insights (augmentation, agents, copilots, or assistants)

Restrictions on disclosure and sharing

- Rules for sharing data, reports, or insights generated by the analytics product
- Restrictions on sharing the product or its functions with third parties

Example 5-4 shows a possible example of an analytics contract for a fictional customer-churn predictor.

Example 5-4. Example analytics product contract in YAML

```yaml
product_description_and_purpose:
  name: "Predictive Analytics Tool for Customer Churn"
  overview:
      "A predictive analytics tool designed to analyze customer data and predict
      potential churn.
      Features include churn likelihood scoring, customer segmentation,
      and churn drivers analysis."
  features:
    - "Customer churn prediction"
    - "Predictive modeling"
    - "Customer behavior analysis"
    - "Trend identification"
  intended_use: "To predict potential customer churn and assist in retention
      strategies"
  augmentation_type: "High-confidence augmentation based on predictive analytics"

findability:
    catalog_location: "http://company-analytics-catalog.com/churn-predictor"
    product_listing_page: "http://intranet.company.com/analytics-tools/
      churn-predictor"

addressability:
  unique_identifier: "churn-predictor-001"
  metadata:
    version: "1.2.3"
    release_date: "2023-08-01"
    feature_summary: "Advanced churn prediction using AI algorithms"

  access_instructions:
    api_endpoints:
      - "http://api.company.com/churn-predictor/v1/predict"
      - "http://api.company.com/churn-predictor/v1/report"
    dashboard_url: "https://analytics.company.com/churn-dashboard"
  integration_notes: "Compatible with CRM and ERP systems via API"

trustworthiness_and_truthfulness:
  data_quality_standard: "ISO 9001:2015 Certified"
  data_sources:
    - "Customer Relationship Management System"
    - "Customer interaction logs"
    - "Transaction history"
    - "Support tickets"
  method_description: "Uses supervised machine learning algorithms to analyze
  patterns in customer behavior"
  model_performance_kpis:
    accuracy: "93%"
    precision: "90%"
```

```
    recall: "88%"
  performance_constraints:
    - "Optimal performance in datasets with at least 10,000 customer records"
    - "Requires at least 2 years of historical data for accurate predictions"

semantics_and_syntax:
  documentation:
    api_interface: "http://docs.company.com/churn-predictor"
    user_guide: "https://docs.company.com/churn-predictor/user-guide"
    faq: "https://docs.company.com/churn-predictor/faq"
    sample_analyses: "https://docs.company.com/churn-predictor/samples"
  terms_and_metrics:
    - "Churn Probability: Likelihood of a customer leaving within the next month"
    - "Retention Factors: Key factors influencing customer loyalty"
  data_structure_explanation: "Data is by default structured in JSON format with
  fields for customer ID, transaction details, and interaction metrics"
    data_formats:
      - "json"
      - "csv"

interoperability:
  data_integration_guidelines: "http://docs.company.com/churn-predictor/integration"
  standards:
    - "Follows GDPR for data privacy"
    - "Adheres to OpenAPI Specification for API standards"

security_and_access_control:
  security_measures: "Data encryption in transit and at rest"
  access_control: "Role-Based Access Control (RBAC) with SSO Integration"

support_and_maintenance:
  support_channels:
    email: "support@company.com"
    phone: "+1234567890"
  update_schedule: "Quarterly updates and maintenance"
  issue_reporting_procedure: "http://support.company.com/report-issue/churn-predictor"
  response_time: "Initial response within 24 hours"

performance_and_sla:
  uptime_sla: "99.9% Service Uptime"
  performance_metrics:
    - response_time: "Under 2 seconds for API requests"

user_responsibilities:
  ethical_use_policy: "Use in accordance with company ethics guidelines"
  data_handling_compliance: "Adhere to GDPR and CCPA standards"
  violation_consequences: "Access revocation and potential legal action"
  limitation: "not allowed for automated processing in agents"

restrictions_on_disclosure_and_sharing:
  sharing_rules: "Data and insights generated are for internal use only"
  third_party_sharing_restriction: "No sharing of the product functionalities with
  external parties without prior authorization"
```

This is just one example of a possible structure for an analytics product contract; ultimately, this contract must be adapted to the circumstances and requirements of your own company.

Conclusion

The technical challenges of introducing AA into your organization's core systems are not trivial. Think them through and plan well. In summary, our three key recommendations are:

- Involve IT decision makers to align with IT's roadmaps. This is particularly important when dealing with legacy technology. Business analysts should learn to think in terms of automations in order to consider functionalities in future workflows.
- Rely on APIs as endpoints for integrating augmentations into workflows. Establish programmatic analytical solutions to future-proof and ensure the organization's vendor independence.
- Regulate the use of analytical solutions in workflows by introducing common rules and commitments.

In the end, AA is more about software engineering than analytics: establishing infrastructure and techniques that unite analytical use cases with core processes to effectively augment corresponding workflows. The interaction between analytical and business capabilities now extends to include IT capabilities. Software developers and analytics engineers are thus more important during this phase than analysts and data scientists.

## CHAPTER 6

Augmented Frames

Now that you understand the challenges of integrating augmentation into workflows, we're going to introduce you to a concept that goes beyond simply providing a technical infrastructure to help you tackle these challenges successfully. This concept, called *Augmented Frames*, is rooted in the TRICUS principles of workflow augmentation: timeliness, relevance, insight, credibility, unobtrusiveness, and specificity.

Augmented frames provide a dynamic, flexible way to view, analyze, and manage different segments of an organization's requirements. This is a more nuanced and detailed approach than traditional data access, static business classifications, or pre-defined dimensions (such as divisions, business units, and product groups). With this approach, you analyze data through different lenses, or "frames," each representing a different perspective or subset of your company's business objects. This approach is designed to bring information about key business-object types into workflows and use that insight to automate parts of business processes.

This concept is not limited to being part of comprehensive workflows; you can also use it to integrate these insights and capabilities directly into tools and processes, making them more like embedded analytics.

Before we dive into this concept, let's look at what business objects are and why we need to focus primarily on them when we talk about augmentation.

Business Objects and Frame Units

Business objects are fundamental units that represent something essential to conducting business activities, either tangible or intangible. They encapsulate relevant data and attributes that relate to a specific aspect of business operations, such as financial details, operational parameters, or customer information. Each one has a specific purpose and function that contributes to the organization's activities, strategy, and goals. Here are some examples of business objects in different industries:

Insurance
> Contracts, customers, agents, claims, locations

Manufacturing
> Products, machines, supply chain partners, inventory, production orders

Ecommerce
> Customer profiles, orders, products, payments, reviews

Industrial manufacturing
> Raw materials, production schedules, machinery, quality-control reports, worker records

Business objects can typically be integrated with broader business systems, such as inventory, CRM, management information, or analytical systems, for efficient processing and analysis. They often interact with other elements of the enterprise ecosystem, like transactions, processes, and workflows, and can influence or be influenced by other business activities. They can evolve over time as you update, extend, or otherwise modify their attributes and data to reflect changes in the business environment or organizational needs.

In most cases, business objects are associated with descriptive attributes that are organized in dimensions and hierarchies. For example, a particular policy belongs to a particular line of business and industry; a product belongs to a specific product group, manufacturing site, or brand.

Traditional data-provisioning systems often rely on this single, linear approach to categorizing and analyzing data, but these predefined dimensional aggregations typically fall short of delivering the desired value. *Augmented frames*, by contrast, let you define a custom, individual, multidimensional view of the data. This allows you to frame your business objects for a specific purpose, and you can freely select their scope. Figure 6-1 illustrates this difference.

For example, instead of looking at the performance of an entire business unit, you could use augmented frames to examine a specific group of product types, a customer group, a geographic area, or a combination of these attributes within the business unit. You set the parameters of individual subset and dimension *frames* based on specific criteria or business-object IDs for a deeper, more targeted analysis, generating insights through advanced algorithms and AI or gen AI. The technically refined, specific, and aggregated results can be seamlessly integrated into specific workflows for immediate interpretation.

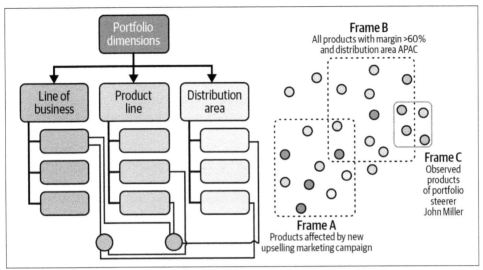

Figure 6-1. Traditional multidimensional data provisioning (left) versus self-defined custom frames (right)

It is therefore possible to set filters on specific attributes that do not correspond to a BI system's hierarchy of defined dimensions. We know that filtering, slicing, and dicing portfolios does not seem revolutionary, even with self-defined dimensions. But what if you want to add special criteria to your selection, such as customer retention or response rate—that is, not dimensions of classifications, but rather dynamic KPIs? Your BI system won't define these criteria as dimensions—or perhaps even consider them at all—because they result from a very domain-specific workflow. If you create a set of products not classified in your reporting system's actual dimensions, would it be difficult to calculate complex KPIs that focus on this particular subset of business objects? You might even want to reuse this framed subset as the basis for other reports and calculations that are not included in your BI system. Filtering on specific attributes makes all that possible.

Throughout this book, we've emphasized that AA's real benefit for businesses isn't delivering *data* but delivering *reliable insights,* the transition from data-driven to insight-driven. This is a paradigm shift that fundamentally changes the traditional understanding of data liberalization, moving the focus from accessing data to gaining concise, immediately applicable insights. In this framework, it's not just the data views that are critical to augmentation but also the out-of-the-box, customizable insights that the data can generate.

Using augmented frames gives you technically refined, specific, aggregated results that you can integrate into distinct workflows for immediate interpretation. This flexibility is critical for organizations dealing with complex and rapidly changing requirements.

We use the term *frame unit* when we talk about a business object that is used in a frame. *Frame unit* is a synonym for business object, but this doesn't correspond to the entirety of all existing business objects in the company; rather, frame units are those business objects that can be processed using the Augmented Frames concept. In the next section, we will explain exactly how their containment by frames and their processing by frame engines, the analysis components, work.

Understanding Frames

In our experience, traditional data and information systems don't always deliver the specific thing you need, which is likely to change often. What they deliver are existing, firmly defined portfolios: consolidated data classifications and structures, according to current or past circumstances. But businesses need the freedom to test analytical solutions on individual subsets of objects in order to adapt to new realities quickly.

Frames are defined subportfolios that group business objects thematically within a broader enterprise context. In this context, a frame is like a customized lens that focuses on a specific aspect of the business, allowing for targeted and nuanced analysis. Any kind of thematic grouping is possible. Some examples are:

- All contracts with a risk rating between 6 and 9
- All customers of the Siemens Group
- All contracts in tunnel construction and reservoir construction
- All contracts with locations in Florida
- Loss-leader contracts of the Milan, Barcelona, and Porto branches
- Small and medium enterprise customers
- Products with materials from supplier XYZ
- Products with a return rate of 25% or more
- Clients with a turnover above $10,000
- Customers with a loss ratio of more than 50%

This concept is central to working with augmented frames because it goes beyond traditional organizational structures, such as departments or branches. The metaphorically rich term *frame* was not chosen at random. Like a picture frame that highlights the image within, a frame in data analytics provides structure and boundaries. It implies focus and context. It delineates the scope of data analysis, highlights specific areas of interest, and gives deep insight into specific segments of data.

Frames provide a focused view and isolate important subsets of data for precise analysis. They can be reshaped or resized to adapt, evolve, expand, or contract based on changing criteria, reflecting the fluidity of business landscapes.

The other basic components are the *frame engines*. A single frame engine is a component that performs specific domain-related evaluations, algorithms, or calculations.

Figure 6-2 shows various frames that are entered into specific engines to expand the scope of the analysis to four frame units in frame 123 and to 13 frame units in frame APAC_1.5m. The performance and data quality engines are frame engines that perform the individual analyses.

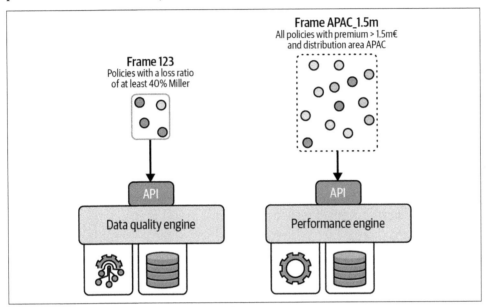

Figure 6-2. Augmented frame: frames and engines

So the frames describe the scope of frame units while the frame engines perform specific tasks based on this selection. Augmented frames integrate analytics, algorithms, and AI models by running them on the same *framed* (defined) subset of business objects (frame units). This allows for a wide variety of insights. With augmented frames, you can drill down into *subportfolios* in addition to existing portfolios, try new combinations of dimensions, and bundle portfolios based on individual thematic dimensions.

In sum, using the Augmented Frames concept lets you do three basic things:

- Offer access to analytics capabilities
- Design and reuse defined sets of frame units
- Ensure governance by executing analysis by responsible owners of the engines

The two main components that make it possible to get started with this concept are frames and frame engines. These components are strongly interdependent, but before we dive deeper into their dependency, you need to understand frames in more detail.

Key Features of Frames

Let's look at a few things that make frames especially useful:

Frames are dynamic.
>In traditional data analysis, frame units are typically uniquely categorized into rigid, predefined segments. Frames, however, enable a more fluid approach, in which a single frame unit can belong to multiple frames. This feature enables multidimensional analysis. For example, a single customer can belong to one frame defined by geographic extent and another frame defined by buying behavior, such as "all customers in the state of California who are frequent buyers (with at least five purchases per month)." This dual mapping enables richer, more nuanced analysis of customer data from different perspectives.
>
>Frame units can move between frames over time, when criteria or business needs change. This dynamic mapping ensures that the analysis remains relevant and can be adapted to current scenarios.

Frames can be reused.
>Frame persistence enables standardization and consistency in data analysis across the enterprise. Once you define a framework, you can save its criteria and structure for reuse, integrating it into multiple IT systems and reporting tools. This integration and interoperability enable different applications and systems to access data easily and generate insights and analysis. Integrating framework definitions into reporting systems also makes creating specific reports more efficient. Business professionals can quickly retrieve data from relevant frames, accelerating the reporting process and ensuring the specificity and relevance of reports.
>
>Say a portfolio manager wants to analyze the individual profitability of certain contracts. They could define and save a frame of interesting contracts and use that frame with different systems. They can then run the analysis in the performance dashboard, create a data-quality report in the data-quality tool, or select both directly from a favorites list in this tool.

Frames can be shared.
>*Frame sharing* lets teams and departments analyze data together using the same set of definitions, instead of each re-creating similar groupings of data for analysis. Sharing frames provides consistent interpretations and conclusions by ensuring that everyone is looking at the same data through the same lens. Not only does this save time, but it's also critical to avoiding errors and inconsistencies in data-driven decisions.

In a large company, different departments can benefit from shared insights. For example, marketing and sales can jointly use frames on customer behavior to coordinate their strategies. Shared frames can also serve as benchmarks. Sharing frames based on company KPIs helps make monitoring and reporting consistent across the company; a frame with the top 100 most profitable customers, for instance, might be used in several business areas.

Frame Types

Frames fall into two basic categories, each with unique properties and applications: free frames and defined frames. This section breaks down each frame type, as shown in Figure 6-3.

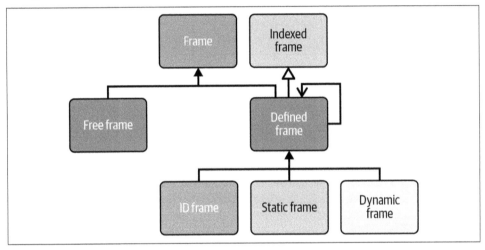

Figure 6-3. Frame types

Free frames are collections of frame units that allow you to categorize and analyze data in the initial stages without rigid structures. They encourage users to explore and learn how to use frames. You can handle them in different ways, even in a simple Excel sheet. A free frame consists of an arbitrary set of entities. Free frames are flexible and can be used for ad hoc analysis. They do not require a formal definition or persistence in the system. They simply enumerate the unique identifiers of individual frame units of a particular type—for example, a list of contract numbers to be evaluated individually by different engines.

Defined frames fall into three main categories. These three types are classified as defined frames because they are based on strict definitions and can thus be identified, maintained, persisted, and shared using a frame ID. You can even combine several defined frames. The three types of defined frames are:

ID frames

> *ID frames* contain only direct frame units—for example, business object IDs, such as policy numbers, customer IDs, or product codes. This type of frame is particularly useful for precise, targeted analysis of specific, individual business objects, rather than categories or attributes. Their simplicity and directness make them ideal for operations that require identifying unique frame units, such as tracking particular transactions, customers, or assets. For instance, a frame with specific policy numbers in an insurance company would allow detailed tracking and analysis of those policies. Therefore, an ID frame represents nothing more than a set of frame units.

Static frames

> *Static frames* are defined once, using static (unchanging) object attributes, and change only when they are manually updated or when the fixed attributes on the frame units change. They are useful for analyzing data sets that remain constant and need to be monitored over time, such as a portfolio of "all contracts in risk category 10" or "all contracts in channel A related to products in the consumer-electronics product segment."

Dynamic frames

> *Dynamic frames* are similar in structure to static frames but are defined with dynamic attributes that change over time and require ongoing evaluation. These attributes may need to be calculated or may be the output of an individual engine. A dynamic frame would be well suited to an attribute like "all customers with a poor credit rating," as the credit ratings are updated constantly, or "all contracts with a loss rate of over 40%," as this rate changes over time.

The distinction between ID, static, and dynamic frames is important because their introduction into the Augmented Frames concept is complex in different ways and will be dealt with later in different iteration stages of the introduction. Ultimately, however, all types are a filter of criteria that can be directly assigned to a business object.

Defined frames can also be classified as *indexed frames*, which is ultimately nothing more than this one officially managed by qualified moderators. This is similar to exchange-traded funds in the finance world, where moderators combine stocks in a portfolio that specific stock indices track. An example could be products affected by a new marketing campaign. The marketing department would be the official owner, responsible for defining and updating the frame, which anyone can use.

Single frame units can be used in different frames. This nonunique assignment coupled with the ability to store and integrate frame definitions into other systems make augmented frames a highly versatile and powerful tool. Augmented frames allow organizations to move away from traditional linear data-analysis models and embrace a more dynamic, multidimensional approach.

Frames provide a focused view and isolate important subsets of business objects for precise analysis. They're flexible and can be reshaped or resized to adapt to evolving business needs. They can evolve, expand, or contract based on changing criteria, reflecting the fluidity of business landscapes.

Frame Engines

A *frame engine* is a component designed to perform domain-related evaluations, algorithms, or calculations for defined frames. Each frame engine is tailored to process specific data types or perform specific analyses, like aggregating figures or calculating KPIs. You can develop different frames to meet different business or analytical requirements. For example, your system might have a performance engine that delivers net results and loss ratios, a customer engine that evaluates customer turnover, and a report engine that generates a report consisting of all facts about the customers in a given frame.

The engines do not process the frames directly; they use only the *identifiers* (frame units) defined in the frames. This means that the individual engines are completely disconnected from the individual frame definitions, which ensures loose coupling. They can even be used outside of the Augmented Frames concept, as long as the interface deals with frame units.

The input to frame engines is *always* a set of frame units. For example, some engines expect a set of policy numbers, and others expect customer numbers. Even if one engine's business logic could process both, it's better for each engine to specialize in one input type and prioritize reusability over processing speed. But both are possible. In the end, it's a practical decision that you can adjust in later iterations of the framework.

Keeping frame engines very small and specific makes them modular and retains their loose coupling, which makes them easier to scale. The organization, business units, or even external developers can develop and integrate new custom frame engines as business requirements evolve without having to overhaul the entire system.

This design, in particular its loose coupling, allows for third-party development of frame engines. This means that external developers or business units can create custom engines specifically for their needs and deploy them across the organization, increasing versatility of the whole Augmented Frames infrastructure. Frame engines provide complete analytic business logic *with domain-specific governance* across the enterprise, advancing the maturity of the analytics transformation and driving data liberalization.

The biggest disadvantage of data liberalization is that *providing* data does not automatically ensure that everyone will *use* it correctly. Let's take another insurance example: even if you provide data on claims, premiums, expenses, and other data fields, along with the correct performance metric to calculate with, the user of that data might not know which calculation to make—or might simply make an error. In other words, with a conventional data supply, you can't guarantee correct use of the data. Frame engines are designed in such a way that the business logic remains within them, and their credibility is guaranteed by their developers and experts.

Engines also enable deeper penetration into the structure of the transferred portfolios, and functionalities, such as aggregation levels and slicing mechanisms, can be applied. Often it is not only calculations at the individual object level that are complex but also aggregations according to certain attributes and classifications. The engines ensure that complex calculations and aggregations returned to the user have been calculated according to the internal validated rules. Users do not have to invest time or effort in understanding the intricacies of the calculations and are prevented from performing them incorrectly on their own. This has a significant positive impact on the governance insights used. Table 6-1 describes some frame-engine use cases from different industries.

Table 6-1. Frame-engine use cases

Engine	Input frame units	Industry	Purpose
Inventory demand forecaster	Product IDs	Wholesale	Predicts future product demand to optimize inventory levels
Vendor performance evaluator	Vendor IDs	Wholesale	Evaluates vendor reliability and performance to improve supply chain efficiency
Price optimization model	Product types	Wholesale	Determines optimal pricing strategies based on market demand, competitor pricing, and cost data
Quality control optimizer	Production workflow IDs	Manufacturing	Monitors production processes to identify and correct quality problems
Maintenance prediction system	Machine IDs	Manufacturing	Predicts machine maintenance needs to minimize downtime
Production efficiency tracker	Business object workflows	Manufacturing	Analyzes production workflows to identify bottlenecks and improve efficiency
Data quality reports	Policy IDs	Commercial insurance	Generates a single data-quality report for a given subportfolio
Net performance	Policy IDs	Commercial insurance	Generates local net performance for a given subportfolio
NatCat engine	Policy IDs or client IDs	Commercial insurance	Returns a list of locations and their corresponding NatCat (natural catastrophe) evaluations

This is diverse enough that you *could* use one engine for all reporting and analytical business requirements. But the concept is not limited to this: an engine can also be transactional and handle business processes and workflows. For example, it can trigger a processing task to send an email to a specific group of customers. The original intention, however, is to support the augmented workflows with analytics.

Frame Engine Types

What do you want your frame engines to *do?* They're designed to run sets of business IDs, but this may not be suitable for all types of engines in your context. For example, during a claims-handling process, you may want to extend a workflow by adding additional information to the claim. In general, we recommend starting with engines that are designed to support reporting and analysis rather than individual operations.

Let's investigate the four general types of engines:

Analytical engines
> *Analytical* engines are used to calculate KPIs based on data within a framework. They are mainly based on a solid foundation of company data in the form of structured data sources, such as relational databases or data lakehouses. Their output is in a structured, multiple-tabular form that addresses individual frame units and enriches them with key figures. Many outputs are close to the standard data provision offering, but you can use them more effectively by integrating them into augmented frames. The focus is on making the data available and on correctly applying and calculating relevant KPIs.

Predictive engines
> *Predictive* engines use advanced AI models to predict future trends, behaviors, or outcomes based on historical and current data. Their outputs are usually predicted values, probability distributions, or trend forecasts. Like analytical engines, they output tables at the level of individual results.

Gen AI response engines
> *Gen AI response* engines use generative AI and data in a frame to create response content, such as text, summaries, or insights, that is contextually relevant to the frame units. Their knowledge base can include structured data sets and/or unstructured data resources, such as document management systems and document spaces. The main challenge is to maintain contextual accuracy and ensure the relevance and quality of the content they generate.

Data-visualization engines
> *Data-visualization* engines translate data into visual formats, such as charts, graphs, or reports. They perform image generation by using engines like Python, R, and Markdown to output visual representations of data, like charts, graphs, and infographics. This is similar to the concept of embedded analytics.

Attribute Aggregation

Frame engines produce individualized results of various types, depending on the type and capabilities of the engine. Some return structured formats, such as lists of tables, while others return unstructured text or even images. We are currently focusing on machines that create structured tables, typically referring to analytical engines. In our experience, these engine types provide the most significant benefit to the entire company.

First, all engines must return a comprehensive result object, starting with a single data table with one record for each requested frame unit in the given subset. This is usually no different than traditional data provisioning, but each record may contain a complex calculation. The engine's interface description should specify which types of variables it generally provides and which can be used for aggregation.

Another functionality is providing domain-specific aggregation levels for results. For example, a second results data set could give aggregated results for certain aggregation levels. The engine itself provides possible aggregation variables. In addition to the frame units, a request to the engine could also contain a *parameter vector* that defines the variables in the result data frame for which the aggregation is to be performed.

If that sounds confusing, let us clarify with an example. Imagine a net performance engine in a commercial-insurance environment, as pictured in Figure 6-4.

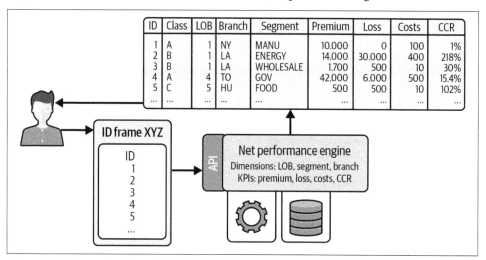

Figure 6-4. Example of a net performance frame engine using internal grouping attributes

This engine is designed to determine, for each of a set of policies, the written premium, the allocated costs, and all actual or ultimate claims for a given operating year. The default output is a table containing all of these values per policy and a calculation of the claims and commission ratio (CCR).

Your implementation might offer further aggregation functions, such as rollup or cube functions, but this capability ensures that you, the user, apply the CCR calculation and attribute aggregation correctly, as defined by the engine's creator. This makes it impossible for you to make mistakes. If you want a consolidated result for portfolio drilldowns, you can simply specify the required frame units.

Don't underestimate these advantages! While it's true that users can perform simple aggregation after the fact, they still have to know *how* to aggregate comprehensive KPIs correctly. But even the simple aggregation of numerical variables can often lead to errors—for example, if they cannot simply be added up but must be aggregated using a special aggregation, such as `maximum` or `quartiles`, or even if weights have to be taken into account for the aggregations. This functionality ensures very strong governance in knowledge generation. It also increases the gain in knowledge, as users slice and dice the aggregation levels into new subportfolios that offer more differentiated interpretations.

But we've missed one important feature. It's great to get an aggregated, consolidated result using the grouping variables each engine provides. But the goal here is to prepare the business for future challenges, not just analyze frame units in a predefined dimension today. A key feature of frame engines is therefore that they accept frame units with user-defined grouping variables or attributes to perform individual aggregations and drilldowns. What does this look like?

Let's revisit the net performance engine from the previous example. This time, the user isn't interested in breaking down an aggregated result into the grouping variables given by the engine but wants to use their *own* definitions of policy segmentation. So they define an ID frame and extend each individual policy ID with an attribute that describes the policy classification, including permutations A, B, and C, for example (shown in Figure 6-5). (It doesn't matter what this classification means semantically— it's in the interest of the user, and that's all that matters.)

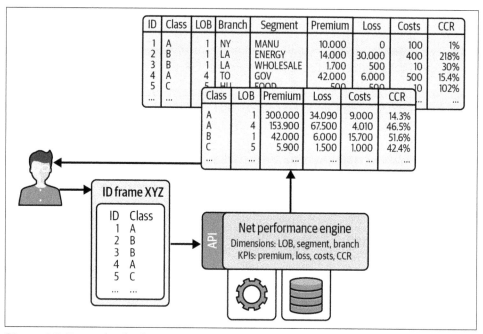

ID	Class	LOB	Branch	Segment	Premium	Loss	Costs	CCR
1	A	1	NY	MANU	10.000	0	100	1%
2	B	1	LA	ENERGY	14.000	30.000	400	218%
3	B	1	LA	WHOLESALE	1.700	500	10	30%
4	A	4	TO	GOV	42.000	6.000	500	15.4%
5	C	5	HU	FOOD	500	500	10	102%
...	...							...

Class	LOB	Premium	Loss	Costs	CCR
A	1	300.000	34.090	9.000	14.3%
A	4	153.900	67.500	4.010	46.5%
B	1	42.000	6.000	15.700	51.6%
C	5	5.900	1.500	1.000	42.4%
...	...	...	...	...	...

ID frame XYZ

ID	Class
1	A
2	B
3	B
4	A
5	C
...	...

API

Net performance engine
Dimensions: LOB, segment, branch
KPIs: premium, loss, costs, CCR

Figure 6-5. Example of a frame engine using external grouping attributes

The engine can obtain these classifications for each policy ID, use them to enrich the internal data set for evaluation, and correctly calculate the KPIs for this grouping variable. It can also combine internal and external grouping variables. For example, the results aggregation data frame could contain the CCRs for a combination of line-of-business (LOB) and policy classifications.

This is not necessarily easy to handle internally, in part because internal and external variables can have identical names. But there are dozens of ways to do this kind of grouping and implement it in the right technology.

This capability ensures a high level of credibility and control, and its results are fully customized to the user's needs. Not only is it convenient, but it also relieves the user of the burden of implementation and of verifying the technical correctness of the results. Such governance ultimately leads to greater acceptance and adoption of the solution.

Engine Interfaces

How users interface with the engines is a very important factor in their success. Once defined, the interfaces will, ideally, be consistent and give engine developers direction on designing engines to integrate with augmented frames.

All engines should provide meta information about their purpose, functionality, required and optional inputs, and outputs (which need to be defined in the executable endpoints). This is a good approach for later use of frame engines in service catalogs or in the *frame agent*, an orchestration component that we'll introduce in Chapter 7.

How might you define a possible implementation of an engine interface? Take a look at the JSON in Example 6-1.

Example 6-1. An abstract frame-engine interface description in JSON

```
{
  "id":"id of frame engine",
  "units":"pol_num",
  "label":"label of engine for listings",
  "description":"short description about functionality",
  "additional_groups":"key value pair of label and actual attribute name in
      result set",
  "Params":"array of parameter which can be processed by the engine"
}
```

In addition to the usual meta-attributes of an engine ID—its required frame unit types, names, and descriptions—each engine must provide an overview of its additional grouping variables. This overview gives callers of the engine an overview of the selections available.

If the engine offers additional parameters for specifying the execution, it must also provide an overview of these parameters. Example 6-2 shows the interface description of the claims overview engine, which contains an additional date-range parameter. This offers the option of restricting the result to damage that occurred within a certain period of time.

Example 6-2. Frame engine interface description as JSON

```
{
  "id":"frame_engine_claims_overview",
  "units":"pol_num",
  "label":"Claims Overview",
  "description":"Generates an overview of all claims for a set of given policies,
    including payments, reserves and total claims. The parameter can be used to
    specify and filter the result.",
  "additional_groups":{
    "Underwriting Year":"uy","Loss Year":"ly","Notifying Year":"ny"
    ,"Claim Line of Business":"claim_lob","Cumul Number":"cumul"
    ,"Claim Cause":"claims_cause_id"
    ,"Claim Type":"claim_type","Cumul Type":"kumul_type"
    ,"Claim Status":"claim_status"
    ,"Claim Location":"loc_region_id"
    ,"Large Loss":"is_ll"
  },
  "params":{
```

```
    "date_range":{
      "description":"date range, if given all claims with loss_date between
                     these values will be selected '[]'",
      "type":"daterange",
      "widget":"dateRangeInput",
      "widget_params":{
          "label":"Date range:", "language":"en", "start":"2011-01-01"
          ,"weekstart":1
      }
    },
    "claim_perspective":{
      "description":"Value perspective of 100%, Gross or Net",
      "type":"character",
      "widget":"checkboxGroupButtons",
      "widget_params":{
        "label":"Perspectives"
        , "size":"sm"
        , "choices":{"100%":"oh","Gross":"gr","Net":"ln"}
        , "selected":["ln"]
      }
    },
    "claim_value_fields":{
      "description":"Value Fields",
      "type":"character",
      "widget":"pickerInput",
      "widget_params":{
        "label":"Value fields"
        , "choices":{
            "First Reserve":"first_reserve"
            ,"Peak Reserve":"peak_reserve"
            ,"Remain Reserve":"remain_reserve"
            ,"Payment":"payment"
            ,"Losses Incurred":"losses_incurred"}
        , "multiple":true
        , "selected":["remain_reserve","payment","losses_incurred"]
        , "options":{"actions-box":true}
      }
    }
}
...
```

The appropriate interface description depends on your needs and your environment—this is just an example of one possible implementation.

We also included in the description some information about how the parameter should be presented in a consuming UI (the widget attributes). This is because we use the engines not only explicitly, as web APIs and R package calls, but also for testing in R Shiny applications or other UI frameworks. (We'll show you more in the next section, "The Frame Agent.") Writing rendering instructions to the generic interface certainly isn't the cleanest approach in software development, but the point is to find an approach that fits your infrastructure and environment. We want to encourage you to be creative in realizing your needs.

You've seen how to describe the interface for a frame engine, but what about the execution endpoint for all engines? To keep these engines' interfaces concise and flexible, we suggest focusing on only two basic input parameters: the input data frame (consisting of frame units with additional grouping variables) and a parameter object, which we will talk about in detail.

We can't tell you very strictly how to design the input data table because it is so flexible in terms of additional grouping variables—your design will depend on how you use it.

The *parameter object* is complex. To give the engine everything it needs to perform seamlessly, you will need to address:

- The expected grouping variables provided by the frame
- The expected grouping variables provided by the engine itself
- Control parameters to instruct the engine to perform grouping tasks
- Control parameters to force the engine to perform optional advanced analysis, if implemented in the engine

For example, the claims engine may be able to provide additional analysis of claim operation types or specific additional statistics.

Example 6-3 is an example of running an engine in R by passing a small input data frame to the execution endpoint.

Example 6-3. Using a frame engine in R

```
library(tibble)

input <- tibble::tibble(
  ids = c(1234, 3456, 3456, 7890, 6789),
  segment = c("A","A","C","C","B")
)
#
# A tibble: 5 × 2
#     ids segment
#   <dbl> <chr>
# 1  1234 A
# 2  3456 A
# 3  3456 C
# 4  7890 C
# 5  6789 B

groups <- "segment"
#grouping variables provided by the engine
additional_groups <- c("ly", "iso3")
date_range <- c("2022-01-01", "2023-12-31")

params <- list(
  groupings = list(
    additional_groups = additional_groups,
    groups = groups
  ),
  parameter = list(
```

```
    date_range = date_range
  ),
  aggregation = T,
  operations = T
)

r <- frame_engine_claims::execute(input = input ,params = params)
```

An input data table is created using the tibble package in R as an example. It contains two columns: ids, with unique identifiers for each entry, and segment, which categorizes each entry into groups A, B, or C.

This input data table is prepared for processing with specified parameters for a function call to frame_engine_claims::execute. Parameters include grouping variables (segment as the primary groups provided by the input data set and additional_groups including "ly" and "iso3" provided by the frame engine), a date_range from January 1, 2022, to December 31, 2023, and flags for aggregation and operations set to true (T). The execute function of frame_engine_claims is then called with the input and these parameters to perform a data analysis based on the specified groupings, date range, and other settings.

The challenge is to implement more dynamic and generic inputs and to handle all inputs with suitable standard parameters. For example, if aggregation has not been set, the required additional parameter must be handled by a default parameter. If there is no restriction on the temporal scope, the engine must handle that. In the end, the principle of augmentation also applies here: the engine makes assumptions automatically and only aborts processing in exceptional cases, such as if inputs are missing.

One approach is to define a generic function that we'll call meta_execution, which should be called at the beginning of all execution functions within all engines to make a complete parameter object available for all further processing. This is shown in Example 6-4 and as R documentation in Figure 6-6.

Example 6-4. Implementation of meta_execution function to provide a meta object

```
#' Creates a meta execution object with given parameters for frame engines
#'
#' This function performs meta execution with the given parameters. It combines
#' optional parameters with default engine parameters to customize the execution.
#' The function returns a list merging the default parameters with the provided
#' parameters.
#'
#' @param input A data.table containing frame units (default: NULL).
#' @param default_engine_params A list of default engine parameters (default: empty list).
#' @param frame_params A list of additional parameters for modifying the default
#' engine parameters (default: empty list).
#'
#' @return An object with a list of parameters for the meta execution. This includes
#' modified default parameters, the number of units,
```

```
#' and the execution date. The structure of the returned 'meta' object is as follows:
#'
#' \itemize{
#'   \item \code{groupings}: A list containing:
#'     \itemize{
#'       \item \code{groups}: A vector of type \code{string} or NULL, indicating the
#'         variables for groupings provided by the frame.
#'       \item \code{additional_groups}: A vector of type \code{string} or NULL, indicating
#'         additional groups provided by the engine.
#'     }
#'   \item \code{parameter}: A list placeholder for engine-specific parameters.
#'   \item \code{aggregated}: A logical value indicating whether the data should be
#'     additionally aggregated (default: FALSE).
#'   \item \code{extended}: A logical value indicating if additional analysis should be
#'     extended by the engine when available.
#'   \item \code{unknown}: A logical value indicating whether unknown units should be
#'     reported (default: FALSE).
#'   \item \code{clean_pii}: A logical value indicating whether personally identifiable
#'     information (PII) should be cleaned (default: FALSE).
#'   \item \code{keep_names}: Specifies how to rename attributes of groups and
#'     additional_groupings with the same name. If TRUE, the same variable names are given
#'     the suffix '_from_engine'.
#'   \item \code{clean_names}: Specifies how attributes of result tables should be represented;
#'     FALSE for technical attribute names, TRUE for defined labels if available.
#' }
#' Additionally, in the root of the object:
#' \itemize{
#'   \item \code{num_units}: An integer indicating the number of observations in the
#'     'input' data.table.
#'   \item \code{execution_date}: A POSIXct object indicating the date and time of execution.
#' }
#'
#' @examples
#' meta_execution()
#' # Returns a list with default parameters, num_units as 0, and the current execution date.
#'
#' @export
meta_execution <- function(input = NULL, params = list(), default_engine_params = list()){

  default_params <- list(
    groupings = list(
      groups = NULL,
      additional_groups = NULL
    )
    , parameter = list()
    , aggregated = T, extended = F, unknown = T
    , clean_pii = F, clean_names = F, keep_names = T
    )

  default_params %<>% modifyList(default_engine_params)
  default_params %<>% modifyList(params)

  default_params$num_units <- ifelse(is.null(input), 0, nrow(input))
  default_params$execution_date <- Sys.time()

  return(default_params)

}
```

Creates a meta execution object with given parameters for frame engines

Description

This function performs meta execution with the given parameters. It combines optional parameters with default engine parameters to customize the execution. The function returns a list merging the default parameters with the provided parameters.

Usage

```
meta_execution(input = NULL, params = list(), default_engine_params = list())
```

Arguments

input	A data.table containing frame units (default: NULL).
default_engine_params	A list of default engine parameters (default: empty list).
frame_params	A list of additional parameters for modifying the default engine parameters (default: empty list).

Value

An object with a list of parameters for the meta execution. This includes modified default parameters, the number of units, and the execution date. The structure of the returned 'meta' object is as follows:

- groupings: A list containing:
  - groups: A vector of type string or NULL, indicating the variables for groupings provided by the frame.
  - additional_groups: A vector of type string or NULL, indicating additional groups provided by the engine.
- parameter: A list placeholder for engine-specific parameters.
- aggregated: A logical value indicating whether the data should be additionally aggregated (default: FALSE).
- extended: A logical value indicating if additional analysis should be extended by the engine when available.
- unknown: A logical value indicating whether unknown units should be reported (default: FALSE).
- clean_pii: A logical value indicating whether personally identifiable information (PII) should be cleaned (default: FALSE).
- keep_names: Specifies how to rename attributes of groups and additional_groupings with the same name. If TRUE, the same variable names are given the suffix '_from_engine'.
- clean_names: Specifies how attributes of result tables should be represented: FALSE for technical attribute names, TRUE for defined labels if available.

Additionally, in the root of the object:

- num_units: An integer indicating the number of observations in the 'input' data table.
- execution_date: A POSIXct object indicating the date and time of execution.

Examples

Run examples

```
meta_execution()
# Returns a list with default parameters, num_units as 0, and the current execution date.
```

[Package *frame.engines.core* version 1.0.0 Index]

Figure 6-6. Displaying meta_execution *in R interface*

Example 6-5 demonstrates the use of the meta object with the execution function of the claim engine. First, the expected internal necessary default parameters are defined, which are overwritten by meta_execution when they are provided by the user call to the engine.

Example 6-5. Using a frame engine to create a `meta_execution` object in R

```
#execution function of claims engine
execution <- function(input = NULL, params = list()){

  # default parameter of claims engine
  default_engine_params <- list(
    aggregated <- F,
    parameter = list(
        date_range = c("2020-01-01", format(Sys.Date(), "%Y-%m-%d"))
      , operations = F
      , claim_perspective = c("gross", "net")
      , claim_value_fields = c("remain_reserve", "payment", "losses_incurred"
    )
  )


  # creation of meta object with all necessary information for further execution
  meta_exec <- meta_execution(
      input = input
    , frame_params = params
    , default_engine_params = default_engine_params
  )

# all processing code follows here
...
}
```

Importantly, Examples 6-4 and 6-5 and Figure 6-6 are pseudocode implementations in R. However, they give you an idea of how to approach a possible implementation in a programming language of your choice.

Result Objects

Next, let's look at the interface for the execution endpoint of each frame engine. As you've seen, the input is quite dynamic due to the grouping variables. The same is true for the response. It depends heavily on the type of engine and operation, but the result can be almost anything: structured data in one or more data tables, semi-structured data, or completely unstructured information, such as text or even images. Especially for results that are actually returned as binary, but also for operations that have long runtimes, for example, you will need alternative strategies that are required for the service endpoints and the consumption of the results.

Two possible solutions would be to return transaction IDs in order to access information later or to return binary files through a specialized service endpoint. Here, though, we will focus on returning structured or semistructured data and additional text that can be represented in JSON. Example 6-6 shows the structure of a high-level standardized return object.

Example 6-6. Exemplary interface description of frame engine

```
{
  "$schema": "http://json-schema.org/draft-07/schema#",
  "type": "object",
  "title": "name of engine / endpoint",
  "description": "short description about the endpoint",
  "properties": {
    "return_object_1": {
      "type": "array",
      "description": "An array of premium related records.",
      "items": {
        "type": "object",
        "properties": {...},
        "required": [...]
      }
    },
    "return_object_n": {...},
    "unknown": {
      "type": "array",
      "description": "An array for unknown frame units.",
      "items": {
        "type": "object",
        "properties": {...}
      }
    },
    "meta_fields": {
      "type": "array",
      "description": "Metadata fields describing various variables of the results.",
      "items": {
        "type": "object",
        "properties": {...}
      }
    },
    "meta_execution": {
      "type": "object",
      "description": "Metadata about the execution or processing of the engine.",
      "properties": {...},
      "required": [...]
    }
  },
  "required": [
    "return_object_1", "return_object_n", "unknown", "meta_fields", "meta_execution"
  ]
}
```

We recommend using a schema that briefly describes what the interface does, then describes the result in detail. This could be a bit redundant because you use a similar description for the frame engine itself, but it depends on your design—if you want to provide more than one endpoint per engine, it's necessary. It's best practice to include at least one fixed element in the schema, or `meta_object`, to give an overview of the execution parameters, the input units, and some parameters of the execution, such as time, date, and default settings.

There is sometimes disagreement on this point. Some argue that, in a direct response system, the caller needs to know what information it is sending, and time, date, and default settings are superfluous, useless information. But think about the design of the concept. Agent calls to engines need to be orchestrated at some point and could take longer to execute than expected, so you need a strategy for handling that properly. At least for documentation purposes, an object in the response with all the necessary information can help you understand the character of the call. Example 6-7 shows an example of a claims engine's meta-object schema, and Example 6-8 shows an example of a concrete form for this. The fields claim_value_fields, claim_perspective, date_range, and operations are individual parameters required by the engine.

Example 6-7. The meta_execution object JSON schema of a claims engine

```
{
    "$schema": "http://json-schema.org/draft-07/schema#",
    "type":"object",
    "properties":{
        "clean_pii":{
            "type":"boolean",
            "description":"Indicates if personally identifiable information has
            been cleaned."
        },
        "keep_names":{
            "Type":"boolean",
            "description":"Specifies how attributes of groups and additional_groupings
            with the same name are to be renamed, if TRUE the same variable names
            are given the suffix '_from_engine', if FALSE '_from_engine'."
        },
        "aggregated":{
            "Type":"boolean",
            "description":"Indicates if aggregation data is included."
        },
        "unknown":{
            "Type":"boolean",
            "description":"Indicates if unknown data is included."
        },
        "num_units":{
            "Type":"number",
            "description":"Number of units or entries in the data set."
        },
        "execution_date":{
            "type":"string",
            "format":"date-time",
            "description":"Date and time of the data execution start."
        },
        "execution_date_finish":{
            "type":"string",
            "format":"date-time",
            "description":"Date and time of the data execution finish."
        },
        "parameter":{
            "type":"object",
            "Properties":{
```

```
                "claim_perspective":{
                    "type":"array",
                    "items":{
                        "type":"string"
                    },
                    "description":"Fields related to the claim perspective, such as
                    'net' and 'gross'."
                },
                "claim_value_fields":{
                    "type":"array",
                    "items":{
                        "type":"string"
                    },
                    "description":"Fields related to the claim value, such as
                    'remain_reserve', 'payment'."
                },
                "date_range":{
                    "type":"array",
                    "items":{
                        "type":"string",
                        "format":"date"
                    },
                    "description":"Date range for the data, formatted as 'YYYY-MM-DD'."
                },
                "operations":{
                    "type":"boolean",
                    "description":"Indicates if operations are included or considered
                    in the data."
                }
            },
            "required":[
                "claim_value_fields",
                "date_range",
                "operations"
            ]
        },
        "groupings":{
            "type":"object",
            "properties":{
                "groups":{
                    "type":"array",
                    "items":{
                        "type":"string"
                    },
                    "Description":"used grouping parameters provided by frame."
                },
                "additional_groups":{
                    "type":"array",
                    "items":{
                        "type":"string"
                    },
                    "description":"Used additional grouping parameters, provided
                    by engine"
                }
            },
            "required":[
                "groups",
                "additional_groups"
            ]
```

```
    }
  },
  "required":[
    "clean_pii", "clean_names", "keep_names", "aggregated", "unknown",
    "num_units", "execution_date", "execution_date_finish", "parameter", "groupings"
  ]
}
```

Example 6-8. An example of the `meta_execution` object from the claims engine

```
{
  "clean_pii": false,
  "clean_names": false,
  "keep_names": true,
  "aggregated": true,
  "extended": true,
  "unknown": true,
  "num_units": 1000,
  "execution_date": "2024-01-03 11:34:54",
  "execution_date_finish": "2024-01-03 11:35:03",
  "parameter": {
    "claim_perspective": ["gross", "net"],
    "claim_value_fields": ["remain_reserve", "payment"],
    "date_range": ["2021-01-01", "2023-12-31"],
    "operations": true
  },
  "groupings": {
    "groups": ["target_group"],
    "additional_groups": ["loss_year", "iso3"]
  }
}
```

Another good practice is to have the engine return a data table of all unknown frame units, which includes all units that cannot be accessed or are not affected by the engine's operation. For example, say you have an engine that analyzes claims for insurance contracts—we'll call this the "claims engine." Not all contracts will have observed claims so far. The contracts without claims are frame units that the engine cannot process. If you have the engine return an "unknown data" table, that table would list those contracts. This helps the caller interpret the results of each individual engine by understanding which selections the results are based on.

Users may also name frame units in a free frame that might not even exist. Consider what exactly you want the engine to return for these objects: it could just list the individual IDs of the unknown units or include the additional attributes transferred with the frame units. The second variant certainly improves interpretation afterward, but it also means that the structure of this `meta_execution` object will be dynamic: a table with a fixed column for the IDs and one column for each additional field.

We also recommend having the engine return a data table called `meta_fields` that describes the individual columns and variables of the result data tables (as shown in Example 6-9). It should specify the data types in more detail and describe the individual fields and some of their characteristics, such as whether individual variables contain personally identifiable information (PII) or a certain subject-related data type, such as a score, ratio, or currency. This isn't mandatory, but it's helpful if you have a large number of engines delivering results as tables.

Example 6-9. Structure of a `meta_fields` object

```
"meta_fields":{
   "type":"array",
   "description":"Metadata fields describing various aspects of all result data.",
   "items":{
      "type":"object",
      "properties":{
         "context":{
            "type":"string",
            "description":"The context or engine."
         },
         "domain":{
            "type":"string",
            "description":"The domain or result table."
         },
         "field":{
            "type":"string",
            "description":"Field name or identifier."
         },
         "label":{
            "type":"string",
            "description":"Readable label for the field."
         },
         "description":{
            "type":"string",
            "description":"Detailed description of the field."
         },
         "type":{
            "type":"string",
            "description":"Data type of the field."
         },
         "domain_type":{
            "type":"string",
            "description":"Additional classification or type information."
         },
         "pii_type":{
            "type":"string",
            "description":"used strategy to ensure the confidentiality of a
            pii field."
         },
         "position":{
            "type":"number",
            "description":"Position or order of the field in the context."
         }
      }
   }
}
```

Example 6-10 shows a result object that lists the specific characteristics of the meta_fields object. It shows a description of the two data tables returned by the claims engine, result and aggregate, with five and four individual columns, respectively.

Example 6-10. Example meta_fields object in engine result

```
$meta_fields
# A tibble: 47 × 9
   context    domain         field pii_type type    domain_type position label
   <chr>      <chr>          <chr> <chr>    <chr>   <chr>           <int> <chr>
1 fe_premium result        pol_num NA       int     NA                  1 ID
2 fe_premium result           name hash     string  pii                 2 Customer
3 fe_premium result       industry NA       factor  NA                  3 Segment
4 fe_premium result          value NA       double  currency            4 TSI
5 fe_premium result        premium NA       double  currency            5 Premium
6 fe_premium aggregate     industry NA       factor  NA                  1 Segment
7 fe_premium aggregate        value NA       double  currency            2 TSI
8 fe_premium aggregate      premium NA       double  currency            3 Premium
9 fe_premium aggregate    mean_prem NA       double  currency            4 Mean Prem
```

While meta_execution and meta_information are almost static and have fixed attributes, each engine will have its own individual and variable number of result tables within their result object. You will need to document each engine's individual structure in the interface description. In Example 6-6, we used a placeholder: return_object_1. Later in this chapter, we'll show you a concrete representation of the entire interface description for a specific frame-engine execution function.

To summarize this complex section on result objects: the result object of a motor call can contain various elements. In our implementation, there are three mandatory elements with a fixed interface:

unknown
    To list the frame units that could not be processed in the engine

meta_execution
    An object with all parameters and key figures for the execution of the engine

meta_information
    A table that describes the actual result tables in more detail

How many individual result tables each engine returns varies; in our example, we have called them return_object_1 or return_object_n, with n indicating that there can be an arbitrary number.

Please note that this is just one way to design and structure the individual interfaces of frame engines. Find out what works best for you as you implement your own engines.

Implementation Challenges

Implementing frame engines is highly customized. Depending on the use case, you'll need to adapt their individual logic to the requirements of augmented frames. The most important point is processing the IDs of the relevant frame units.

However, there are several challenges you'll need to address during implementation:

Data access

Engines that analyze data have access to the persistent data they need for the analysis. The calls to the engines only concern the frame units that can be processed by the engine and the optional grouping variables. If in doubt, other types of frame units must be transformed into the corresponding types beforehand— for example, an engine expects claim IDs, but the call has a set of customer IDs. All data retrievals and calculations take place in the engine.

API infrastructure

The engines are ideal for API web services in a microservices architecture. Ultimately, the runtime of the individual engines does not matter as long as they guarantee the corresponding interfaces, functionality, and accessibility as a web service. This approach is about loose coupling, both on a technical and an infrastructural level. In case of doubt, the challenges of APIs are the runtimes and asynchronous calls.

Interface definition

It's vital to agree upon a clear interface definition for the engines, which affects not only the input but also the output. While the input can be standardized in principle (excepting the usage of self-defined grouping variables), the output's structure is very different: only the top level of each result object can be defined. For analytics engines, at least, the result set should contain:

- An individual result data table

- An aggregated result table (optimal but not mandatory)

- An "unknown data" frame with all objects that were passed in the input set but could not be referenced or evaluated

The output is different for other types of frame engines, of course; a gen AI engine will produce a document, or at least unstructured text, while visual engines will produce images in various file formats. Just remember the original purpose: to gain valuable insights based on data, we recommend starting with analytical engines. They are usually easy to implement, have standard development features, and guarantee a gain in immediate insights.

Orchestrating calls

Some frame engines can process data quickly while others take longer due to the complexity of their tasks. You'll need to take a flexible approach to using these engines because, given this variance, it's not always feasible or efficient to call a frame engine synchronously at runtime. Instead, you may need to schedule calls to a particular engine or execute them asynchronously. This prevents time-consuming processes from degrading the system's overall functionality and user experience.

Frame Agent

The *frame agent* acts as an orchestration component, mediating between the user and the frame engines. It schedules, invokes, and coordinates these engines and handles the complexity of asynchronous operations and varying execution times. It effectively shields the user from the intricacies of the engine's operations. It simplifies the user experience and makes using the Augmented Frames concept easier and more seamless, democratic, and user-friendly. Users can interact with the system without having to understand or directly consume the detailed workings of each frame engine.

Figure 6-7 shows a standard workflow of a frame agent that is triggered by a call. The first step is to retrieve the frame and the name of the frame engine to be processed as well as the parameters to be taken into account. The next several subsections describe the key functions of the frame agent.

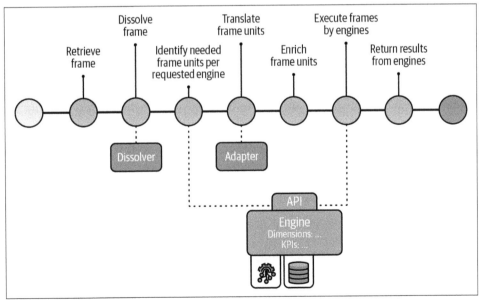

Figure 6-7. Workflow for handling a request by the frame agent

Dissolving Frames

If the transferred frame is a defined frame, it must still be resolved into its individual frame units. As a reminder, frame engines only accept frame units and not frame definitions. The frame agent organizes the resolution of the defined frames in their respective frame unit IDs. This process is not performed directly by the frame agent, though; it delegates the task to the *Frame Dissolver*, which is responsible for retrieving the actual business entities from various data sources based on the frame definitions. (We'll discuss the Frame Dissolver in detail later in this chapter.)

Identifying Types

When the Frame Dissolver dissolves a frame, it always returns a set of frame units. As a reminder, engines only consume frame units of a type that matches that engine. The frame agent checks whether the type of the units of the respective resolved frame matches the type of the engine. If their descriptive meta-attributes don't match, the units must be converted into a suitable format.

Translating Frame Units

The frame adapter comes in as a supporting construct. It takes frame definitions based on specific unit types and translates them into requirements that the engines can understand. This ensures that the data is in a format the engines can process and that different engines can process a wide variety of frames.

Enriching Frames

With static and dynamic definitions, no grouping variables explicitly defined on the business objects can be saved, as these are not explicitly named but are part of the frame because of their attributes. However, it may be necessary to enrich the resolved units with standard grouping variables to be able to use them when processing the engines, which may also be of interest for ID frames and free frames.

If, for example, a frame is defined with all products that belong to the "Toys" product type, it is not possible to add self-defined grouping variables to the individual product IDs. That's because the IDs could not be named directly when the frame was defined and therefore could not be assigned individual variables.

The frame agent provides standard grouping variables for different ID types and enriches the IDs in the frames before sending them to a frame engine. For example, policy IDs are enriched with an "industry segment" attribute so that they can be grouped in an engine that does not have "industry segment" in its own set of available group variables. The agent does not use its own business logic to do this; instead, it uses dedicated engines that provide these specific attributes for various ID types.

Orchestrating Calls

The frame agent organizes the engines' processing flow, ensuring a consistent methodology that includes coordinating the sequence and timing of processing steps. The challenge is how to handle engines with longer execution times. Engines must inform the agent about their execution patterns at runtime so that the agent can define mechanisms, such as processing identifiers for polling, to create a lean architecture without having to set up callback functions to the caller.

Standardizing Results

The frame agent compiles the results of the various processing operations and returns them to the user in a standardized format. Of course, individual engines are structured differently, but you could combine multiple engine uses dynamically in a request to create a holistic response object. Doing so would be a major challenge for the system, though. With multiple requests, you can't implement a static interface description of the agent's endpoints, since the structure now depends dynamically on the engines used and their order in the request to the agent. However, you can define a body for the return that at least contains meta-information for the agent processing the request. This uniformity is essential to ensuring that the output is understandable and usable, regardless of the complexity or diversity of the processes involved.

Central Repository

The frame agent acts as a central repository or library for multiple frame engines to facilitate easy access. It catalogs and indexes the available frame engines so that users can more easily identify the engine they need. This system can include metadata about each engine, such as its capabilities, result structure, performance metrics, usage policies, and any dependencies or prerequisites. However, it does not actively manage the version control for the frame engines but relies on that being provided in their respective runtimes in an up-to-date and correct state.

Monitoring and Performance Analysis

The frame agent monitors the performance of each frame engine. It can collect data on usage patterns, efficiency, and any problems or errors that are critical to maintaining system reliability and making future improvements. It can also provide valuable insight into the needs of individual engines, including their consumption of specific frames. For example, in a later iteration of the framework implementation, you might consider incorporating caching capabilities that allow for fast, resource-efficient delivery of high-traffic frames and engines.

User Access and Security

The frame agent manages users' access to frame engines, including authentication and authorization, to maintain data security and integrity. Do this with a sense of proportion so as not to restrict enterprise-wide insight generation too much. In any case, consider implementing GDPR-relevant data cleansing, whether centrally in the agent or in the individual engines. A best practice is that engines can accept a GDPR flag when called with frame units, then individually anonymize or even remove specific fields in the results.

User Interface

The frame agent also serves as a GUI between users and the frame engine. This makes the system more accessible and easier to use, especially for nontechnical users. Users can load their own lists of free frames into the system in the form of Excel lists and execute individual engines.

The engines themselves are listed in the frontend, and their individual input fields are generically mapped so that they can be queried individually. The frontend also lists the results of the individual engines and offers the user the option of further processing the results.

Figure 6-8 is an example of a user interface for a frame agent.

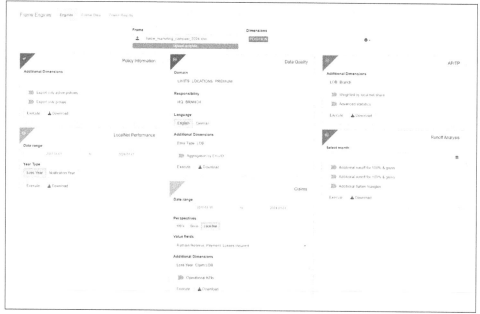

Figure 6-8. Frame agent GUI for a data-quality engine

A free frame can be uploaded via the interface, and the listed frame engines can be executed directly. The individual frame engines are listed with their defined input variables, which users can set and customize. In this example, the agent uses the UI definitions of the individual frame engines to create a parameter selection form. All engines contain an Execute button, which then causes the agent to send the uploaded frame to the selected engine.

The example shows a data quality (DQ) engine, which returns the current data-quality status of individual policies in the inventory system. This engine is connected to a data source that contains specific data-quality rules violations for all policies in the inventory system, including missing mandatory functional requirements for the correctness and completeness of policy attributes. The engine creates a data-quality assessment to report any violations of the quality rules.

To get an understanding of which defined errors are reported for different policies and/or groupings, you can ask the engine for a summary of specific policies. The engine calculates a DQ score and a portfolio score for all the specified policies and optional groupings.

The engine acts primarily as a data provider that selects the policies concerned and calculates the DQ score. However, this is not just simple selection of data from an existing database; the engine also calculates the score individually based on predefined parameters. For example, the user can instruct the engine to take into account only errors belonging to significant error types, such as missing information on the sum insured, relevant customer turnover, or a missing expiration date.

The user can also specify a specific context for their request. For example, they might request only errors that are directly under the responsibility of the corresponding branches. The machine must therefore evaluate the selection individually. This illustrates that frame engines are more than simple data-provision tools. They are designed to fulfill individual requirements and ensure the correct calculation of additional KPIs, such as a reduced DQ score.

In addition, the engine calculates a correct aggregation for the requested portfolio. The portfolio score is more than an aggregation and average of all the policies' DQ scores; it is a comprehensive KPI that accounts for factors like the total sum insured. The engine's complex algorithm is built in, ensuring that users can trust the system to deliver accurate results as intended by the engine's provider.

In a second view (Figure 6-9), the agent lists all frame units and additional attributes in the uploaded frame. In this example, we have uploaded a sample frame with 28 policies and variables describing the policy's position on a top policies list and the assigned broker: two potential grouping variables that can be used to get an aggregated DQ score, position, and/or broker. In addition, the agent shows the fill level for each variable so that the user can check the completeness of the frame definition.

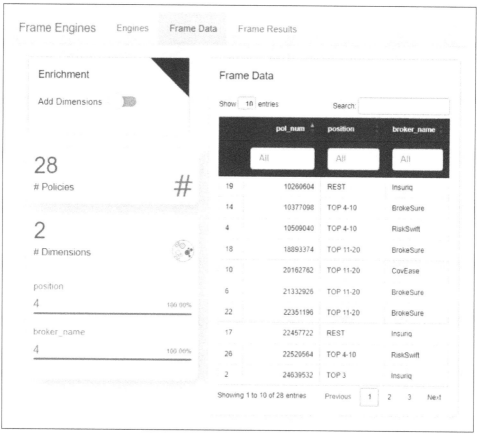

Figure 6-9. Frame agent frame unit overview

Once the engine has been executed, the agent displays the result. It should be able to handle different result formats, including dynamic formats. In Figure 6-10, the result object contains two result tables. One shows a summary of errors per policy; the other shows the aggregated result per broker, which was passed to the engine as an aggregation variable. In addition to the recommended result attributes of `meta_execution` and `meta_fields`, the engine can freely define the structure. In our GUI example, the frame agent can dynamically identify and display all result data tables. This example was developed in R and Shiny.

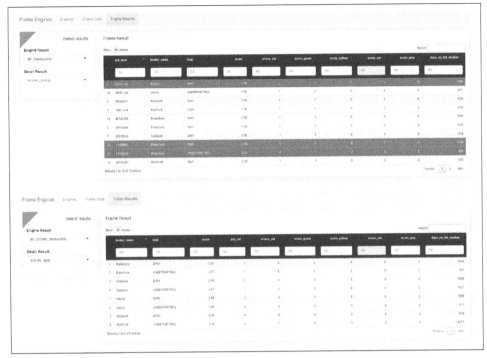

Figure 6-10. Engine result displayed in the frame agent

The frame agent should definitely be equipped with a frontend. Not only does this help test the engines, but it also gives everyone access to analytical insights through simple handling. This makes users more likely to accept and adapt the concept and request its functionalities in augmented workflows.

Frame Dissolver

The *Frame Dissolver* is designed to transform theoretical or abstract definitions of frames (which can be specific business aspects or categories, such as customer segments or policy types) into concrete, actionable frame units. It acts as a bridge between the abstract concept of frames and the frame units that need to be extracted from different data sources and accepted as input by the frame engines.

The Frame Dissolver works with defined frames according to a specific pattern. Unlike free frames, defined frames are persisted; the call to the frame agent only passes a frame ID. The Frame Dissolver extracts the corresponding frame definition from an internal database and uses it to decompose the frame definition into individual frame units.

Depending on the frame definition, the Frame Dissolver then proceeds differently. While resolving ID frames requires only a list of frame units and possible groupings, dissolving static and dynamic frames is much more extensive. Initially, these frames provide a definition only based on business-object properties and filter criteria. The Frame Dissolver must understand this definition and then apply it in the appropriate data system to obtain the corresponding frame units.

Here, it is possible to store the definition in the form of a domain-specific or configuration language in a dedicated storage location, then select the units using a specially built data-access engine. While this can be done with reasonable effort for static frames, it becomes more complex for dynamic definitions and must be well thought out. We will not discuss storage strategies and suitable technologies for parsing and interpreting frame definitions here. But data sinks that can handle semistructured definition objects in particular, such as object databases, and flexible programming languages like R or Python are useful.

Let's first illustrate handling static frames. Let's say the frame agent passes a frame with the ID FR345 to the Frame Dissolver. The Frame Dissolver retrieves all necessary definitions for this frame from an internally managed persistence, such as an object database, used to store, index, and organize frame definitions. As mentioned previously, frames should be well defined, with names, tags, and an optional description for sharing and reuse.

Only when the definition is selected from the database does the Frame Dissolver recognize that it is a static frame that defines policies as a frame unit type, which wants to consider only currently active policies from the company's New York branch. The Frame Dissolver uses these selection criteria to extract the frame units from an appropriate data source.

With a dynamic definition, the whole thing becomes more complex. For instance, the definition here could be "all customers with a credit score worse than 3." This attribute isn't available in a standardized factual customer data set from the inventory system, as customers' names or addresses might be. It comes from a KPI, which is stored in a separate reporting system. The KPI is based on a regular dispositive calculation. This ranking can change at any time, which is why it is called "dynamic."

The dissolving component has an elementary function in later maturity levels of the concept but is not necessarily relevant in early iterations, and it can also be started without this component. We will go into this in more detail later in this chapter.

Frame Adapter

The *frame adapter* acts as a translator. In frame definitions, frame units and information are often available in different types, so the frame adapter's main task is to convert those different types into a standardized format that the respective frame engine can process. This ensures that the data can be used multiple times within the Augmented Frames concept, regardless of its original form or source.

In any data-driven framework, data consistency and compatibility are critical. The frame adapter translates frame units into the required unit type as much as possible. To ensure this, you should use business objects with dependencies in the concept whenever possible, as these can be translated for a larger number of engines and can therefore be used more widely. For example, if the types in a business data model can reference one another, the frame adapter can handle them; the only challenge is to identify these relationships and eliminate any duplicates during generation.

Figure 6-11 shows a simple example of a business data model that the frame adapter could resolve.

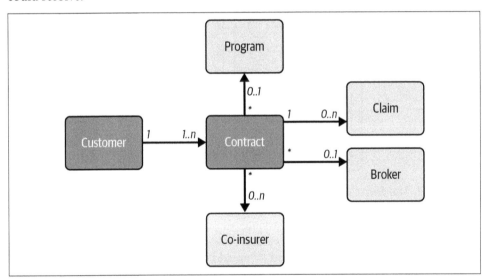

Figure 6-11. Example of frame units' structure and dependencies

All the objects shown in Figure 6-11 are related. For example, you could transform a frame consisting of units of type `Customer` into a set of frame units of type `Claim` by referring to the contract.

The practical application here would be to evaluate a defined frame with *all customers from the wholesale segment* in terms of how *their claims are processed*. The claims-processing engine only accepts claim IDs that the adapter can identify. It then transfers them to the engine. (You could also consider adding the customer number as an additional attribute to the claim IDs, which would allow the claims engine to perform domain-specific aggregation directly at the customer level.)

Let's look at another example, in which a set of `ClaimID` numbers (14, 8, 27, 9) is translated into defined sets of other types as the definition of a frame: in this case, `BrokerID` or `PolicyID`. These represent the brokers and contracts that match the set of transferred claims. The definition of the business model creates defined frame-unit structures whose relationships are mapped and can be resolved. Figure 6-12 shows the input, a rule set for mapping, and the result of the mapping.

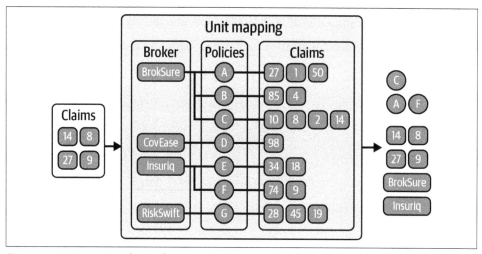

Figure 6-12. Mapping claims frame units into other units

However, any additional grouping variables defined in the claims are lost because the higher-level contracts and brokers cannot hold them uniquely. Let's stick with our example and give Claims 8, 9, 14, and 27 an additional grouping variable, which we'll call `ClaimClass`, to classify their claim type.

Dealing with Group Variables

Two scenarios are now conceivable. In the first scenario, the frame adapter multiplies the variable out and enriches all mapped frame units with the `ClaimClass` variable. The mapped frame units are thus duplicated (BrokSure appears three times), as illustrated in Figure 6-13.

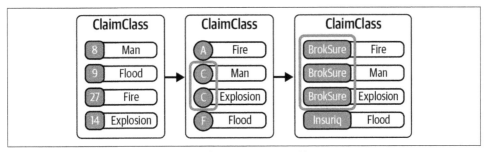

Figure 6-13. Frame-unit mapping with grouping variables

In the second scenario, shown in Figure 6-14, the attributes expire, so they can't be transferred to the subsequent engines.

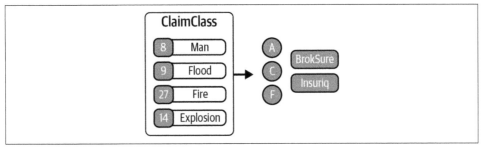

Figure 6-14. Frame unit without grouping variables

Both scenarios are compromises, and both would be possible, but they present different challenges. The implementation of the engines provides for a unique set of frame units, not a set with redundant frame units. The implementation could also be done differently, but this could lead to difficulties or even errors in the internal evaluations of the engines. Frame engines should therefore always ensure the uniqueness of their frame units. A good practice here is to carry out a standardization process at the beginning of the execution of an engine to ensure that it really is a set of frame units.

In the second approach, the granularity of the evaluation is lost as the grouping variables are eliminated. But is granularity really necessary at all in these cases? Is it still meaningful?

What's the best way to deal with nonunique assignments? We recommend designing the grouping variables in such a way that nonunique assignments are only possible if there is uniqueness in the respective translated sets, as in Figure 6-14. The adapter implements this by checking the uniqueness of the returned units and, in case of doubt, removing the grouping that leads to redundancy. Uniqueness is easy to ensure if it is translated from a generalist frame unit to a more specialized one. As shown in Figure 6-15, for instance, you can uniquely transfer additional attributes of the frame-unit broker to other frame units.

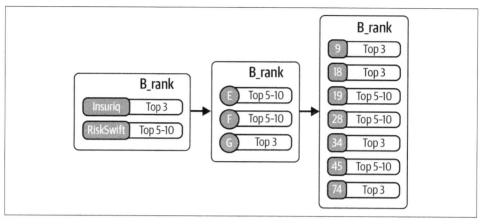

Figure 6-15. Mapping clearly assignable grouping variables

In this example, the mapping makes sense and is intended to be translated into claim units, since here you directly access the results of the claim-centered engines to get dedicated claims analysis for exactly this selection of brokers (Insuriq and RiskSwift). Especially when you first start working with frames, we recommend using just a few elementary frame units to reduce the transformations' complexity and increase traceability in processing individual components.

Dealing with Bottom-up Business Object Structures

Let's assume that our frame with the four claims (in Figure 6-14) has been technically defined to use claim-centric engines for analysis. You could translate this frame into broker units so that you can execute it using broker-centered engines. But would this make sense?

The broker engines process operations for the transferred brokers, regardless of their relationship to the individual claims. This means that the result from the broker engines is detached from the four claims and does not restrict its results to them, which would certainly not be possible in many broker engines.

This is because the broker engine naturally refers purely to the IDs of the brokers and not to the original definition—in this case, the claim IDs. This means that all information and KPIs for these brokers are now determined without restricting them to the claim IDs or the contracts associated with them.

This can be optionally implemented in engines for broker frame units, of course, but that is probably not useful from a business point of view and makes the implementation of individual engines very complex. Such engines would have to interact with many more different data sources (the broker, the contract, and the claims data, in this case). This increase in complexity would destroy the lightweight nature of frame engines. In addition, individual engine providers would be less willing to take responsibility as they would also be responsible for the correct interaction between complex data structures.

In our example, the engine determines the average brokerage fee, and its results would not be limited to claims 8, 9, 14, and 27 or to the related contracts A, C, and F. Its results would include all contracts belonging to brokers BrokSure and Insuriq (including contracts A, B, C, E, and F). However, it may be useful to know exactly how the brokers associated with this set of claims behave in general. If you are looking for this, you need to be aware of the limitations of this engine: in this case, the result is not specialized but provides all associated contract information.

Dealing with Unconnected Business Objects

It also becomes problematic when business objects that do not depend on one another are included in the framework. The adapter won't be able to translate, which means that individual frames cannot be executed on all engines; this would certainly not make much sense because the business objects do not belong together (see Figure 6-16).

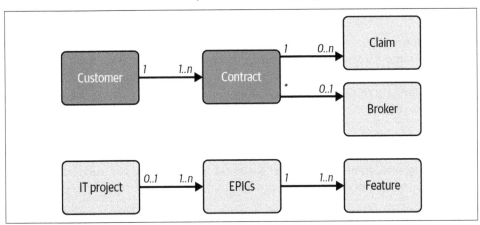

Figure 6-16. Introducing unrelated business objects

The frame adapter is designed to be flexible enough to handle mappings from different sources. This adaptability is critical in a business environment, where data structures and types can vary widely. The frame adapter is a key function of the Augmented Frames concept; as a central component, it ensures that all frames are available for execution on many engines. However, there is a great deal of complexity here.

In the simplest case, the implementation looks like this: the object mappings are kept in related structures, translated into individual data sets by data-wrangling operations, and then returned to the agent. There are no limits to the creativity you can bring to analyzing and mapping this relationship—anything from simple table mappings to complex graph structures. Our only recommendation is to fall back on existing structures, such as from the reporting and BI infrastructures, since individual fact and dimension tables likely already offer dependencies in an analyzable structure.

Frame Creator

The *Frame Creator* facilitates creating and organizing frames and making them accessible to all users. While it's possible to create defined frames without a special application, having one makes creating frames more accessible. The Frame Creator is essentially business users' entry point into the Augmented Frames concept. By defining and organizing frames, it lays the foundation for subsequent analysis, allowing the frame engines to perform domain-specific evaluations and the frame agent to orchestrate the entire concept. Its purposes include:

Defining frames
> The Frame Creator allows users to define what constitutes a frame. This includes selecting specific criteria or attributes that group business objects together, such as "all policies in a particular product line" or "all customers in a particular geographic region."

Organization
> The Frame Creator also organizes frames to ensure that they are stored, retrieved, and managed efficiently. This can include categorizing frames, labeling them for easy retrieval, and integrating them with other parts of the Augmented Frames concept.

GUI and accessibility
> The Frame Creator has an interface that guides users through the process of defining and organizing frames. It should have intuitive controls, templates, or wizards to simplify the creation process, making it as user-friendly as possible.

Once you create a frame, you need to make it accessible to other components of the framework, such as frame engines and the frame agent. The Frame Creator formats and structures frames and ensures their compliance with governance so that other components can use them effectively.

The Frame Creator can be used as a platform for sharing frames within the company. In addition to enabling access to indexed frames, which have an official character, the Frame Creator allows users to copy, collaborate on, or subscribe to frame definitions so that they can create their own frames. For example, multiple editors might share and modify a portfolio defined specifically for later review.

The Frame Creator is an important tool within the Augmented Frames concept that allows you to define, customize, organize, and manage frames. It is central to the analytical capabilities of the framework. Because of its high complexity, it can be implemented in a later iteration.

Case Study: AP/TP Frame Engine

In this section, we'll show you a brief fictitious example of how to use a specific frame engine to demonstrate how return types can be structured. As we have mentioned, each engine has a very individual return structure. This makes it all the more important to document the interfaces well, to ensure proper use in highly automated workflows. Here, we'll give you an example of an engine for analysis in an insurance context.

First, what is AP/TP? In commercial insurance, the term *achieved premium* (AP) refers to the actual income that an insurance company receives for providing insurance coverage. It reflects the real pricing of insurance policies. The term *target premium* (TP), on the other hand, refers to the income that the insurance company *wants* to achieve based on its risk assessment, its pricing strategies, and market conditions. The AP/TP is a ratio of the two. A ratio above 1 is optimal for profitability. OK, enough of the insurance-specific digression—let's look at how the engine works.

This engine determines the actual premium information for specific policies and calculates the AP/TP. You may wonder why this should be a special engine. After all, isn't the point of engines to encapsulate complex calculations and ensure governance? This doesn't seem to be a high-complexity calculation—just simple division. Couldn't you just do it yourself? You could, but here are three reasons not to:

- The engine acts as an official and reliable data provider.
- While the calculation for individual policies is simple division, aggregations must account for the additional weights of the individual contracts. This complicates obtaining the result, and you would need to ensure governance for a valid result.
- You don't *have* to do it yourself. Engines encapsulate not only complex tasks but also time-consuming and repetitive ones, which are the best use cases for workflow automation.

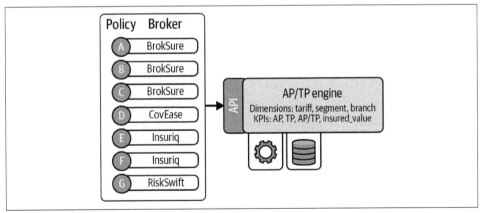

Figure 6-17. Using an AP/TP engine

For the example in Figure 6-17, we select the list of policies defined in Figure 6-12 and add the corresponding brokers as an additional attribute to use as a grouping variable in the result. So the simple workflow is to select the frame of seven policies, enrich it with broker information, and send it to the AP/TP engine. The detailed workflow does not matter in this case, but basically, after receiving the frame units, the engine collects all necessary premium information from internally accessible data sources and filters them according to the seven policies. The next step is to select only the necessary attributes and calculate the result at the level of individual policies and the desired aggregation. In our example, the aggregation is defined by only one external variable: the specified broker. The engine also aggregates and returns the result (Example 6-11).

Example 6-11. Result output of AP/TP engine

```
$premium
# A tibble: 7 × 8
  policy broker   tariff.      achieved_premium target_premium  aptp lead_share insured_value
  <chr>  <fct>    <chr>                   <dbl>          <dbl> <dbl>      <dbl>         <dbl>
1 A      BrokSure  TARIFF I              103077.         86932. 1.19        0.3     114122681
2 B      BrokSure  Compact                 2717.          3804. 0.714       1         2490020.
3 C      BrokSure  XoL                    46002.         57503. 0.800       0.260   153128895
4 D      CovEase   PropertyCal.           23740.         30762. 0.772       0.5      21000000
5 E      Insuriq   TARIFF II               1659.          1412. 1.17        1         2353534.
6 F      Insuriq   XoL                   316408.        316408. 1           0       854615112.
7 G      RiskSwift TARIFF I              103077.         86932. 1.19        0.3     114122681

$aptp_agg
# A tibble: 4 × 5
  broker        n achieved_premium target_premium  aptp
  <fct>     <int>            <dbl>          <dbl> <dbl>
1 BrokSure      3          151796.        148239. 1.02
2 CovEase       1           23740.         30762. 0.772
3 Insuriq       2          318067.        317820. 1.17
4 RiskSwift     1          103077.         86932. 1.19
```

The return object from the engine will have the structure shown in Example 6-12.

Example 6-12. AP/TP return object structure

```
{
  "premium": [
    {
      "policy": "A",
      "broker": "BrokSure",
      "tariff": "TARIFF I",
      "achieved_premium": 103076.7,
      "target_premium": 86932.3,
      "aptp": 1.1857,
      "lead_share": 0.3,
      "insured_value": 114122681
    },
    ...
```

```json
  ],
  "aptp_agg": [
    {
      "broker": "BrokSure",
      "n": 3,
      "achieved_premium": 151796.42,
      "target_premium": 148239.34,
      "aptp": 1.0171
    },
    ...
  ],
  ...,
  "meta_execution": {
    "clean_pii": false,
    "clean_names": false,
    "keep_names": true,
    "aggregated": true,
    "extended": true,
    "unknown": true,
    "num_units": 7,
    "execution_date": "2024-01-03 11:55:00",
    "execution_date_finish": "2024-01-03 11:55:03",
    "parameter": {
      "weighted_by_ln": true,
    },
    "groupings": {
      "groups": ["broker"],
      "additional_groups": []
    }
  }
}
```

The interface definition for the general result object will look something like Example 6-13.

Example 6-13. AP/TP result object interface definition

```json
{
  "$schema": "http://json-schema.org/draft-07/schema#",
  "type": "object",
  "title": "AP/TP Engine",
  "description": "Achieved / target premium engine, to report the actual AP/TP",
  "properties": {
    "premium": {
      "type": "array",
      "description": "An array of premium related records.",
      "items": {
        "type": "object",
        "properties": {...},
        "required": [...]
      }
    },
    "aptp_agg": {
      "type": "array",
      "description": "An array of aggregated AP/TP records.",
      "items": {
        "type": "object",
```

```
      "properties": {...},
      "required": [...]
    }
  },
  "unknown": {
    "type": "array",
    "description": "An array for unknown frame units.",
    "items": {
      "type": "object",
      "properties": {...}
    }
  },
  "meta_fields": {
    "type": "array",
    "description": "Metadata fields describing various variables of the results.",
    "items": {
      "type": "object",
      "properties": {...}
    }
  },
  "meta_execution": {
    "type": "object",
    "description": "Metadata about the execution or processing of the engine.",
    "properties": {...},
    "required": [...]
  }
},
"required": [
  "premium",
  "aptp_agg",
  "unknown",
  "meta_fields",
  "meta_execution"
]
}
```

Let's examine the interface description for this example. Here, two data tables are defined in the interface for this engine: premium and aptp_agg. As you can see, the injection of the broker attribute makes the individual interfaces of both data result tables dynamic. The possibility of adding your own group variables prevents the execution function from having a uniform fixed interface. The engine can't know which additional variables will be used in the result until execution because they'll be passed through the frame (in this case, the broker frame).

In addition, variables in the engine's data tables can be renamed dynamically, when the frame sends a grouping variable to the engine with a name that the engine is already using (for instance, tariff). The keep_names attribute, in the parameters passed to the engine, tells the engine to rename one of the variables.

As you can see in Example 6-14, the broker attribute is not documented in the interface but appears in the result data tables in Example 6-10. The fact is that this variable is documented in the meta_attribute object, but the interface description is "violated," and meta_information does not recognize it either. This means that the interface descriptions do not correspond to the resulting output in case of doubt. Although all these circumstances are reported via the `meta_execution` object so that it is possible to trace what is in the result and how it is known, this can lead to restrictions, especially in very inflexible environments.

Example 6-14. Interface of AP/TP engine `premium` and `aptp_agg` objects

```
{...,
  "premium": {
    "type": "array",
    "description": "An array of premium related records.",
    "items": {
      "type": "object",
      "properties": {
        "policy": {
          "type": "string",
          "description": "Identifier for the policy."
        },
        "tariff": {
          "type": "string",
          "description": "Tariff code or name."
        },
        "achieved_premium": {
          "type": "number",
          "description": "The premium amount actually achieved."
        },
        "target_premium": {
          "type": "number",
          "description": "The target premium amount."
        },
        "aptp": {
          "type": "number",
          "description": "Ratio of achieved premium to target premium."
        },
        "lead_share": {
          "type": "number",
          "description": "The lead share percentage."
        },
        "insured_value": {
          "type": "number",
          "description": "The total insured value."
        }
      },
      "required": [
        "policy",
        "tariff",
        "achieved_premium",
        "target_premium",
        "aptp",
        "lead_share",
        "insured_value"
      ]
    }
  },
  "aptp_agg":{
    "type":"array",
```

```
    "description":"An array of aggregated APTP records.",
    "items":{
      "type":"object",
      "properties":{
        "n":{
          "type":"number",
          "description":"Number of records aggregated."
        },
        "achieved_premium":{
          "type":"number",
          "description":"Total achieved premium amount across aggregated records."
        },
        "target_premium":{
          "type":"number",
          "description":"Total target premium amount across aggregated records."
        },
        "aptp":{
          "type":"number",
          "description":"Aggregated ratio of achieved premium to target premium."
        }
      },
      "required":[
        "n",
        "achieved_premium",
        "target_premium",
        "aptp"
      ]
    }
  }
},
...}
```

Dynamic handling of the results is required to use the engines correctly and to their full extent. You decide how you want to handle the dynamic naming and structure of the data objects. At the very least, you can avoid the dynamic naming of variables that are named in interfaces. The caller can check the variable names of the result tables of the engine beforehand and adapt its frames accordingly or control them via the keep_names parameter.

If you want to use the option of using your own grouping variables, adding more information, then you must accept the dynamic structure of the results. It is a compromise between insisting on static structures and maintaining high flexibility in augmentation. Our recommendation is to create flexible processes that can handle dynamic structures, but try to be as precise as possible in the documentation. Ultimately, flexible responses to user requirements will bring the desired benefits to the extended workflow.

Infrastructure and Technology

For a better understanding, we would like to present a thematic architectural sketch. The frame agent is the central component that internally uses the Frame Dissolver and the frame adapter and organizes the described execution process. The agent makes API calls to the engines and transmits resolved frames (frame units). Users interact directly with the engines through the agent's GUI and an API that serves as an endpoint for the surrounding workflows, as shown in Figure 6-18.

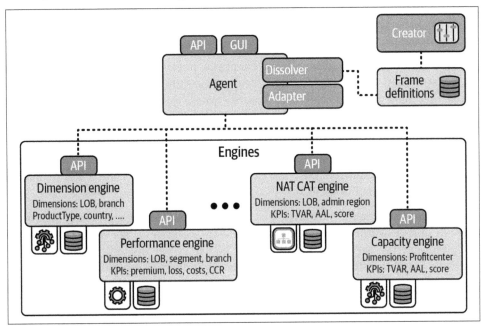

Figure 6-18. Augmented Frames components and infrastructure

The engines can also be used for augmentation without an agent in the infrastructure. They have an individual interface and are deployed as APIs. Their ability to handle frame units makes them independent of the rest of the Augmented Frames concept.

Frame engines themselves are independent artifacts, ideally implemented as executable packages (as described in Chapter 5). This means that not only are they available as APIs, but they can also be programmatically integrated as a reference into other applications, scripts, or workflows. Since they have the corresponding meta-information and interface descriptions, which are ideally delivered with the packages, nothing stands in the way of programmatic integration in suitable runtime environments. You need only the required runtime environment variables to use them.

This approach can be very effective when you're implementing a large number of workflows in the same programming language. Implementation is fast and easy, but it also has its drawbacks. In particular, changes in individual engines' implementation are not readily apparent in programmatic workflows. Programmatic package references usually have to be updated manually but let you decide which version of an engine it should use to build the workflow. The corresponding API provides the internal optimization of the engine but does not explicitly reference the current version. Interface adjustments to individual APIs, in turn, necessitate adjustments to the workflow. As you can see, both types of consumption have advantages and disadvantages. That's why it's important to establish adequate version management for individual packages and APIs.

Because the engines will ultimately be integrated into many workflows, try to make as few structural changes as possible. Ideally, you should deploy individual engines when they have reached a level of maturity where you only expect to implement changes internally.

The frame agent's cataloging capabilities can help orchestrate version resolution. For example, if individual engines provide different API endpoints for different versions, the agent can communicate this. You can also specify a version when you invoke an individual engine via the agent.

However, such a system requires good maintenance and governance; the more engines and consuming workflows there are in the system, the higher its level of coupling and the lower its flexibility. In Chapter 7, we will discuss strategies for individual workflow types to deal with changes in individual dependencies.

For this reason, it is also important to maintain clean interfaces. If in doubt, consider the analytics contract approach described earlier in this chapter. A central contract service can also serve as a "trading platform" by concluding contracts in the truest sense of the word, making it possible to track which workflow requires which engine/API in which version. You can use such a list to clarify which engines/APIs are being used where and to inform users of planned adjustments.

This also brings us to the possibility of third-party, or *federated*, specific domain providers. Ultimately, the framework concept is no different than a data-mesh approach, where different parties offer their solutions and take responsibility and ownership for them. When these domain-specific engines are offered via APIs (whether they are frame engines or any other executable analytic solution), they can be listed in the agent if they meet the requirements of the Augmented Frames concept and if their contracts can be published centrally. This means that different domains can now offer their analytical products and be integrated into the central system of analytical solutions.

For instance, consider the following situation: the risk management department has implemented its own analytical service to simulate natural hazards for insured locations. As the experts on such simulations, they deliver a high-quality, reliable result. They provide their engine as a frame engine, which expects contracts as frame units. This service is not centrally managed and operated by the CoE; instead, it's offered in a federated manner via "third parties"—that is, risk management. The API is also published as a contract so that all conditions and deliveries are communicated. Risk management's product is now used in other workflows and processes through the Augmented Frames concept.

Although the frame agent serves as the central listing component, it should *not* be the central listing service for analytics contracts, as these are broader in functionality and interface than the managed frame engines. This includes contracts for frame engines and for any other analytical APIs or augmented workflows that expect different inputs and serve different purposes. It is even conceivable that entire workflows could be provided through APIs that have their own contracts with the outside world. When used in this way, contracts should provide information about the types of engines or workflows they represent.

In Figure 6-19, you can see an example infrastructure that integrates augmented frames into a holistic analytical product infrastructure. All services are registered in a centralized analytics contract library. Various APIs work together in this approach by using the centralized analytics contracts as a rule system for agreements on inputs, deliveries, and terms of use.

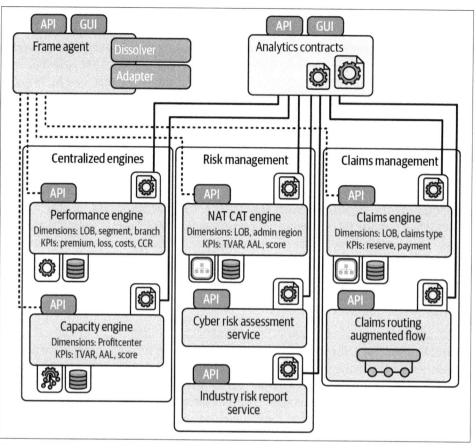

Figure 6-19. Augmented frames and analytics contracts repository

As you can see, the whole thing can be extended and implemented in any number of complex ways. If overengineered, it can lose its flexibility and lightness. Therefore, our advice is to start small and fast, be pragmatic, and iteratively approach an optimal but manageable level of maturity. The next section describes what such an iterative approach to augmented frames might look like.

Different frame engines can be used in different augmented workflows and other analytical products. For example, the claims routing augmented flow can leverage the claims engine and the capacity engine and ultimately act as a way to leverage decentralized analytics capabilities and assemble them effectively for its own purpose. This gradually creates a neural interdependency of analytics capabilities within the organization and lays the foundation for higher excellence for business processes. Of course, this interconnection also brings challenges, but it is necessary to gradually augment workflows and transform the company from data-driven to insight-driven.

An Iterative Approach to Introducing Augmented Frames

Introducing the Augmented Frames concept to an organization requires a structured, iterative approach. Each phase should extend the overall concept in a way that adds value. Figure 6-20 illustrates a proposal for six possible iterations.

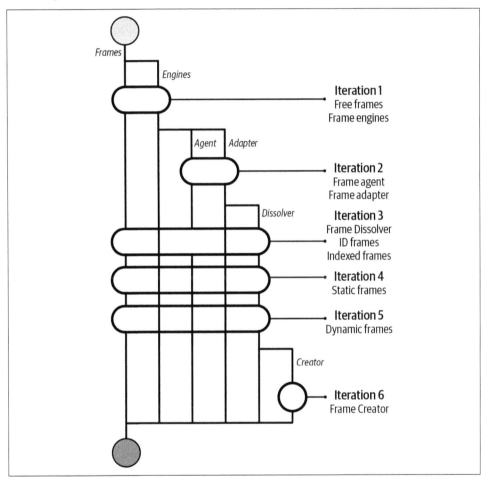

Figure 6-20. An iterative approach to introducing augmented frames

Let's break this down, iteration by iteration.

Iteration 1: Free Frames and Frame Engines

As you learned at the beginning of this chapter, *free frames* are collections of frame units that allow you to categorize and analyze data in the initial stages without rigid structures. They encourage users to explore and learn how to use frames. You can handle them in different ways, even in a simple Excel sheet.

You'll need to implement frame engines at this stage, too, to process and analyze data in free frames. The engines may need significant customization and effort to provide meaningful insights. In this first iteration, their basic structure is defined and unlikely to change. Loosely coupling the engines to the overall framework makes them nothing more than processing services that take a set of business-unit IDs and process them in a domain-specific way. Whether these later originate from a construct called a "frame" is irrelevant for the engines, which only accept frame units regardless of how they were originally identified. Thus, further iterations won't require any adjustments to the frame engine's infrastructure.

This early iteration will have challenges. Free frames will still be an abstract construct, so users will need to learn how to use them. Further, the frames will not yet have an Augmented Frames UI: the concept will only be available as a web service API at this stage. This is a first step toward introducing these possibilities into workflows, but business users may find it difficult to accept.

At the end of this first iteration, the engines can be integrated into workflows and used with free frames (a set of 1 to n frame units) to add value to workflows. For example, in the policy inventory, you could call the claims engine to display the current status of the current claims situation. Or the system could send a customer number to the returns engine in the background and immediately display the ratio of returns to orders for that customer.

At the end of this iteration, the system is still in a "proof of concept" state. It demonstrates augmented frames' potential for data analysis but is not yet fully integrated into daily operations. The frame engines, in particular, are still somewhat loosely and poorly cataloged. In principle, however, the system is already creating fundamental added value.

Iteration 2: A Frame Agent and Frame Adapter

In the second iteration, you'll introduce the frame agent as a centralized gateway to the frame engines. You'll begin using the frame agent to orchestrate interactions and manage data flow, translate frame units, and provide unified, consolidated user access. The frame adapter also ensures that data from different frame units is compatible with different frame engines so that individual engines can be used much more broadly.

The challenge during this phase is to integrate the frame agent into the existing IT infrastructure. This will be complex as the frame agent must fulfill the design and interface requirements of the infrastructure. As the central access point, it must ensure the consistency of the engines' interfaces. This can require considerable effort when implementing the infrastructure, since the interfaces are generally harmonized in terms of input, but their result objects are highly individual. Have the frame agent pass configurative interface descriptions directly from the engines to the callers.

To ensure data compatibility, you may need to do extensive mapping and give the frame adapter access to appropriate data sources. This means embedding it in existing data systems; the framework will lose its lightness and must accept dependencies on established structures.

At the end of this iteration, the system will be ready for basic orchestration and data-integration tasks as well as more extensive use by workflows.

Iteration 3: The Frame Dissolver, ID Frames, and Indexed Frames

The third iteration introduces the Frame Dissolver, which makes it possible to retrieve relevant frame units based on defined frames, including new frame types. Starting to work with frame IDs and indexed frames enables you to perform centralized, moderated queries of the engines. Users can use and communicate frame IDs without needing to know their specific composition.

Developing a robust Frame Dissolver can be technically challenging and time-consuming. The advantage, in this iteration, is that the defined frames' structure is still very rudimentary: it's just a stored list of frame units. This sets up the initial persistence mechanisms, but the Frame Dissolver does not yet need to be interoperable with other data sources or sophisticated business logic to dissolve complex filters.

The system becomes more powerful and efficient during this iteration, allowing for targeted data analysis and retrieval. You can use it for more advanced analysis within specific business areas or workflows. Business experts in one area can define a frame perfectly, implement it, and then share its identifiers for use in different workflows. For example, the marketing department could create a frame of products for a new campaign and share it across the organization. Any other workflow could then use that frame ID with different frame engines to query and integrate KPIs.

Iteration 4: Static Frames

The next iteration introduces *static frames*, which provide a stable structure for consistent analysis over time. This is important for tracking and comparison. Static frames are good at addressing individual stakeholders' needs. They can be defined by their attribution, not just by fixed frame units, which helps users define and adopt them. Users no longer have to search manually for all frame units in a system (such as "all customers belonging to the group of sole proprietors"). They just define that characteristic, and the Frame Dissolver resolves the corresponding frame units at runtime.

You can extend the frame agent by, for example, allowing frame definitions as input in addition to the frame IDs. This allows external definitions to be transferred directly from the frame agent to the Frame Dissolver. This functionality comes at a high price, though: you need to extend the frame agent at its interfaces, The Frame Dissolver already has sophisticated business logic as it has access to data systems that can link features to frame units. However, the advantage would be significant as calls can now not only trigger executions with predefined frame IDs but also query evaluations for frame units with certain attributes on demand. This low-threshold access increases flexibility as well as usage rates.

Carefully consider how you define characteristics in the static frames. The definition should be stored in a separate persistence and described in an accessible format. To retrieve the corresponding frame units from an appropriate data source, the Frame Dissolver can reformulate a domain-specific language (a dedicated language for defining and describing filter criteria for frame units), describing the characteristic in specific queries. We recommend that you implement this using dynamic languages that can be interpreted at runtime, such as SQL or R.

Introducing static frames is a milestone in a company's augmentation and automation efforts. Imagine the impact: when a new customer is created in an inventory workflow, you can automatically query KPIs for that customer's characteristics based on the attributes entered. The workflow does not need to know the comparison customers directly; it simply uses the defined characteristic to query valuable information from frame engines at runtime. The user is informed right in the workflow that, for example, customers in this category are particularly profitable or prefer to consume certain products.

Iteration 5: Dynamic Frames

Dynamic frames increase frames' flexibility so that they can better adapt to changing data or business requirements. They behave similarly to static frames, except their properties are subject to changing circumstances. For example, a dynamic frame that contains "all customers with an annual revenue of $100,000" will certainly have a changing number of frame units throughout the year.

The challenges here are immense. To guarantee these dynamic attributes during runtime, the Frame Dissolver must be deeply integrated into the company's data infrastructures. This is complex and will cause long execution times during the dissolution process.

Resolving dynamic frames is similar to resolving static frames. Both definitions must be resolved against data sources in an interpretable way. You could consider using predefined, regularly generated reference data and base the resolution of these frames on certain time cycles, such as weekly or daily KPI updates. Of course, if the KPIs you use for the definition are updated in real time, then a real-time resolution would be more interesting since you could use a single engine (querying without IDs to get all references). Use caution, however: this requires a lot of traffic, execution time, and resources.

A good starting point for this iteration is to have a dedicated team manually define the internal frame definitions of complex dynamic frames. This isn't the most scalable solution, but it makes frame resolution more manageable. It's also a practical way to test functionality and determine whether the organization actually needs these types of frame definitions.

The ability to respond to dynamic KPIs in the definition takes frames to a whole new level, setting new standards for insight-driven decision making—if the cost of such a complex implementation is justified by the value it adds.

Iteration 6: The Frame Creator

The Frame Creator allows end users to create and manage frames independently, democratizing their use. Developing an intuitive Frame Creator that balances performance and usability is challenging.

You must provide a complete GUI application that covers all aspects of frame definition. In addition to simple ID frames, it must be able to define static and dynamic frames that can be based on complex combinations of conditions. This is a difficult task, but this will be the ultimate access point for all users.

With a guided GUI process, you can limit the scope of the definition or steer it in a certain direction, such as toward simpler conditions that can be resolved later with less effort. Although this doesn't give the highest degree of flexibility, it can be a good balance between not realizing anything at all and a comprehensive implementation. Defining the UI will be challenging, but further functionalities, like listing, sharing, and collaboration, are manageable and of standard complexity for transactional IT systems.

The sixth iteration brings the augmented frames system to its highest level of maturity yet. It is fully dynamic and can handle maximum involvement of all business users and stakeholders. Individual extensions can now be integrated into the workflows.

Iteration Wrap-up

This is one possible approach for introducing the Augmented Frames concept iteratively. You can evaluate after each iteration to see if it makes sense to take it to the next iteration, given the resources you have available.

The fourth iteration, in particular, provides a good foundation for driving augmented workflows. It lets you persist definitions, translate different frame units, and dissolve static frames into frame units, which will have a huge impact on the organization's insight capabilities. After each iteration, you'll have an executable, value-added solution to augment your workflows.

The loose coupling of the individual components minimizes the adjustments you'll need to make later to already complete functionalities. For example, complete frame engines, frame adapters, and frame agents will not change as the overall system expands. This makes it easier to implement and helps when experimenting with new functionalities in later iterations: only the Frame Dissolver will need to be adapted.

We recommend that you start small and then gradually scale up. Always start with engines that cover a critical business need. Because engines are implemented independently of the Augmented Frames concept, they can support a wide variety of use cases and can even be integrated into internal technical data pipelines. This means that the effort involved in the first iteration is definitely not wasted.

If you are satisfied with the functionality of the core framework in a particular iteration, stop maturing it and focus instead on implementing new frame engines and integrating the existing implementations into your workflows. See what's possible with your company's internal resources, then get creative.

Conclusion

Do you absolutely *need* augmented frames to establish AA in your workflows and drive the analytics transformation? The honest answer is no. There are many different approaches, some of which do not fit well into this concept. We will present some of these approaches in the next chapter.

However, the Augmented Frames concept has numerous advantages because it focuses on analyzing the most important business objects in your company so that it can answer most questions from business users. This technical concept provides a standardized approach that helps integrate proven analytics into existing IT infrastructures. The infrastructure is easily extensible and lets you reuse complex data structures and context mappings. Once implemented, you can extend the concept with domain-specific frame engines.

Users can define and apply filters (frames) to all engines to gain increasingly granular insights. The frame agent, Frame Dissolver, and frame adapter will process, enrich, and transform frame units into a defined, engine-specific format, while the frame engines are more isolated and detached from complex data infrastructures and can focus on high-quality, reliable analytics.

It is easy to integrate third-party solutions from other business domains and their results into the analysis infrastructure. This supports efforts to federalize analytics across the organization and promotes deep ownership for analytics results in these domains.

Because business experts define the domain-specific engines, the employees who use them can rely on the results being calculated correctly, which enables analytics governance within the organization. With these engines, you can integrate complex forecasting, sophisticated analytics-engineering tasks, and comprehensive KPIs into workflows.

Augmented frames empower users to make decisions because users can enrich frames with domain-specific groupings, share them with one another, and drill down into their portfolios to understand correlations that previous BI systems could not map.

To pilot this concept iteratively, you'll need a small team of one to three developers, a good analytical infrastructure, and a suitable programming language (such as R or Python). We recommend that you consider doing so. In the final chapter of this book, we'll examine some use cases to show you how this plays out in practice.

## CHAPTER 7

Applied Examples

This chapter explores practical examples of applied augmented analytics, demonstrating how the concepts you've learned throughout the book are solving real-world problems in a variety of industries. We begin with a close look at the insurance industry, focusing on the underwriting process: the procedure by which an insurance company decides whether to offer someone insurance and at what price. But we'll go beyond insurance to look at project management and sales workflows, showing how the same tools can lead to better decisions, faster work, and more accurate results. The goal is to show you the power of AA, no matter what industry you are in.

As we explore these examples, you'll see that the ideas we're talking about—augmenting workflows with AI and automation—aren't limited to one type of job or industry. They can be adapted to many situations, helping you solve a wide range of business problems and opening up new opportunities for innovation and progress. By the end of this chapter, you'll not only understand how to use AA in real-world scenarios, but you'll also have ideas about how to apply it to your own work to make it more efficient and forward-thinking.

The Underwriting Process

The insurance industry is deeply rooted in assessing and managing risk through the *underwriting* process: a critical and complex series of steps through which insurers evaluate and price the risks associated with insuring an asset. This is traditionally a labor-intensive process that requires a delicate balance among actuarial science, personal judgment, and risk management.

An underwriter's job is to review the insurance application, consider the company's risk appetite, assess the applicant's risk profile, and decide on the terms and pricing of the insurance policy offered. This requires a comprehensive analysis of extensive and diverse data sources, ranging from personal information and historical data to complex geographical and socioeconomic factors.

The ever-increasing amount of data, the complexity of the factors to be considered, competitive pressures in the market, and the increased expectations of policyholders and brokers have made it necessary for the industry to optimize this holistic process. The need for efficiency and precision has never been greater. That's where augmented workflows come into play.

Types of Augmented Workflows in Underwriting

Augmented workflows are encapsulated, self-contained, comprehensive subprocesses within a larger overarching workflow that are designed to improve users' efficiency, accuracy, and decision-making ability. These subprocesses can be divided into different types, each of which fulfills a specific function in the underwriting process:

Fully automated augmented workflows
These workflows are designed to work autonomously and perform precisely defined tasks without human intervention. By automating routine and repetitive tasks, underwriters can focus on more complex aspects of the underwriting process.

Augmented workflows to gain insights
These enhancements are analytical powerhouses that bring together data from disparate sources to provide actionable insights. They help underwriters overcome bias and consider information that may not have been previously accessible or obvious. They improve the underwriter's ability to make informed, consistent, and understandable decisions. They are generally not suitable for strict automation.

Conversational augmented workflows
With the advent of LLMs and gen AI, underwriters can create natural language output, when creating policy proposals, personalized customer communications, and other text, for example. This speeds up the process and ensures consistency and quality in customer contact.

If you recall the types of augmentation discussed in Chapter 5, augmented workflows (AugFlows) are based mainly on processes that fall into the fixed-rule augmentation category. These workflows give users a high level of confidence in the results. Insight-generation workflows are based on fixed-rule augmentations as well as on augmentations that support idea and insight enrichment. Ideally, these workflows can themselves be used in the infrastructure as independent components, which have their own contracts that regulate their use. Regardless of the type of augmentation, these processes can be provided in the infrastructure as frame engines and APIs to enrich individual workflows.

The Workflows in Detail

Let's take a detailed look at the underwriting process to better understand its work-flows, how they interact, and what components underlie them. The process as we present it here is somewhat simplified for the sake of clarity. In real life, not only is the process more complex, but it's also not strictly linear—various parallel tasks and subprocesses arise due to circumstances and branches and specifics in the workflow. The aim of these case studies is to show you how to extract individual subprocesses from the overall workflow, process them in isolation, and use their output for augmentation. This should give you an idea of how to develop these workflows for your own processes and how to transfer these concepts. In the augmented flows as well as in the service architecture, the same principle applies: divide and conquer, which means separate complex processes into smaller parts that can be handled individually.

Figure 7-1 illustrates the tasks of the underwriting process.

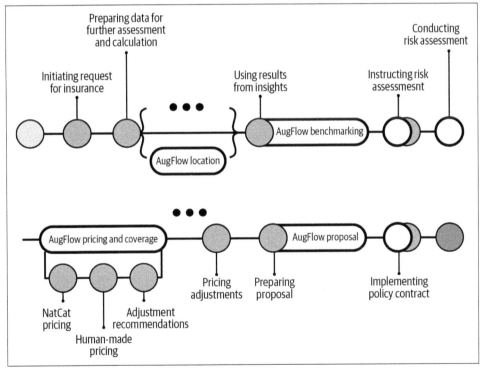

Figure 7-1. A basic overview of the underwriting workflow

We pay particular attention here to the four AugFlows that are part of the overall process chain and enable the underwriter to make augmentations at certain points. We will examine these in detail, but already you can see how analytics, automation, and AI create an interplay between machines and humans. Of course, the entire workflow could be done manually, as it was for most of the industry's history, but we'll show you how the augmentations optimize the workflow.

We'll begin with a closer look at the nine workflow steps depicted in Figure 7-1. The underwriting workflow in the insurance industry is a meticulous process consisting of several critical steps, each designed to assess risk and make informed decisions about issuing and pricing policies. The process can be summarized into the following key stages that are enhanced by AugFlows to streamline operations and improve outcomes:

1. *Initial insurance application*
   During this first step, potential customers express their need for insurance coverage and provide basic information, such as details of the risks, the type of property or asset to be insured, and the type of coverage required.

2. *Location AugFlow*
   This subprocess assesses geographical and location-related data that may be part of the insurance coverage. It includes:

   - A *location-data quality check* to verify the quality of the information

   - *Value imputation* to estimate any missing values, if necessary

   - Special geospatial operations (such as natural-hazard analysis) to understand the context of the risk

   This workflow is *highly automated* and relieves the underwriter of a lot of manual work.

3. *Benchmarking AugFlow*
   Benchmarking involves comparing the potential policy with existing policies, using frame engines to assess the new policy's expected performance and profitability, and comparing benchmark policies' premiums and terms and conditions. These benchmarks help the underwriter understand how the new policy compares to established metrics and industry standards. This should help them better assess the new policy. This process is not always mandatory, but it adds useful information that enhances the process's depth and quality. This workflow falls into the category of *augmentations to gain insight*. The efficiency of augmented workflows, which we described in Chapter 3, comes into play here: the underwriter does not have to actively take care of the information supply, just interpret the information.

4. *Refinements with results*
   The underwriter uses the insights they gained during the benchmarking phase to refine their underwriting criteria and pricing strategies. This is where the fact that good data literacy is indispensable in addition to specialist knowledge comes into play. The underwriter must have sufficient data literacy as well as specialist

knowledge to correctly interpret these insights. At this point, it becomes clear that augmentations don't take decision making away from underwriters, but they do greatly simplify it by taking care of the tedious technical task of preparing clean results. The specialist must then interpret those results correctly in their entirety; they are still the human in the loop.

5. Risk assessment

Risk assessment is a crucial step during which the underwriter assesses the likelihood and potential impact of a claim. At this stage, the underwriter initiates a comprehensive assessment of the risk based on the information gathered and the AugFlows' insights, analyzing the customer's history, the nature of the risk, and external factors that could affect the policy. This process, greatly simplified, is also enhanced by automated workflows. For instance, LLM processes summarize and interpret complex risk surveys on structural conditions, providing underwriters with a nuanced evaluation basis through abstract or uniform KPIs.

6. Pricing and coverage AugFlow

Based on the risk assessment, this subprocess is crucial for determining the appropriate pricing and coverage options for the policy. It uses the insights gained to make recommendations for necessary adjustments to ensure that the policy is competitively priced and appropriate for the perceived level of risk. The underwriter might adjust the price adjustments to account for natural catastrophe risks (*NatCat pricing*) or human-made risks (*human-made pricing*), depending on the specifics of the policy. This is another highly automated workflow. With appropriate input into the workflow, different components for pricing as well as frame engines (claims history for the contract, for subsequent contracts) are consumed, and different pricing services are used.

7. Price adjustments

After the AugFlow presents its fully automated pricing recommendation, the underwriter manually adjusts it according to the market situation, strategic conditions, and any other new information.

8. Policy proposal

A policy proposal, created by a dedicated automated service, serves as a formal insurance offer to the customer, setting out the terms of coverage, premiums, and all other important details. The underwriter, supported by a separate, integrated workflow, also creates contract documents and reports that document and explain the decision for communication with the client. Conversational augmentations are used here to preformulate the correspondence with the results of the overall process in natural language and are proposed to the underwriter. The contract document itself is also created by automating a dedicated service.

9. Implementation of finalized contract

Once the customer accepts the offer, the final step is implementing the insurance contract. This establishes the terms and conditions and binds both the insurer and the insured person to the agreed-upon conditions. In this final step, the policy and all conditions are settled in the inventory system. This subprocess, too, is augmented with automations that enrich attributes for the inventory system and supply various interfaces.

Example 1: Location Workflow

In this section, we dive into the first subprocess of the comprehensive underwriting workflow: the location AugFlow.

Situation and Problem Statement

During the underwriting process, the underwriter must make a wide variety of assessments of the given risks based on very different data. Much of the data that needs to be translated into insights is provided by the client or broker themselves. This information is usually not available in the format and completeness required for the underwriting process. In commercial property insurance, this includes location information—that is, the location of an insured property, such as a factory, a production facility, or even a building yard. This information must be taken into account to obtain a comprehensive view of the customer in terms of risk assessment, customer service, and pricing. Addresses, location, insured value, type of property, and the content of the risks to be insured are examples of this data. Complex processing of various services is used to convert this data into the correct form and format, so that it can be used for further processes. These tasks include a series of quality and completeness checks, value imputation, and value enrichment.

Solution Overview

Many of these activities are highly repetitive and require a highly consistent approach. Figure 7-2 shows the full location-handling process: a dedicated workflow that accesses distributed web services and orchestrates routing to the relevant components using internal rules. The inputs for this workflow are a set of location information and, if this is a contract renewal, the existing contract.

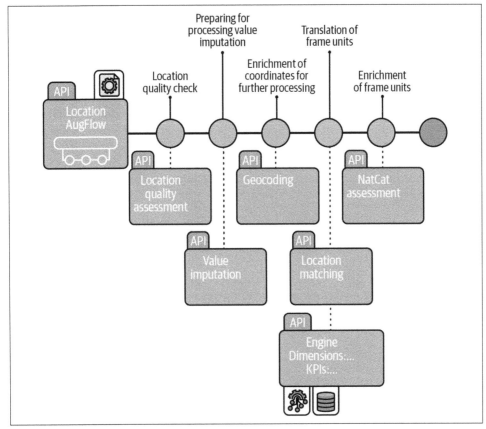

Figure 7-2. Workflow of location handling

The workflow eliminates a certain amount of the repetitive manual work of data cleansing and value enrichment. If the adjustments in the individual steps are manageable, the entire process can take place autonomously, without manual intervention by the underwriter. We are therefore talking about a fixed-rule workflow that offers almost fully automated augmentation and can ultimately act as an agent. This workflow returns a processed data set and insights that the underwriter factors into their recommendations for action. If individual process steps cannot be automated, the underwriter can intervene.

The workflow itself is a package implementation or even a service that is provided via an API and controls the entire orchestration. It accesses distributed services, each of which has been implemented for a specific task. The logic of controlling the workflow depends on predefined rules and is influenced by the results of the individual services that are strung together.

Solution Breakdown

We can dig a little deeper by looking at each step of this subprocess.

Location-data quality assessment

The first component is assessing the quality of the location data. This data might come in many formats, but the most common is Excel. The component reads the data and checks for completeness and data quality—that is, are all the required attributes present and filled with meaningful values? The result of this process is a harmonized data set enriched with quality KPIs.

Value imputation

If the data quality is limited to a defined degree, this procedure makes it possible to automatically cleanse the data and, in case of doubt, impute missing values.

An example of this could be a distribution of the insurance value to individual items. If, for example, only a sum of insurance values is specified for a certain location type, these are distributed to individual operating items (share for buildings, contents, materials) according to a certain distribution logic. This is based on empirical observations from the past and, for example, other locations in this data set. However, it is essential as this separation of values is necessary for subsequent processes. In this step, you'll make several adjustments *if* you have a high degree of confidence in the results *and* you can estimate and justify the implications for processing in further steps.

Georeferencing

The next step in the process is *georeferencing*, in which the locations are translated into a data set of map coordinates. Addresses are cleaned up, adding any missing attributes, correcting misspellings, and the like. This process uses familiar external functionalities, such as the map pin displayed in Google Maps when you enter an address. However, quality KPIs provide information about how accurately the coordinates represent the location, if possible. Of course, if only a city name and a country are specified, no coordinates can be determined that reflect the location at its actual position.

Matching

In *location matching*, a frame engine expands the data set with any information about the location that already exists in the company's inventory systems (especially for contract renewals). The advantage here is that this information has already been refined and is highly reliable.

The frame engine used here is an analytical engine, and the type of frame is a free frame generated at runtime. The engine supplies the data and provides statistical values for this portfolio of locations (fill levels, insurance values, and special contractual conditions for individual locations, such as limitations and deductibles as well as extended individual risk-assessment KPIs). The information is returned to the AugFlow, which then actively compares identical locations and, if necessary, adapts values and transfers them to the new data set. This is an undervalued augmentation because comparing and enriching existing information with new locations is usually time-consuming and labor intensive.

Natural catastrophe assessment

The final step in this AugFlow is evaluating the risk of natural hazards. A *natural hazard* (*https://oreil.ly/2y9gD*) is the threat of an event that will likely have a negative impact. A *natural disaster* is the negative impact following an actual occurrence of a natural hazard in the event that it significantly harms a community. This important information determines whether the location is insurable and it fits the company's risk appetite as well as how the insurance solution will be priced.

The main input for this process is all natural-hazard information for each location, in the form of classifiers and scores. KPIs describe each individual location's exposure to a specific type of natural hazard in terms of return period and intensity. For example, the risk of being affected by an intense earthquake is much higher in California or Istanbul than in London. Each natural hazard has a different global occurrence rate and characteristics and is therefore categorized differently. To provide a uniform picture of the overall situation for each individual location and the entire portfolio, classifications for each type of hazard are scored. (Figure 7-3 shows an example of NatCat classification.)

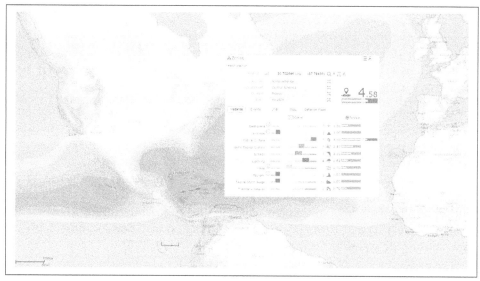

Figure 7-3. NatCat evaluation in ARGOS (https://oreil.ly/Hsq8E) (HDI Global SE)

A dedicated department with specialized knowledge provides the frame engine for this enrichment. This domain is responsible for the correctness and availability of this information via a corresponding contract. This information serves as a decision driver for further automated processes and gives the underwriter a better picture of the risk that informs their decisions.

Example Summary

The result of the entire workflow is a harmonized data set of location information, adjusted for attributes and enriched with geographic location, NatCat identifiers, and additional information about known locations.

This workflow is an excellent example of augmentation. It uses services, rules, and knowledge from the past to automate as much manual work as possible and ensure strong consistency.

Some tasks can't be performed manually, such as enriching the data with natural-hazard KPIs. The user can perform other processes in advance, like value distribution and imputation. However, removing this step and standardizing it in a dedicated process ensures that all distributions, regardless of who initiates them, are carried out according to the same rules and conditions. This ensures data quality and uniformity, regardless of the user.

This is a complex workflow, and a company that uses it will need a certain level of analytical and infrastructural maturity (Data Progressive) to build these processes and integrate them seamlessly. This includes competent employees in analytical roles who are experienced in both software development and data analysis and can correctly define the business cases and evaluate their relevance. Departments should collaborate closely to ensure a comprehensive understanding of the workflows and technical capabilities involved.

Example 2: Benchmarking Workflow

This example corresponds with step 3 in the underwriting workflow, benchmarking, and its AugFlow.

Situation and Problem Statement

Thoughtful underwriting considers the organization's past decision-making experience. It's rare for the nature of the risk being addressed to be completely unknown. It's likely that the company has dealt with a similar client or request in the past (or even currently). However, the problem is often that the individual underwriter may not be aware that others have assessed and insured similar risks. It's important to share these experiences to increase efficiency and uniformity in handling and to strengthen collaboration. In addition, exchanging this kind of information helps inexperienced and new colleagues better understand the risk in question and supports the goal of a data-liberal organization.

The benchmarking process is a workflow that gains additional insights into contracts similar to the new one, consolidates them, and gives recommendations that inform and enrich the underwriter's decisions. It creates a holistic view of past experiences by identifying insurance requests and solutions with similar characteristics, extends the scope to the higher-level portfolios to which these similar solutions belong, and calculates various KPIs for decision augmentation. This process is an idea and insight enrichment augmentation. It isn't mandatory but has enormous potential to improve the underwriting decision.

Solution Overview

Benchmarking can be divided into various subprocesses (see Figure 7-4). Depending on whether a preinsurance policy already exists, the processing workflow splits into subprocesses that collect additional individual KPIs and information about the previous policy. However, the main benchmarking-processing branch deals with the collection of comparable insurance solutions (let's call them "peers"). Its two basic steps are identifying similar solutions and collecting information about them at different levels of aggregation.

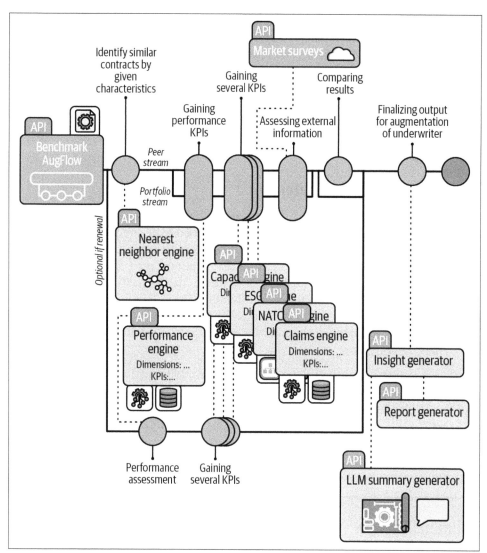

Figure 7-4. The benchmarking workflow

If the client is renewing an existing contract, the benchmarking process splits early on into subprocesses to collect additional individual KPIs and information about the previous policy. This helps the underwriter compare the existing policy with peers to learn if there's anything unusual about the claims situation or if its performance or the insurance conditions differ greatly from the peers.

The main process collects the comparative information of previous solutions, which is valuable information for the underwriter regardless of whether a prepolicy exists, as it gives them an indication of where the policy ranks in terms of claims patterns, performance, ESG development, capacity, or operational expense. The list can be expanded as required, depending on what information is available and suitable for benchmarks.

The result of this workflow is a comprehensive report called a *markdown* that contains all relevant information and direct comparisons, and, if necessary, uses a language model that formulates recommendations for action.

Solution Breakdown

Let's dive into the workflow a bit. (We won't explain the entire process in detail for all components, as that would get repetitive.)

Identifying peers

Let's first focus on identifying peers. This is done through a similarity analysis based on descriptive attributes of the queried insurance solution. You need a set of attributes, and you need to define rules for selecting benchmarks, such as how many peers you want for the comparison and what similarity thresholds are appropriate. The basic input for the entire process is therefore a description of the variables of the proposed solution.

It's a good idea for the underwriter to focus on meaningful attributes that are accessible at an early stage. The process is most valuable if done as near the beginning of the policy initiation as possible. The challenge is that there are often only a few attributes available at the beginning of the policy-initiation process, and a comprehensive selection of these attributes cannot be ensured. The algorithm used to identify peers must therefore be able to work with a diverse and incomplete attribute data set as input.

Let us give you an example: in one case, you have only the total sum insured, the industry segment, and the country available. In another case, you have more detailed information, such as attachment points for deductibles, turnover, and specific coverage information.

Identification can be very complex, but a good starting point is to use a simple, unsupervised ML model: the *k-nearest neighbor* (KNN) algorithm, a cornerstone of machine learning with a straightforward, effective approach to classification and regression tasks. It's a versatile, highly performant algorithm that's often used with dynamic and complex data sets.

We'll simplify here for clarity, but the KNN algorithm classifies a new entry according to how similar it is to existing entries in the data set. This similarity is quantified by a distance metric, such as Euclidean or Gower's (which is used when the data is of mixed data types) distance, which measures the "distance" between the new policy's features (input variables) and those in the existing data set. The algorithm considers a certain number k of the most similar policies (nearest neighbors) of the new entry.

Figure 7-5 shows an example of distance measurement; peers are represented with uppercase letters. Here, only two dimensions are considered: turnover and total sum insured. The algorithm determines distance based on the combined characteristics, then selects the five peers with the smallest distance and thus the highest similarity (C, D, E, H, and I).

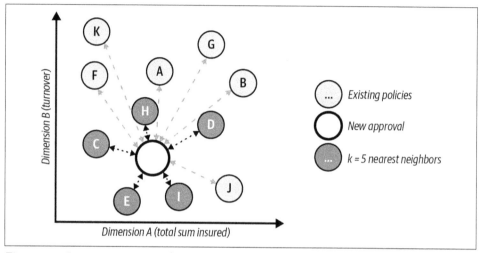

Figure 7-5. Distance measures for benchmarking, calculated by a KNN algorithm

KNN's effectiveness depends on the value of k, the number of nearest neighbors to be considered. This choice represents a significant trade-off:

Higher k (larger distance)
> If you choose a larger value for k, a broader set of measures is included in the decision process. Using a larger sample of the data set minimizes the impact of anomalies and noise. There is a risk of bias, though, especially if the distant neighbors do not accurately represent the category of the new policy, which in turn can lead to less accurate predictions.

Lower k (smaller distance)
> Conversely, using a lower value for k focuses the algorithm on the nearest neighbors. This can be beneficial if these neighbors closely match the new policy. However, this approach is more susceptible to the influence of outliers. A single deviating nearest neighbor can disproportionately influence the classification and lead to erroneous predictions.

Implementing KNN in a dynamic environment such as a commercial insurance portfolio system, where the input variables change frequently, requires a careful balance.

While the KNN algorithm is simple in its basic features, it requires sophisticated application to effectively handle the complexity of real-world data environments. The advantage, however, is that this algorithm is very well suited to identifying peers, even with a limited set of comparison attributes.

The output of this subprocess is a list of policies and their attributes, which can then be used for input as frame units in various frame engines. (This contrasts with the classical KNN, which categorizes based on majority categories.)

Gathering knowledge about peers

The next step is to gather knowledge about the peers. This is where the frame engines come into play. While the KNN engine was only responsible for identifying a sensible selection of comparable peers that meet the requirements of the overall process, the frame engines now determine what the actual KPIs of the benchmarks are. We will not describe these in detail as this has already been done in Chapter 6 as an example. But to understand the process, here is the approach: as a result of the last process, the higher-level process now receives a selection of frame units. As illustrated in Figure 7-4, these units can now be processed in two ways: on direct peers and on overarching portfolios.

The first choice is to select the identified peers as input for individual engines. You combine the frame units into a free frame and address the individual engines via the frame agent to obtain domain-specific findings. You can also select a generic aggregation that queries the KPIs without further differentiation at the overall frame level. The results for each frame engine are the KPIs for the individual peers as well as an aggregation. You can compare the new contract proposal against the peers as a whole and examine individual peers more closely.

The other option is to extend the selection to a comprehensive portfolio. For example, if most of the peers or the new contract itself belongs to a certain industry segment in a certain country, you can define a static frame at runtime that maps all policies in the portfolio with these attribute characteristics and provides them as input for the engines. This ultimately gives the underwriter a more comprehensive, albeit more generic, view of the contract initiation. The result could, for example, be the following insight: "For contracts in industry segment X in country Y, we observed performance below the defined targets and recorded an unusually high number of frequency claims."

This means that benchmarking can be carried out at different levels: on direct peers as well as on their overarching portfolios. Incorporating additional external data sources, such as external rating services or insights from market-research institutes, can further enrich the knowledge base and help provide a more targeted and comprehensive view of the risk.

Evaluating existing policies

The parallel process for renewals typically uses the same frame engines to collect specifics about performance and behavior. The frame engines are used according to the same principle. At runtime, a free frame is defined that contains only the existing policy number as a frame unit.

Once the underwriter has the KPIs and information from both processes, they can optionally merge and compare the attributes of the existing contract with the benchmarks. What is compared and how are individually implemented. This was determined and defined in a separate use case, as were the limits of the KNN comparison, taking into account expert assessments. In other words, this small process step alone was originally a separate use case that was implemented by a multidisciplinary team to generate truly meaningful full comparisons and insights.

The final step generates holistic reporting for the underwriter. All KPIs are transferred into a report that visually explains all the details. We recommend using R Markdown technology here: not only can you provide it as an API endpoint, but it also delivers interactive HTML reports that can be integrated into surrounding applications. The output of the whole process is a report and the evaluation results in tabular form. You may want to save the frames and tables for later benchmarks.

A specialized LLM bot with predefined system prompts generates the report itself. It also provides the underwriter with email templates for text related to benchmarking that can be used in internal and external communications, including one for rejecting the application, if needed. These templates are customer focused; internal communications include very detailed descriptions with reference to KPIs while those for other audiences may be much more generic.

Example Summary

This process is a perfect example of AA using complex algorithms to give the user additional optional insights, freeing users from intensive research.

Smaller components are combined into a holistic workflow, largely enabled by API microservice architectures. Each small engine and service contributes to and is based on the ideas and experiences of business users, usually from their own small analytics use cases.

The insights that this workflow generates include aspects that the underwriter may not even be aware of with regard to their relevance, existence, or accessibility (see also Figure 3-2). The underwriter gets extensive information that they must interpret and use. This again illustrates the original thesis of the book. Augmented analytics does not *replace* analytics awareness, which is still essential to empowering people in the organization. But most people won't need the extensive data literacy required to collect and collate this information if their workflows are comprehensively and meaningfully augmented.

This solution is insight- and idea-generation augmentation. It provides insight to the user but does not trigger further automated processes. The machine does the dirty work consistently and reliably; the human, who can classify the results, adds the finishing touches (see also high integration/low automation copilots in Figure 5-8). Any user, regardless of their skills and analytical abilities, can obtain the same in-depth knowledge with the same quality and reliability.

Example 3: Proposal Workflow

The final AugFlow in the overall underwriting process prepares the quotation. This workflow is the conversational type. It supports standardized communication and documentation of quotation creation through a combination of language models and reporting capabilities.

Situation and Problem Statement

Depending on the business type or product to insure, the communication is customized, with certain mandatory elements. Typical components of an offer are the results from the preceding processes—in other words, details from the needs assessment and risk assessment, information on the recommended insurance solution, and results from the price calculation. The following content is typical:

Coverage details
Precise description of the insurance coverage offered, including the share of participation

Pricing
Detailed breakdown of premiums and costs

Terms and conditions
Exclusions, deductibles, and special conditions

Validity of the offer
No unknown losses before inception

Company information
Information about the insurer and its ability to carry the risks

Customer information
Personalized explanation of how the offer is tailored to the customer's specific needs and risks as well as any special features or ambiguities that may also impose restrictions on protection or require adjustment

The proposal process is time-consuming and involves a lot of repetitive work. The underwriter combines information from the proposal with standard clauses and conditions to give the customer a comprehensive, comprehensible, and reliable offer. Proposals should follow a standard structure since they also serve as internal documentation and governance.

Transparency is essential in this process. Quotations must give customers clear information about all conditions, coverage, and costs. A detailed, professional quotation strengthens trust in the relationship between customer and insurer. The augmented workflow aims to provide efficiency, consistency, quality assurance, and, above all, shorter response times.

Solution Overview

This AugFlow takes the information from the previous process as input and processes it internally, together with other attributes defined by the underwriter, to create an offer. Its result can vary depending on the communication requirements, business type, country, or target group. For example, it could return a PDF containing all the information in a consolidated structure or a simple email that suggests a communication template to request missing information from the customer.

The special thing about this workflow is that, unlike the previous ones, it requires user interaction. It proposes communication texts and individual modules, but the underwriter can change them. However, the general aim at the end of the process is to have all the required documents and information summarized in an offer and to generate proposed text for any additional communications, such as email correspondence.

The solution internally is a combination of different elements: LLMs to generate individual passages of the offer, which can be particularly useful for specific declarations from the risk assessment; predefined text modules to describe mandatory conditions and clauses; and, depending on the type of offer, reporting capabilities to present certain information in structured forms like charts and tables, such as limits and deductibles or the results of pricing or risk assessment.

Solution Breakdown

This workflow is designed to address the complexities and requirements of creating customized insurance quotes while ensuring efficiency, consistency, and a high level of customization. The following is a functional overview of the steps involved in this advanced workflow, as illustrated in Figure 7-6.

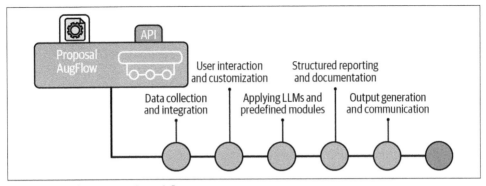

Figure 7-6. The proposal workflow

Data collection and integration

The workflow begins with the aggregation of data from a variety of preprocesses, including the needs assessment, the risk assessment, and the price calculation. This step ensures that all relevant information, such as coverage details, pricing, and terms and conditions, is captured and ready for processing. Integrating different types of data from multiple sources and types is critical for creating a comprehensive and accurate quote.

User interaction and customization

A key feature of this workflow is its conversational interface, which requires active user interaction. The underwriter is presented with suggested text and modules based on the initial data collection. These suggestions are generated using LLMs (e.g., GPT), which are capable of creating nuanced and context-specific content. Recognizing the importance of human expertise, the workflow allows underwriters to modify these suggestions, enabling a high degree of customization and ensuring that the final proposal meets customer needs.

Applying LLMs and predefined modules

The workflow uses LLMs to create individual sections of the proposal. This is complemented by using predefined text modules to describe standard terms and conditions. The combination of LLM-generated content and predefined modules ensures that the proposal is both personalized and consistent with corporate and industry standards.

Structured reporting and documentation

To enhance clarity and professionalism, the workflow includes advanced reporting capabilities. This allows critical information, such as limits, deductibles, and pricing details, to be presented in structured formats like charts and tables. The workflow creates a draft policy that combines clauses and wording from legal texts (predefined text modules) with the input and results of the previous processes. In the end, all policy-relevant information is contained in one document, and an additional report is created for detailed explanation.

Output generation and communication

Depending on the specific requirements of the proposal, the workflow can generate a variety of outputs, including rich PDF documents or simplified email templates. This flexibility ensures that the final product is appropriate for the communication needs of the business type, country, or target audience. In addition, the workflow can suggest templates for subsequent communications with the client to streamline the entire process.

Example Summary

The proposal workflow represents a significant improvement to the overall underwriting workflow, offering a solution that combines technical sophistication with the need for personalized customer service: leverage the power of LLMs and structured reporting yet leave room for underwriting expertise and individualization. This workflow addresses the critical time and repetition challenges of the proposal process. Ultimately, this approach not only increases operational efficiency but also significantly improves proposal quality and reliability, fostering greater trust and transparency between the insurer and the customer.

Example 4: Improved Forecasting in Agile Projects

Forecasting in Agile project management is like trying to predict the weather for a camping trip—it's important but not always easy. Agile projects change a lot, just like the weather, and figuring out how long a project will take can be tricky.

One big challenge is that every task in a project is different. Some tasks are easy, and some are hard, and it's difficult to guess how long each one will take. Also, every team works differently, and things can change quickly in Agile projects. This makes it difficult to plan accurately.

Situation and Problem Statement

Forecasting project schedules is very important. It helps us plan better by figuring out how many people we need for a project and when we'll need them. It's also key in keeping our promises to clients about when we'll finish their projects. Accurate forecasting means we can make smarter choices about the project, like deciding if we can add new features without causing delays. This is really important because it helps us adjust our plans in a way that keeps everything running smoothly and ensures we deliver what we promise.

In Agile projects, we often use "story points" to estimate how much work a task (for example, a user story) will take: a property known as *cycle time*. But these points are more about how complicated the task is than how long it will take. Because teams may see a task differently, it's hard to use these points to estimate time accurately, as you can see in Figure 7-7, which shows the correlation (or better: lack of correlation) between cycle time and story points in an Agile project.

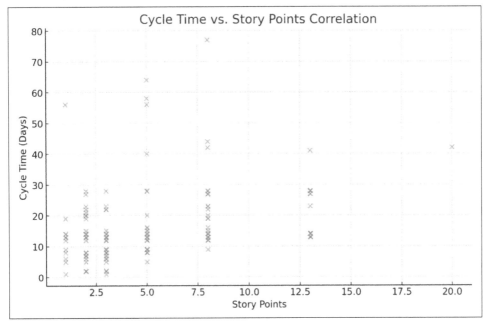

Figure 7-7. Correlation between story points and time completion

In addition, many project owners and managers over-rely on past performance without considering the unique challenges of the current project. This ultimately leads to poor forecasts. A more in-depth forecasting methodology could help, but product owners often lack the time and skills to do so.

Solution Overview

To improve the quality of forecasts, Agile project managers can use an AugFlow that enables them to make better, more insight-driven decisions. At a high level, the solution relies on an LLM-powered chat interface within the process that the project manager or scrum master is currently using. This could be as simple as a dedicated chatbot in Microsoft Teams (where product owners are already discussing the feature requests with other stakeholders) or, in a more elaborate setting, the chat interface could be integrated into a project-planning tool like Jira. The chat interface acts as an "Agile prediction expert." The LLM that powers it acts as an orchestrator to a trusted data source and analysis script or process, assisting the user with asking the right questions and explaining the analysis results in simple terms. Figure 7-8 shows a high-level view of the solution's architecture with the example of using a custom GPT in ChatGPT Team.

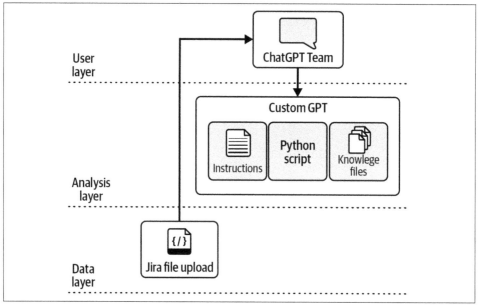

Figure 7-8. High-level architecture

The solution provides versatile forecasting options, from simple throughput-based forecasting to advanced simulations. The chat interface offers unobtrusive user interaction and quick access from the point where the insight is needed.

Solution Breakdown

Let's explore how this solution works by walking through the different stages.

Data layer

First, you need a frame engine that can fetch data from a Jira project given some parameters like project ID and historic time frame. The frame engine should also be able to enforce an analytics contract that checks for compliance with basic data-quality rules and handles predefined data-preparation logics, such as removing duplicate issue IDs and handling issue IDs without a resolution date.

This component delivers a "forecasting-ready" data set that it makes available using a simple API call and documented API schema. Another frame engine in the analytics layer can then consume this data set as an input. An example of such a data set is shown in Figure 7-9.

	A	B	C	D
1	IssueKey	ResolutionDate	StartProgress	StoryPoints
2	AGPT-37134	11/22/23	11/8/23	5
3	AGPT-37001	11/17/23	11/8/23	5
4	AGPT-36930	11/1/23	10/25/23	2
5	AGPT-36891	12/8/23	10/11/23	5
6	AGPT-36714	10/30/23	10/11/23	1
7	AGPT-36592	11/3/23	10/25/23	5
8	AGPT-36485	12/6/23	11/22/23	8
9	AGPT-36484	11/22/23	11/8/23	8
10	AGPT-36483	11/6/23	10/25/23	5

Figure 7-9. A ready forecasting data set

Analysis layer

Within the analysis layer, there are essentially three scripts, which can each be implemented as a single "Agile forecasting" frame engine. Each script takes an input in the form of the forecasting-ready data set described in the previous step, then runs an analytical process on it. The three scripts are:

Advanced data analysis

This script analyzes the historical throughput and velocity of completed tasks from the forecasting-ready data set, which can then be used to further visualize the relationship between the variables. This step helps the user understand how throughput and velocity are correlated, if there are any historical outliers, and which metric—throughput or velocity—is more appropriate for running the forecast. Example 7-1 illustrates what this might look like.

Example 7-1. Code example for advanced data analysis

```
def calculate_throughput_velocity(df):
    import pandas as pd

    # Ensure 'ResolutionDate' is in datetime format for accurate resampling
    df['ResolutionDate'] = pd.to_datetime(df['ResolutionDate'])

    # Calculate monthly THROUGHPUT as the count of issues resolved per month
    monthly_throughput = df.resample('M', on='ResolutionDate').size()

    # Calculate monthly VELOCITY as the sum of story points resolved per month
    monthly_velocity = df.resample('M', on='ResolutionDate')['StoryPoints'].sum()

    # Return the calculated metrics as a tuple
    return (monthly_throughput, monthly_velocity)
```

Simple prediction

The simple forecast script, as shown in Example 7-2, generates a tuple of two lists with time steps and work remaining that can be used to plot a simple burndown chart forecast for a number of story points (velocity-based forecast) or issues (throughput-based forecast), depending on the user's preference. This simple forecast does not account for variability, such as changes in the scope of work.

Example 7-2. Code example for simple prediction

```
def burn_down_forecast(df, total_scope, scope_type):
    import pandas as pd
    import matplotlib.pyplot as plt
    import numpy as np

    # Calculate average throughput per month
    if scope_type == 'throughput':
      throughput = df.set_index('ResolutionDate').resample('M').agg({'IssueKey':
        'count'}).mean().values[0]
    elif scope_type == 'story_points':
      throughput = df.set_index('ResolutionDate').resample('M').agg({'StoryPoints':
        'sum'}).mean().values[0]
    else:
      return("scope_type must be throughput' or 'story_points'")

    # Calculate the time to completion
    time_to_completion = total_scope / throughput

    # Calculate intermediate points
    intervals = 10
    time_steps = np.linspace(0, time_to_completion, intervals)
    work_remaining = total_scope - (np.array(time_steps) * throughput)

    return (time_steps, work_remaining)
```

Advanced forecast

The advanced forecast, as shown in Example 7-3, incorporates variability in the work, assuming a range of 120% to 140% of the original scope, depending on how this function is implemented. The function will then perform a Monte Carlo simulation to obtain a probability distribution of completion times given the expected variability in work. The forecast can be done by either velocity or throughput, depending on which is more appropriate given the advanced data analysis.

Example 7-3. Code example for advanced forecast

```
def monte_carlo_simulation(df, total_scope=None, scope_type='story_points',
  scope_range=None, delivery_pace_variation_factor=1.0, trials=1000, percentile=85):

    import pandas as pd
    import numpy as np
    import matplotlib.pyplot as plt
    import random

    if total_scope is not None and scope_range is None:
        # Assuming a range of 120% to 140% of the original scope
        scope_range = (total_scope * 1.2, total_scope * 1.4)

    # Convert ResolutionDate to datetime and group by time unit (e.g., month)
    df['ResolutionDate'] = pd.to_datetime(df['ResolutionDate'])
    df['TimeUnit'] = df['ResolutionDate'].dt.to_period('M')
    # Grouping by month, can be changed as needed

    # Calculate historical delivery pace
    if scope_type == 'story_points':
        delivery_pace_data = df.groupby('TimeUnit')['StoryPoints'].sum()
    else:  # scope_type == 'throughput'
        delivery_pace_data = df.groupby('TimeUnit').size()

    avg_delivery_pace = delivery_pace_data.mean()
    std_dev_delivery_pace = delivery_pace_data.std()

    # Define delivery pace range
    delivery_pace_range = (max(avg_delivery_pace - std_dev_delivery_pace *
      delivery_pace_variation_factor, 0),avg_delivery_pace + std_dev_delivery_pace *
      delivery_pace_variation_factor)

    # Monte Carlo Simulation
    simulations = []
    for _ in range(trials):
        total_work = random.uniform(*scope_range) if scope_range else total_scope
        time_passed = 0
        simulation = []
        work_remaining = total_work
        while work_remaining > 0:
            delivery_pace = random.uniform(*delivery_pace_range)
            work_remaining -= delivery_pace
            time_passed += 1
            simulation.append(round(max(work_remaining, 0),1))
        simulations.append((time_passed-1, simulation))

    return simulations
```

The frame engine's analysis returns another object that contains a new data set with simulation data, which can be visualized as shown in Figure 7-10.

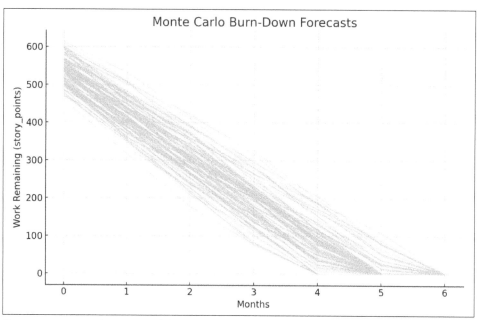

Figure 7-10. Sample output of the Agile forecasting frame engine for the advanced forecast

In addition to the frame engine, the analysis layer includes a frame agent in the form of an LLM that orchestrates the process. For example, the LLM will accept user requests, ask about the relevant project idea and timeframe, and translate this information into the appropriate requests to the data set and prediction script. You could use a custom LLM agent implementation for this or an off-the-shelf solution, like the OpenAI Assistants API (*https://oreil.ly/oS3gU*).

User layer

As noted before, users access the system through a simple chat interface supported by an LLM. This provides several benefits, including:

- Guiding the user through the process (such as asking for the project ID and historical time frame or suggesting doing advanced data analysis first)
- Performing calculations in the background on data coming from the frame engines
- Displaying key insights and graphs from the simulations
- Asking questions and explaining the results to assist the user in interpretation

Figure 7-11 shows an example of such a chat.

 You
So is it fair to say that if I start implementing 500 new story points tomorrow, the chances of getting them done in 6 months or less are pretty good?

 Agility GPT
Yes, it is fair to make that assumption based on the histogram and Monte Carlo simulation results, with some important considerations:

* **Probability**: The histogram gives an estimate of when 500 story points might be completed. If the 85th percentile falls within 6 months, it implies a high probability (85%) of completing the work in that timeframe.
* **Past Performance**: This forecast is based on historical data. It assumes that the team's future performance will be similar to their past performance.
* **Variability and Risk**: The simulation accounts for variability in velocity, but unexpected factors can still impact delivery.
* **Continuous Monitoring**: Agile methodologies emphasize adaptability. Regularly review progress and adjust forecasts as needed.

In conclusion, starting 500 story points tomorrow with the expectation of completion in 6 months is reasonable, but remain adaptable and continuously monitor progress. Would you like to explore any other aspects or have further questions?

Figure 7-11. User question and AI-generated answer from chat interface

Example Summary

This approach addresses the inherent unpredictability and variability of Agile project management by providing a streamlined, data-driven forecasting process. It does so by augmenting an Agile project-planning process with an advanced LLM-powered chat interface that gives insightful analytics to support decision making in real time.

The use case provides a variety of benefits that drive real business value:

Increased forecast accuracy
> By leveraging data from tools such as Jira and applying advanced analytics, the solution gives more accurate forecasts and reduces reliance on subjective estimates, such as story points.

Easy-to-use interface
> The chat interface simplifies interaction, making complex data analysis accessible to those with limited technical expertise.

Real-time insights
> Instant access to forecasting data and analysis within existing workflows (such as Microsoft Teams and Jira) ensures timely decision making.

Adaptability
> Incorporating advanced forecasting and simulation, such as Monte Carlo methods, allows for variability in projects and scope changes.

Education and guidance
> The LLM not only analyzes the data but also educates users and guides them through the forecasting process, improving their understanding and developing their skills.

While this solution can be further improved and extended, it provides a straightforward first approach to improving the planning process for Agile projects—and it brings analytics closer to the user.

Example 5: Quick Sales Intelligence

In modern sales, every second counts. Imagine you're a salesperson about to make an important call to an unknown (at least to you) prospect that we'll call the Acme Corporation. Your mind is probably racing with questions like:

- Has this company been a customer before?
- What is the company currently doing?
- How big is the company?

Finding answers to questions like these has traditionally meant diving into time-consuming manual research that often leaves you with even more questions. To address these questions, you would need to search the CRM for the company, look up its website, and read notes from previous salespeople (if any) who have dealt with the company.

This is where the "Quick Sales Intelligence" use case is designed to augment and streamline the workflow. In this AugFlow, the user gets easy access to all required customer information to start a high-quality sales process without delay.

Situation and Problem Statement

Here are some key challenges that salespeople face when preparing for effective sales calls:

Time-consuming research
Searching for a company in the CRM and finding the right account can be a pain. Even in a midsize company that deals with just a few multinationals, a simple CRM search for a company like "Siemens" can return dozens or hundreds of results. In this case, looking up customer information could leave you more confused than when you started.

Keeping up with the news
If you're calling a company that just held the biggest product launch in history yesterday, you want to know. It can open the door to a deeper conversation, or, if the launch didn't go so well, it might be a topic best avoided. So staying on top of a prospect's news is critical. But how do you keep up? Visiting each company's website for news or updates is a daunting task, especially when you're dealing with a large volume of prospects.

Historical data management
There's nothing worse than looking unprepared on a sales call. But considering the effort it takes to go through previous call notes and recordings, we feel for any salesperson who skips this step. It's probably the most important step, but it's also the most time-consuming.

Analytics
Advanced analytics for customer use cases, like churn prediction, have been around for decades. But too often, their impact is lost because salespeople don't have access to the analytics or the time to dig into them (for the reasons mentioned previously). In the end, the salesperson may end up operating on gut instinct instead of data-driven insight.

These challenges are more than just minor inconveniences. When stacked up, they represent significant roadblocks to effective and efficient sales. There are two possible worst-case scenarios here: either the sales rep shows up unprepared for a call, or they spend *way* too much time researching a prospect before picking up the phone, only to find that no one is answering or the person they need to talk to is on vacation. The bottom line is missed opportunities, wasted effort, and poor performance. What sales teams need is not more data but the *right* data at the right time.

Solution Overview

The Quick Sales Intelligence chatbot is designed to address these challenges. Here's how it works at a high level: the user interacts with the system through a simple chat interface powered by an LLM that's been fine-tuned for chat instructions. This chatbot can be integrated into any application the sales reps are working with: the home page of the CRM system, an Outlook email client, or even a WhatsApp chat on their phone.

The chatbot first asks the user to provide some information about the company they are researching. Its LLM elicits information from the user: "What company are you looking up?"

The salesperson provides some rough information: "Acme Corp, acme.com." The Chat LLM takes this information, validates it, and passes it to another LLM. This model, the Assistant LLM, is fine-tuned for assistant tasks and will act as an orchestrator for calling and managing various API services. (We'll dive deeper into these API services in a moment.) The Assistant LLM queries the appropriate service and returns the information to the Chat LLM, which uses this information to respond to the user. Figure 7-12 depicts this workflow.

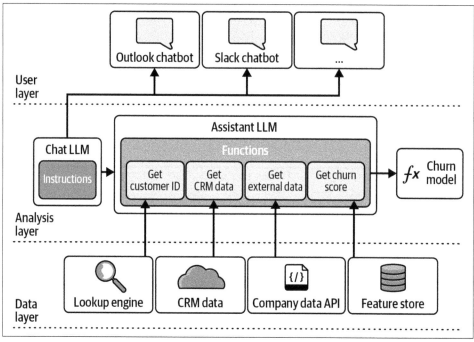

Figure 7-12. Solution architecture overview for Quick Sales Intelligence

If this sounds complicated, don't worry. We'll dive deeper into the individual components next!

Solution Breakdown

Let's look more closely at the core components of this approach.

Data layer

To make this system work, you'll need access to high-quality, easily available data. In particular, here are the services you need:

Lookup engine
> This frame engine takes a search query, such as a string with a company name and domain address ("Acme Corp, acme.com"). It performs a search of companies known to the business. This data will come primarily from the CRM but could also come from external database vendors. The engine returns one or more pairs of IDs, including an account ID if the company is an existing customer or a DUNS number if it's a new customer:
>
> ```
> Example response:
> # known customer
> (1000345, 5-048-3782)
>
> # known company
> (NaN, 5-048-5732)
>
> # unknown company
> (NaN, NaN)
>
> # multiple matches
> [(1000345, 5-048-3782), (1000346, 5-048-2001) ]
> ```

CRM data
> This frame engine takes at least one of a pair of IDs—account ID and/or DUNS number—and fetches relevant information from the CRM. This could contain structured data (such as customer lifetime value, number of won opportunities, or number of contacts) or unstructured data (such as sales notes from the last three contacts associated with this account). Example 7-4 shows what this component's response could look like.

Example 7-4. CRM data frame engine response in JSON

```
{
  "customerID": "1000345",
  "DUNSNumber": "5-048-3782",
  "stats": {
    "customerLifetimeValue": 250000,
    "wonOpportunities": 15,
    "numberOfContacts": 5
```

```
    },
    "callNotes": {
      "salesNotes": [
        {
          "contactID": "C001",
          "note": "Discussed new product features, very interested in the
            upcoming release.",
          "date": "2024-01-10"
        },
        {
          "contactID": "C002",
          "note": "Expressed concerns about delivery timelines, reassured with
            recent project updates.",
          "date": "2024-01-05"
        },
        {
          "contactID": "C003",
          "note": "Requested detailed pricing breakdown for bulk order,
            sent proposal.",
          "date": "2024-01-03"
        }
      ]
    }
  }
```

Company data API

This frame engine accepts a DUNS number and returns a set of predefined metrics retrieved from an external company database, such as the company's number of employees, current revenue, and annual growth rate. Example 7-5 gives a sample of this response.

Example 7-5. External company data frame engine response in JSON

```
"response": {
  "status": "success",
  "data": {
    "companyInfo": {
      "dunsNumber": "5-048-3782",
      "companyName": "Acme Corporation",
      "numberOfEmployees": 450,
      "currentRevenue": "$120M",
      "annualGrowthRate": "4.5%",
      "industry": "Technology",
      "headquarters": "San Francisco, CA, USA"
    }
  }
}
```

Feature store

This augmented frame accepts an account ID and model ID and fetches customer features. For example, given a churn prediction model that requires historic sales data, a possible request and response to this feature store could look like Example 7-6.

Example 7-6. Feature store frame engine response

```
{
  "accountID": 1000345,
  "modelID": "churn_prediction_v01",
  "features": {
    "revenueLast3Months": 120000,
    "revenueLast6Months": 250000,
    "revenueLast9Months": 360000,
    "monthsSinceFirstOrder": "18",
    "monthsSinceLastOrder": "1",
    "customerRegion": "Europe"
  },
  "metadata": {
    "requestTimestamp": "2024-01-16T12:00:00Z",
    "responseTimestamp": "2024-01-16T12:00:05Z",
    "modelVersion": "1.2.4"
  }
}
```

To be clear, setting up the data connectors like this is probably the hardest part. Everything else is easy. That's why we recommend using the AA approach if your organization has reached at least level two of the analytics maturity model (Data Active). Deploying and maintaining such data services require your organization to have good governance, infrastructure, and ownership.

Of course, these services could serve many different use cases. For example, the Feature Store API would serve not only this use case but also any use case that requires real-time customer churn prediction.

Analysis layer

The core of the analytics layer is two different LLMs with different purposes and another service for fetching advanced analytics, such as customer churn predictions, in real time.

Information handling. The Chat LLM's role is as a frontend processor. It simplifies and interprets user inputs and passes structured data to the Assistant LLM. For example, when the salesperson asks for information on "Acme Corp, acme.com," the Chat LLM processes it more or less as follows:

1. The Chat LLM parses the input to identify the company name, "Acme Corp," and the domain, "acme.com."
2. The Chat LLM validates the company name and domain using internal logic to ensure that they're legitimate.

3. Upon validation, the Chat LLM structures the information in a format that the Assistant LLM can process, such as a JSON object:

```
{ "company_name": "Acme Corp", "domain": "acme.com" }
```

4. The Chat LLM passes the structured information to the Assistant LLM.

The Chat LLM is primarily focused on understanding and structuring the user's request. It interacts with the user, interprets their input, and formats it into a structured query for the Assistant LLM. While this requires advanced natural language understanding and some contextual awareness to handle conversational nuances, a cheaper LLM, such as GPT-3.5, or a performant open source model, such as Mistral 7B, could be suitable for this task, reducing the overall cost of the solution.

Task orchestration. The Assistant LLM functions as middleware, coordinating the various API services. Delegating this task to a specialized service is more efficient and scalable than trying to include it in the information-handling stage. On a high level, here's how the Assistant LLM works:

1. The Assistant LLM receives structured information from the Chat LLM.
2. It calls the Lookup Engine API with the domain to get the company's unique ID. If more than one ID is returned, the Assistant LLM responds to the Chat LLM to ask for more information from the user.
3. If it identifies one or both IDs, the Assistant LLM queries the CRM data for any past interactions or records related to Acme Corp.
4. The Assistant LLM may also reach out to the Company Data API to fetch recent news, press releases, or any other external data that could be useful for the sales rep.
5. It compiles all the gathered data into a comprehensive report.
6. It returns the report to the Chat LLM.

The Assistant LLM's response to the Chat LLM could look like Example 7-7.

Example 7-7. Assistant response

```
{
  "response": {
    "customerDetails": {
      "companyName": "ACME Corporation",
      "accountID": "5-048-3782",
      "dunsNumber": "5-048-3782",
      "customerLifetimeValue": 250000,
      "wonOpportunities": 15,
      "numberOfContacts": 5,
      "numberOfEmployees": 450,
      "currentRevenue": "$120M",
```

```
  "annualGrowthRate": "4.5%",
  "industry": "Technology",
  "headquarters": "San Francisco, CA, USA",
  "recentInteractions": [
    {
      "date": "2024-01-10",
      "note": "Discussed new product features, very interested in the
        upcoming release."
    },
    {
      "date": "2024-01-05",
      "note": "Expressed concerns about delivery timelines, reassured with
        recent project updates."
    },
    {
      "date": "2024-01-03",
      "note": "Requested detailed pricing breakdown for bulk order,
        sent proposal."
    }
  ]
},
"status": "success",
"actionItems": [
  "Follow up on the new product features interest shown on January 10.",
  "Address any remaining concerns about delivery timelines from the discussion
    on January 5.",
  "Confirm receipt and understanding of the detailed pricing breakdown sent
    on January 3."
]
  }
}
```

The Assistant LLM's responsibilities are more complex than those of the Chat LLM. The Assistant LLM must understand the purpose of each API, the significance of the data, and how to combine everything into useful output. This implies a higher level of "cognitive" sophistication: it must manage a workflow, understand the context of various data sources, handle potential errors or exceptions from these sources, and synthesize all this information into a coherent response. Thus, a state-of-the-art LLM like GPT-4 or Gemini Ultra may be more appropriate for this task.

User layer

Based on the provided data, the chat LLM reports back to the user with the requested information, as shown in Figure 7-13.

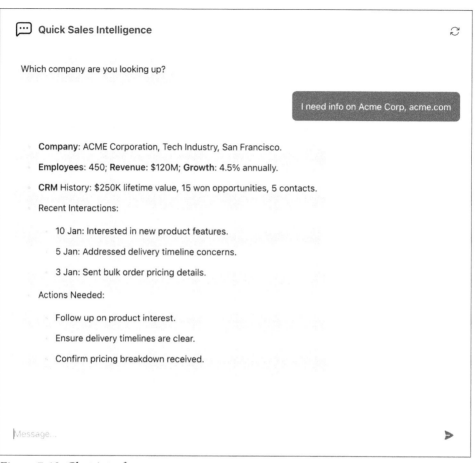

Company: ACME Corporation, Tech Industry, San Francisco.

Employees: 450; Revenue: $120M; Growth: 4.5% annually.

CRM History: $250K lifetime value, 15 won opportunities, 5 contacts.

Recent Interactions:

10 Jan: Interested in new product features.

5 Jan: Addressed delivery timeline concerns.

3 Jan: Sent bulk order pricing details.

Actions Needed:

Follow up on product interest.

Ensure delivery timelines are clear.

Confirm pricing breakdown received.

Figure 7-13. Chat interface

What if the user has a follow-up question? Perhaps they ask, "How likely is it that this customer won't buy from us again?"

The process doesn't restart from scratch. The Chat LLM will remember the message's context, such as the account ID, and pass it over to the Assistant LLM, along with a task description. The JSON object that the Chat LLM passes over to the Assistant LLM would look something like Example 7-8.

Example 7-8. Chat LLM output passed to Assistant LLM

```
{
  "task": "predict_churn",
  "parameters": {
    "company_name": "Acme Corp",
    "domain": "acme.com",
    "account_id": "1000345"
  }
}
```

The Assistant LLM recognizes this as a churn prediction task and queries the feature store for `account_id` `1000345`. This returns a JSON object (like the one in Example 7-8) in the data layer. The Assistant LLM takes this response and calls the churn prediction model API with the JSON object in Example 7-9.

Example 7-9. Assistant LLM request to churn prediction model

```
{
  "modelID": "churn_prediction_v01",
  "features": {
    "revenueLast3Months": 120000,
    "revenueLast6Months": 250000,
    "revenueLast9Months": 360000,
    "monthsSinceFirstOrder": "18",
    "monthsSinceLastOrder": "1",
    "customerRegion": "Europe"
  }
}
```

The churn model API returns a response like the one in Example 7-10.

Example 7-10. Churn prediction model response

```
{
  "account_id": "1000345",
  "churn_probability": 0.30,
  "top_features": ["monthsSinceLastOrder"]
}
```

This response would indicate a low probability of churn because the customer just recently made a purchase. The Assistant LLM passes this information over to the Chat LLM, which generates the final user-facing output shown in Figure 7-14.

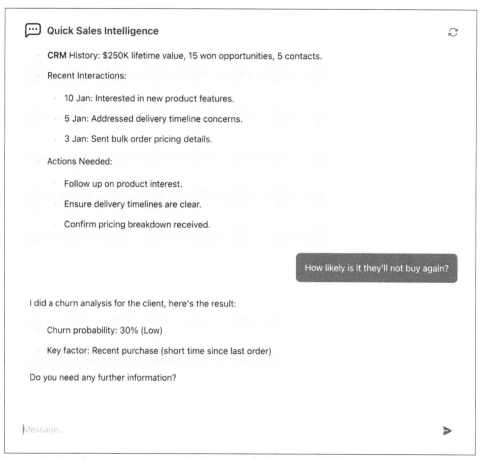

CRM History: $250K lifetime value, 15 won opportunities, 5 contacts.

Recent Interactions:

    10 Jan: Interested in new product features.

    5 Jan: Addressed delivery timeline concerns.

    3 Jan: Sent bulk order pricing details.

Actions Needed:

    Follow up on product interest.

    Ensure delivery timelines are clear.

    Confirm pricing breakdown received.

> How likely is it they'll not buy again?

I did a churn analysis for the client, here's the result:

    Churn probability: 30% (Low)

    Key factor: Recent purchase (short time since last order)

Do you need any further information?

Figure 7-14. Chat conversation with churn probabilities and follow-up question

Example Summary

In conclusion, the Quick Sales Intelligence chatbot shows an effective way to augment the sales process with relevant data and optimize the overall workflow. Key outcomes from these data-driven insights include:

Efficient sales-call preparation
> The system drastically reduces the time that sales representatives spend on manual research, allowing them to focus more on strategic aspects of the sales process.

Enhanced customer interaction

The chatbot enables sales teams to approach calls with a comprehensive under-standing of the prospect, leading to more informed conversations and better sales outcomes. With direct access to a prospect's recent activity, historical interactions, and other relevant data, sales reps can personalize their approach, increasing the likelihood of a successful engagement.

Predictive analytics

Features such as churn prediction provide forward-looking insights that help sales teams proactively address potential problems and capitalize on opportunities.

Easy-to-use interface

The conversational interface simplifies the process of obtaining complex business intelligence, making it accessible to those with limited technical or analytical expertise.

Scalability and adaptability

The modular design of the system allows for easy integration with existing CRM platforms and can be scaled to meet the growing needs of the organization.

Overall, this system addresses core challenges that many sales teams face and empowers them to operate with greater intelligence, agility, and effectiveness.

Conclusion

As we wrap up this final chapter, we hope the examples and case studies have shown you the transformative power of AA. Our journey through the pages of this book was designed not only to showcase the theoretical foundations of bringing insights into various business workflows but also to inspire you to envision and apply these principles within your own organization.

This chapter doesn't just mark the conclusion of our exploration but also a moment of achievement for you: *congratulations*!

By completing this book, you've taken a significant step toward steering your organization toward becoming an insight-driven entity. Throughout our discussions, we've explored the increasing importance of analytics in the modern business landscape, identified the primary challenges that organizations face, and outlined strategies for leveraging AA to bridge the analytics chasm. This approach enables the integration of insights at scale across a wide range of processes, helping your business to thrive through improved decision making at every level and managing the analytics transformation.

It was important to focus on two different topics: the business perspective in the first half of the book and the technical perspective in the second half. Realizing that you can't build an augmentation with a snap of your fingers is critical. It's not just a technical implementation; your organization must already have a higher maturity level in analytics transformation. It requires a holistic approach that also focuses on business strategy, people, organization, and culture. Successfully implementing both aspects simultaneously will set your company up for a successful transition to an insight-driven organization.

It's crucial to remember that at its heart, AA is about people, with technology serving as a powerful enabler. Adopting a human-centric approach to AA paves the way for success, ensuring that your initiatives are both impactful and sustainable.

Don't hesitate to take the first step by assessing your current position and setting realistic goals. Adopt an Agile mindset and a culture of experimentation as you iterate toward your goals, allowing for regular reflection and course correction. This adaptability is key to navigating the road ahead. As the saying goes, "Start small but think big." Achieving early success lays the groundwork for more ambitious projects, making the path forward smoother and more navigable.

We wish you all the best for the exciting journey ahead! Feel free to share your experiences and successes with us and foster a community of knowledge and innovation in the field of augmented analytics. Here's to a future of making better decisions together. Good luck!

Index

B

behavior, changing, 4-5
benchmarking, 222
benchmarking workflow applied example, 229-235
bias
    overcoming with augmented analytics (AA), 51, 53
    types of, 53-55
Big Data, 8
bottom-up business object structures, 198, 199
business analysts, 81
business integration, 100-101
business objects
    bottom-up structures, 198-199
    defined, 159-162
    unconnected, 199-200
business transformation
    cultural changes needed, 7-10
    data-driven versus insight-driven decision-making, 18
    defined, 1
    factors in, 1-5
    industries affected by, 5-7
business value assessment, 118-119

C

Casebase, 134-136
center of excellence (see CoE)
centralized approach (CoE), 90
change management, 28
    Influence Model, 94-97
change management specialists, 81
change, speed of, 2
chatbots, 248-256
clustering, 122
CoE (center of excellence), 27
    centralized organization, 90
    creating, 86-88
    decentralized organization, 89
    federated organization, 90-93
    tasks of, 94
cognitive bias, 53
collaboration support, 29
collaborative augmentation, 112
commercial insurance

analytics in, 15
benchmarking workflow applied example, 229-235
location workflow applied example, 224-229
proposal workflow applied example, 235-238
underwriting process, 219-224
competitor expectations, 12
complexity in analytics, 8
computer vision, 57, 61-62
concept phase (use-case approach), 115-118
confirmation bias, 53
consumers, changing behavior, 4-5
contextual augmentation, 112
contracts, 152-156
convergence of multiple technologies, 2
conversational augmentation, 111-112
Conway's Law, 87
copilots, 131
cultural change (SPEC framework), 20
    cultivating data literacy, 97-101
    Data Active stage, 24
    Data Fluent stage, 37
    Data Progressive stage, 32
    Data Reactive stage, 21
culture of learning, 35
curse of knowledge, 95
customer centricity, 4-5
customer expectations, 12
customer service representatives, 76
cycle time (Agile), 239

D

data
    ease of locating, 34
    importance of, 2-4
    unstructured, 4
data access for frame engines, 186
data access layers, 147
Data Active stage (analytical maturity model), 17, 23-31
data analysts, 80
data analytics (see analytics)
data architects, 81
data awareness, 98
data competencies measurement, 35

About the Authors

Willi Weber is head of data analytics at HDI Global SE, a leading German industrial insurer, who has been at the forefront of transforming the business from a data-reactive company to a data-progressive one and paving the way to an insight-driven future. With a background in information systems, Willi was an early believer in the power of data analytics to drive business success. He is on a mission to create broad analytics awareness, drive transformation through use cases, and establish a culture of analytics in a decentralized approach at HDI Global SE.

Tobias Zwingmann is a leading expert, speaker, and author on artificial intelligence. In his role as managing partner of the German AI advisory firm RAPYD.AI, he helps B2B companies around the world innovate and grow their businesses with AI and machine learning. Prior to cofounding RAPYD.AI, he worked for more than 10 years in a corporate setting where his responsibilities included creating a company-wide data strategy and building out data science use cases. He also authored the book *AI-Powered Business Intelligence* (O'Reilly).

Colophon

The animal on the cover of *Augmented Analytics* is an aardvark (*Orycteropus afer*), a burrowing mammal native to Africa.

A long snout and a stout, medium-sized body with an arched back and coarse hairs give the aardvark a pig-like appearance, although it has a more elongated head than a pig does. The aardvark's rear legs are longer than its forelegs, and its front feet have only four toes while its rear feet have five.

The aardvark lives in savannas, rain forests, thickets, and woodlands, and it avoids particularly rocky places. It lives in a burrow and digs new burrows frequently, leaving its burrow occasionally during the day to sunbathe despite being nocturnal. An aardvark will travel along stretches of miles in a zigzag motion in search of food, pressing its snout against the ground to sniff. The animal's diet consists almost entirely of ants and termites, but it will occasionally eat beetle larvae. An aardvark grinds food up in its stomach instead of chewing it.

With stable, robust numbers in populated areas, the aardvark has a conservation status of "Least Concern." Many of the animals on O'Reilly covers are endangered; all of them are important to the world.

The cover illustration is by Karen Montgomery, based on a black and white engraving from *Braukhaus Lexicon*. The series design is by Edie Freedman, Ellie Volckhausen, and Karen Montgomery. The cover fonts are Gilroy Semibold and Guardian Sans. The text font is Adobe Minion Pro; the heading font is Adobe Myriad Condensed; and the code font is Dalton Maag's Ubuntu Mono.

O'REILLY®

Learn from experts.
Become one yourself.

Books | Live online courses
Instant answers | Virtual events
Videos | Interactive learning

Get started at oreilly.com.